WORLD SECURITY

THE NEW CHALLENGE

To Danny Barron
— good friend & my
"family" member in
Calgary — and
I hope a future
colleague —
With admiration
& best
"Uncle" Bill
Epstein

WORLD SECURITY
THE NEW CHALLENGE

Edited by
Carl G. Jacobsen, Morris Miller, Metta Spencer and Eric L. Tollefson
for
CANADIAN PUGWASH GROUP

Project Editor: Derek Paul
Science for Peace

Prepared with administrative and editorial assistance for the Canadian Pugwash Group by Beverley J.T. Delong, and editorial assistance for Science for Peace by Shirley Farlinger and George Hathaway

Printed and bound in Canada by Best Gagné Printing Ltd., Louiseville, Quebec

Canadian Cataloguing in Publication Data

Main entry under title:

World security

Includes bibliographical references and index.
ISBN 0-88866-952-6

1. Security, International. 2. International relations. I. Jacobsen, C.G. (Carl G.)
II. Paul, Derek. III. Canadian Pugwash Group.

JX1952.W67 1994   327.1'72   C94-931260-6

Science for Peace
University College
University of Toronto
Toronto, Ontario M5S 1A1

Distributed by:

Dundurn Press Limited	Dundurn Distribution	Dundurn Press Limited
2181 Queen Street East	73 Lime Walk	1823 Maryland Avenue
Suite 301	Headington, Oxford	P.O. Box 1000
Toronto, Canada	England	Niagara Falls, N.Y.
M4E 1E5	0X3 7AD	U.S.A. 14302-1000

Contents

Preface

Books submitted to Science for Peace for publication in the new Dundurn series are published on their merits having regard to the purposes of Science for Peace, and the timeliness of the subject matter. Generally a typescript is submitted to a process of peer review prior to acceptance. Authors wishing to publish through Science for Peace should write in the first instance to the Publishing Committee, Science for Peace, C/O Professor Veronica Dahl, Department of Computer Science, Simon Fraser University, Burnaby, B.C. V5A 1S6.

The present volume brings together great diversity of subject matter and many authors. We have tried to preserve the full range of individuality of their writings, even where this prevents uniformity of convention.

Views expressed in this book are those of the authors, and do not necessarily reflect those of the granting agencies who supported its publication.

Derek Paul
President
Science for Peace

Foreword

The authors and project editor of this book are all participants in the international Pugwash movement and members of the Canadian Pugwash Group. The latter is the official arm of the international movement that is rooted in Canada. The movement, officially called *The Pugwash Conferences on Science and World Affairs*, began in Nova Scotia in 1957, with a small conference hosted by Cyrus Eaton at his vacation home in the village of Pugwash. On that occasion 22 prominent nuclear scientists were invited to discuss the dangers of nuclear war and the imperatives of doing something to reduce and eventually eliminate that menace. Over the intervening years the movement has grown, and today hosts frequent specialized workshops and symposia worldwide, on numerous vital subjects, as well as one annual international conference having a broader scope.

This book reflects many concerns of the Canadian Pugwash Group about the future of human society on this planet, in both near and medium term. The nuclear bombs have not gone away; but we have come to see the global predicament in a new light. This volume throws some of the new issues into relief.

The authors make no pretence that they have covered the entire field of Pugwash concerns, but they do remind us, in a terse and readable fashion, of what needs to be done in order to shape a world less frightening than the present one. The challenge is enormous. It is correspondingly important that we meet it.

John Polanyi

Acknowledgements

Thanks go to the following for significant assistance to the editors, or for opinions on one or other of the chapters: Norman Epstein, Franklyn Griffiths, Trudy Govier, John Hewitt, Susan Leniczek, Joanna Miller, Jean Olthuis and Jean Tollefson. Theodora Foster and Dennis Howlett undertook detailed reviews of selected chapters, for which we are most grateful. For assistance with proofreading we thank Janet Creery.

The publication of this book has been made possible by the financial support of the Cooperative Security Competition Program, the Pugwash Park Foundation, and Tollefson Engineering Enterprises Ltd. Our thanks go to all these organizations.

Part I

TOWARD A SUSTAINABLE PEACE

CHAPTER 1

From Conflict to Community

Douglas Roche

The new era of history that opened up with the end of the polarizing Cold War has produced not euphoria but a profound anxiety. Hardly had the Berlin Wall been breached, signalling the coming end of Communism as an international political force, than the Gulf War broke out. The brutal dismemberment of Yugoslavia followed with shocking acts of systematic rape and other atrocities under the revolting term *ethnic cleansing*. Clan warfare in Somalia and other parts of Africa resulted in the starvation of hundreds of thousands of people, mostly children. The number of refugees has doubled since 1989, and migrants, forced off their lands, now total nearly 100 million [1]. Terrorism and political assassinations dominate the news.

The regular, and non-newsworthy, plight of hundreds of millions of people, victims of the widening gap between rich and poor, worsens [2]. This anomaly in a world of ever-enrichening technology is seen most vividly along the North-South fault line but exists at increasing levels within the rich societies too. The stock market soars and the unemployment lines grow. *Jobless recovery* has entered not only the language but the economic models. Deficits mount and social programs are cut. What used to be described as *aid weariness* has turned into meanness as a characteristic of the post-Cold War society. Help is begrudged, whether to restore the Russian economy, to assist a beleaguered Africa, or even to get the homeless off our own streets. So far this decade, heralded as the entry into the 21st century, has been marked by chaos, confusion, rejection, and self-protection. The taste of the early 1990s is sourness.

An assessment of our times must also record positive developments. Democratic regimes are spreading, with world-wide electronic communication infusing peoples everywhere with the energy of self-determination. The stranglehold of apartheid in South Africa has been broken and all Africa may benefit economically. Drastic reductions in nuclear weapons are occurring. The Clinton Administration's decision to extend the nuclear testing moratorium has brightened hopes that a Comprehensive Nuclear Test Ban is within reach; the prospects for the extension of the Non-Proliferation Treaty beyond 1995 have brightened. A treaty banning the production of chemical weapons has entered into force.

Despite under-financing and the continuing problem of determining where the right to national sovereignty ends and the global right to humanitarian protection begins, United Nations' peace-keeping missions are growing and the United Nations itself is being re-defined as a manager of global security. The East-West partnership, developing through the aegis of the Conference on Security and Cooperation in Europe (CSCE), may be the forerunner of regional associations backing up the UN.

These developments have a sweetness to them. But the sourness of brutality and rejection seems, within public attitudes, to overcome the sweetness of human progress.

Positive trend lines, welcome as they are, cannot obscure the dangers to the future of human civilization. These dangers lie, of course, in the uncontrolled expansion of weaponry, nuclear and conventional, through crisis-ridden regions of the world, but they lie most deeply in the atrophy of the political systems unable, or unwilling, to build the conditions for peace with the same intensity that they prepare the weapons of destruction. What the end of the Cold War revealed was the paucity of machinery for peace in the various regions of the world.

This paucity has its roots in the lack of a shared vision for an international community sharing an increasingly despoiled planet. There is not yet a political comprehension of the social injustice caused by the traditional growth economy crashing against the limitations of a biosphere. The latter is clearly cracking under the strain of a swelling, poverty-stricken humanity. An international system providing equitability rather than exploitation is the central need of our times. But the forces of greed, fear, and dominance, fed by a supine media and political hierarchy, overwhelm, at least at this period of the 1990s, the movements for change.

The implications of the ecosphere stress factor for continuation of human society on the planet are widely known, but not yet ingrained into the political consciousness. Only here and there can we see the appropriate reaction to the emergency — for an emergency it certainly is. The ecosphere stress is a general result of population (see Chapter 7), grossly magnified by the fact of one quarter of the global population having control over three-quarters of the Earth's technology, wealth and resources, and being responsible for a similar proportion of pollution, while three-quarters have access to only one-quarter of the wealth. Also the disproportionate population growth, where 95 percent of babies are born in the South, intensifies the struggle for survival of the poorest societies [3] — see also Chapters 7, 8. With weaponry spreading at an alarming rate through these areas, more conflicts seem inevitable — unless a system fostering human community can be built.

To move from conflict to community will require a surge of creativity that will only come from a synergy of human actions. Neither the political order nor the economic order seem capable of lifting up humanity to its potential for equitable development. A vision of peace, sponsored by multitudes (even if these numbers of activists still represent a minority of populations) is needed to overcome the fatalism now infecting so many, especially the young.

First, we must reject the simplistic notion that violence is an inevitable part of human nature and that, consequently, war is a necessarily recurring phenomenon in history. It is scientifically incorrect to claim that war or violent behaviour is genetically programmed into our human nature [4]. Sweden and Japan are but two nations that have overcome a warring past and now pride themselves on a peaceful order.

Biology does not condemn humanity to war. Civilizations clash because of struggles over resources and land. The phrases *ancient hatreds* and *evil empire*, used to explain the irrationality of warfare, obscure complex motivations of needs exploited by political leaders. Preventive diplomacy, advanced by UN Secretary-General Boutros Boutros-Ghali in An Agenda for Peace [5], is a way to put into practice the new recognition that peace must begin in our minds.

If the exigencies of the Cold War spawned peace movements, the added complexities of the post-Cold War era demand a renewed engagement for peace. Fortunately, the new understanding of the common ground of the planet has provided an intellectual breakthrough. While the fracturing of nations and societies is one consequence of the rejection of authoritarian rule, it is the globalization of world society that presents a more powerful challenge. For, by understanding the wholeness of humanity, we can deal with the global clamour for development in equitable terms. This is not to suggest that equality among humans or an end to conflict are within reach; but the gross distortions that characterize the North-South split, with their consequent dangers, provide a new imperative to repair the injustices of the past. The dangers now revealed by the continued Western dominance of the economic systems of the world are accompanied by a new realization that the comfort of the few can no longer be bought at the expense of the affliction of the many.

No one can predict the years ahead. The present is too volatile. Venality may, indeed, overcome altruism. The power of this moment, however, comes from an enlightenment replacing the shadows of the bipolar gloom of the Cold War. Certain signs of progress can be discerned, which offer the potential of multiplication.

A new definition of security

The work of the Brandt, Thorsson, Palme, Brundtland and Nyerere international commissions of the 1980s provided a new definition of security [6]. For a very long time, security was measured in arms capacity. But the commissions, grappling with the consequences of poverty, militarism, environmental destruction and North-South inequalities, presented a holistic view of the modern, wired world. They challenged the political order to approach security with an integrated agenda. They said it was no longer enough to decelerate the arms race, nuclear and conventional; it was also essential to promote economic and social development, environmental protection, and the extension of human rights. In short, implementing disarmament and sustainable development would promote global security.

Their findings, pushed aside during the Cold War, have now come into the open and, indeed, have been propelled forward by the declaration of the UN Security Council Summit of January 31, 1992:

> The absence of war and military conflict among States does not in itself insure international peace and security. The non-military sources of instability in the economic, social and humanitarian and ecological fields have become threats to peace and security. [7]

This declaration, at the highest political level, provides a basis for reforms of great magnitude.

In identifying the *sources of instability*, we are led, first of all, into the area of nuclear weapons. During the Cold War, the focus was on the relative military strength of the two superpowers. The West always insisted it had to compensate in nuclear weapons for the conventional military superiority of the Soviet Union. The end of the Cold War brought to the forefront the resentment of a number of States proscribed from acquiring nuclear weapons while the five permanent members of the Security Council maintain their *right* to possess such weapons. This discrepancy threatens the extension of the Non-Proliferation Treaty (NPT) — see Chapter 4.

At the 1995 Review Conference, which will determine the future of the NPT, many non-nuclear States will demand a non-proliferation regime that bans the possession and deployment of nuclear weapons by any State. The nuclear weapons powers show no signs of accepting this demand. But there are signs that a Comprehensive Nuclear Test Ban (CTB) can be successfully negotiated by 1995. A CTB will be an indication that nuclear weapons development can at least be brought under control. Without an effective international non-proliferation regime that addresses both vertical and horizontal nuclear weapons development, the horizontal proliferation, one of the greatest instabilities of the present moment, will undoubtedly grow worse [8].

The Clinton Administration has turned US policy away from the Reagan-Bush hostility to an immediate ban on nuclear testing. President Clinton, in a courageous decision, extended the moratorium on testing as a contribution to obtaining a negotiated test ban. That is clearly an important step forward. But the fundamental discrepancy and instability will not be resolved until the nuclear weapons powers agree to the institution of a global ban on the possession of nuclear weapons.

Abolition of nuclear weapons has usually been considered a dream or the ultimate consequence of a permanent peace. But, as the authors of the new Pugwash book, **A Nuclear-Weapon-Free World: Desirable? Feasible?** [9], point out:

The idea of a nuclear-weapon-free world should no longer be dismissed as fanciful. It is an idea which deserves serious study.

It is time to divert a good part of the immense research effort which is still going into nuclear development to work on the problems of a nuclear weapon-free world.

A Working Group at the 43rd Pugwash Conference on Science and World Affairs (Stockholm, 1993) reaffirmed "the conviction that nuclear weapons are the primary threat to global security ... Nuclear proliferation cannot be halted as long as some States claim nuclear weapons as 'their' legitimate instruments for 'their' security". The Pugwash meeting, which advocated a treaty on the elimination of nuclear weapons, concluded:

A truly cooperative and global security order can only be brought about after the elimination of nuclear weapons. [10]

This was the same conclusion reached by prominent world figures launching the Rajiv Gandhi Memorial Initiative for the Advancement of Human Civilization (New Delhi, 1993):

Nuclear weapons pose the greatest threat to human civilization and to humankind's survival. Their elimination is, therefore, the first pre-requisite for the advancement of human civilization. [11]

The alternative to a nuclear-weapon-free world is not the status quo, for it is already clear that near-nuclear states (i.e., states which already possess the technology to build nuclear weapons) will not accept *second-class* status in the world community. The alternative is a world in which a large number of States eventually have nuclear weapons. Then it will become inevitable that nuclear weapons will be used.

The elimination of nuclear weapons is feasible, given an international body with the power to contain all weapons-usable material, plutonium-239 and uranium-235. The dismantling of all installations dedicated to the production of nuclear weapons would have to be assured along with a verification system to prevent a State from hiding a cache of weapons-usable material. The technical aspects of verification can be mastered once the world community has joined in a determination that the maintenance of nuclear deterrence is incompatible with global security. Though we seem to be still a long way from such recognition, the efforts to have the International Court of Justice rule on the legitimacy of nuclear weapons and the moratorium on testing are steps in the right direction.

The Gandhi Foundation has issued (along the same lines as Mikhail Gorbachev's approach and the speech by Rajiv Gandhi to the UN Third Special Session on Disarmament in 1988) an action plan leading, in stages, to the elimination of all nuclear weapons not later than the year 2010, based on a comprehensive verification system that precludes the production of any nuclear weapons. The Foundation succinctly stated the answer to the nuclear weapons dilemma of our time:

A comprehensive test ban would reduce the discriminatory nature of the NPT and such discrimination will only be fully overcome when the existing nuclear weapons States renounce reliance on nuclear weaponry and move expeditiously to accomplish its elimination. [12]

The reduction of conventional forces to minimum defensive levels is also a necessary step in building the conditions for global security. The post-Cold War record in this area is mixed.

The implementation of the Treaty on Conventional Armed Forces in Europe (CFE) has begun. Given the history of warfare in Europe in past centuries, the reduction of armaments and soldiers is an accomplishment. Yet the inability of NATO, the sole surviving military alliance, to deal with the genocidal aggression in Bosnia and Herzegovina puzzles the world community. The re-structuring of NATO forces is clouded by the economic recession and the lack of a clear plan for the role of NATO in the European security structure designed by the CSCE.

Though world military expenditures fell by fifteen percent in 1992 [13], NATO's expenditure actually rose, as a result of the Gulf War; the main reason for the world fall was the halving of defence spending in one year by the successor states of the USSR. The global arms trade fell by about 25 percent in 1992, but the USA retained the position it achieved in 1991 as the dominant arms-exporting country, accounting for 46 percent of all transfers in 1992.

Though military expenditures by developing countries as a whole have been falling, the nations of East and Southeast Asia are engaged in accelerating arms races. China and Taiwan are upgrading their military programs. Indonesia, Japan, Malaysia, Singapore, Thailand and North and South Korea are involved in major arms acquisition programs and the development of high-tech military industries. These Pacific Rim countries are importing not only complex weapon systems but, more important, the technology with which to manufacture them. Michael T. Klare, Director of the Five College Program in Peace and World Security Studies, says, "Without arms control and regional security measures, the Pacific Rim could one day be the site of a major conflagration." [14]

Meanwhile, arms transfer contracts are outstanding with almost every Middle Eastern state, the post-Gulf War effort to limit the sale of arms into this volatile region proving as feeble as in the past. Large orders for arms have been placed by Egypt, Israel and several States located around the Persian Gulf. Greece and Turkey have imported large volumes of weapons. Even Canada, a relatively minor player in the world arms trade, has jumped into the Middle East market. In 1992, Canada exported $227 million in military goods to Saudi Arabia, including $217 million in armoured vehicles [15]; Canada expects to sell an additional $1 billion worth of armoured vehicles over the next few years.

In the principal supplier states — the USA, Russia, Britain, France, Germany — overcapacity has intensified the economic motivation to sell arms. The aim is to obtain hard currency, preserve the defence industrial base, keep military production workers employed, and bring down the unit cost of production of sophisticated equipment by increasing the production run.

The new United Nations Register of Conventional Arms constitutes the only current international effort in which both supplier and recipient states cooperate to address the excessive accumulation of weapons worldwide. Though weak because it is not mandatory and covers only certain classes of weapons with skeletal information, the Register at least provides the beginning of an international accounting of conventional arms; transparency is a precondition for control.

The picture that emerges out of these cross-currents of facts about weaponry in the post-Cold War era is one of continued reliance on militarism as the guarantor of security. Though world totals have declined from the heights of Cold War spending, arms production is driven by a repetition of the idea that it is necessary. This condition will likely linger in world consciousness for some time — at least until the other components of global security are given as much attention in public policy as military production. The peace dividend awaits.

The search for human security

In addition to the proliferation of arms, there are three other major impediments to humanity's well-being and progress: dehumanizing poverty in large parts of the world, environmental degradation, and the relative absence of democratic values within nations and in relations between nations. These elements point to the security of people, not just the security of territory, as a critical need today. It is not just security through arms but security through development, job security, security for education and health, security for the sustainability of the planet's life-support systems that are now uppermost.

The Global Summit on Social Development, to be held in 1995, provides the opportunity for governments to seal a global compact on basic human development to ensure universal access to primary health care, basic education, safe drinking water, child nutrition and family planning services by the year 2000.

Considering what is still spent on arms despite the end of the Cold War, it is clear that the world community has the means at hand to end mass malnutrition, preventable disease and widespread illiteracy, particularly among children. UNICEF estimates the additional cost for such a program would be about $25 billion a year [16]. For this sum, major childhood diseases could be controlled, the rate of child malnutrition halved, clean water and safe sanitation provided to all communities, family planning services made universally available, and every child provided with at least a basic education. A fraction of existing military budgets would provide this money.

> The time has ... come to banish in shame the notion that the world cannot afford to meet the basic needs of almost every man, woman and child for adequate food, safe water, primary health care, family planning and a basic education. [17]

Aid by itself cannot provide the equitable development needed to stabilize life in the developing countries. Those who support a movement to meet basic human needs must also be aware that action on debt, trade, loans and on trading relationships is a necessary part of the development struggle. The developing world needs investment: in its peoples' health and education; in the infrastructure of transport, communications, and energy; in its industrial enterprises. Yet large parts of the developing world are not able to make that investment. The cause is not only high levels of military spending but the enormous debt load — $1.3 trillion — requiring 20 percent of all export earning just to service. Capital and interest repayments are three times as much as the aid received from all sources. Investments and loans from outside the South have almost ceased as more than $100 billion has gone to Eastern Europe, especially Russia, and to reconstruction in the Persian Gulf.

Some developing countries are acquiring the technologies to enable them to increase exports and create jobs and incomes at home. But that opportunity is being denied them by the tariffs, quotas, and other restrictions imposed by the industrialized nations. Such barriers are today costing the developing world $50 billion a year in lost earnings. Moreover, as UN figures show, the gap between the richest and poorest peoples of the world has widened dramatically in the past 30 years, indicating that market forces alone do not help the poorest. Specific government policies are needed not just to promote the right kind of growth but to translate that growth into improvements in the lives of the disadvantaged.

Mahbub ul Haq, chief editor of the Human Development Report, published annually by the UN Development Programme, lists a five-point agenda concentrating on these developing country needs:

First, freeze military expenditures in the South by phasing out military bases and assistance; the North to reduce subsidies to arms merchants.

Second, develop regional alliances for peace in the developing world.

Third, re-direct the money saved by freezing military spending in the South to a $50 billion peace dividend investment. For its part, the North to restructure aid so that it goes to the people who need it most.

Fourth, make the link that as military spending declines, social expenditures rise.

Fifth, the UN to set up a new Economic Security Council, composed of representatives of the North and South with no veto, to take up issues bound to dominate early 21st century life: food security, humanitarian assistance, environmental degradation, drugs, AIDS, and migration.

Dr. Haq adds:

The new challenge is human security. It demands new concepts, new policies, new institutional initiatives. [18]

An ethical perspective

The 1992 Earth Summit in Rio put a global spotlight on the relationship of the environment and development as key components of global security. While falling short of expectations, the Earth Summit established an agenda for the 21st century (*Agenda 21*) dealing with a vast range of issues affecting the environment and the economy, such as: protection of the atmosphere and of the oceans; combatting deforestation, desertification and drought; the role of indigenous peoples and of women in implementing sustainable development; the meeting of basic human needs, such as health, education and housing; the eradication of poverty; and the transition to patterns of production and consumption in the industrialized countries, which would significantly reduce their disproportionate contribution to the deterioration of the earth's environment.

Agenda 21, carried forward by the UN Commission on Sustainable Development, requires not just adjustments in national policies and more money than was committed at Rio but a change in thinking. Changes in economic policies will only come about through a holistic approach to sustainability and equity. And educating the public to this wider vision is only beginning.

The 1993 Pugwash Conference studied the crucial issue of sustainable development and noted that prevailing attitudes driving an ever increasing expansion of markets and consumption would have to be overcome. Improved technology should mean that everyone has a sufficient standard of life to reflect human dignity. But widespread political resistance to global equitability stands in the way. This is very much an ethical question not likely to be resolved until there is increased participation of people in shaping their own destiny.

A full pursuit of Agenda 21 would explore four sets of relationships that must become the basis for public policy to uphold an equitable world order providing sustainable development [19]:

Relationship with the Earth. Each human being is a unique and integral part of the Earth's community of life and has a special responsibility to care for life in all its diverse forms.

Relationship with each other. Each human being has a right to a healthy environment and access to the fruits of the Earth, along with a duty to preserve those rights for future generations.

Relationship between economic and ecological security. Since human activity is rooted in the natural process of the Earth, economic development, to be sustainable, must preserve the life-support systems of the Earth.

Governance and ecological security. The protection and enhancement of life on Earth demand adequate legislative, administrative and judicial systems at appropriate local, national, regional and international levels.

The intersection of spiritual values and pragmatic imperatives, represented by the above four principles, was put most succinctly by Maurice Strong, Secretary-General of the Earth Summit:

> Changes in behavior and direction called for here must be rooted in our deepest spiritual, moral and ethical values. ...Caring, sharing, cooperation with and love of each other must no longer be seen as pious ideas, divorced from reality, but rather as the indispensable basis for the new realities on which our survival and well-being must be premised. [20]

Despite theological divergencies, there is a widening effort to affirm a holistic world view and the sacredness of the planet and the universe. There is also a growing agreement that humanity must respect life in all its diverse forms. The literature on this subject is growing rapidly [21].

Vested interests, of course, put tremendous pressure on the political machinery everywhere to protect the powerful. Yet the idea of global equitability is slowly gaining credence. It is this idea that lies at the base of the reform of the United Nations.

In order to sponsor democracy, the UN itself must practice democracy, which is certainly not the case in the permanent membership of the Security Council. For the rule of law and justice to prevail in international relations, the democratization of the international system is necessary. As a first step, the permanent membership of the Security Council must be enlarged to reflect the fundamental changes that have taken place since the Organization's inception. At present, Africa and South America are not represented and Asia is under-represented. A suitably enlarged Security Council should play its proper role in hastening the elimination of nuclear and other weapons of mass destruction. There is also clear need for an enlargement of the UN General Assembly's role in global security matters — especially in conflict resolution, including the socio-economic causes of conflicts within nations. A strengthened collective security system requires major advances in international law, including acceptance by all States of the compulsory jurisdiction of the International Court of Justice, and the establishment of a permanent international criminal court. Proposals for a permanent UN peace-keeping force and a UN Parliamentary Assembly are gathering momentum and are reflections of the perceived need to reform the UN.

Examining world needs from an ethical, or at least a more human, perspective leads to the key question of the governance of the planet. World government may or may not become a viable idea in the future. Today, it is not. But management of the inter-locking problems that transcend national borders has now become essential. This is the starting point for the Commission on Global Governance, a body of 28 international figures headed by former Swedish Prime Minister Ingvar Carlsson and former Commonwealth Secretary-General Shridath Ramphal, which will submit a report in 1994 aimed at reforming and strengthening global institutions. Recognizing that the era of absolute national sovereignty is over, the Commission has taken on the task of articulating a vision of global cooperation to institute political and economic solutions to global problems. Carlsson says:

The tasks before the world community will put great demands on us all, intellectually, but even more so, I would say, spiritually. We need to develop our identities, our feelings of belonging, of citizenship. If no nation can handle the issues facing it, on its own, then our identity as citizens must develop as well to reach out across borders. What we need now is a new global civic spirit. [22]

The Commission's real power lies in its potential to animate people to take, or retake, control over their destinies. This is the only cure for the sourness of this moment. When people organize, they increase their level of participation and increase influence over their own lives. The shift to democracy across the developing world has led to an explosion of participatory movements and nongovernmental organizations. The 1993 UN Development Report says that NGOs today benefit more than 250 million people, compared to 100 million a decade ago [23]. NGOs are often able to reach the poorest in society, where governments have not.

Global awareness is, in fact, leading to global involvement. And this may be the most fortuitous of all the signs of change at this transformation moment in world history. Though the scarcity of political leaders with vision and courage is appalling, at the same time the horizontal energizing of the world has reduced dependency on top-down leadership. Today, people in every walk of life have the knowledge, the updated information, the communication skills to influence people and events around them. These new leaders — the people who are committed to the equitable development of humanity — embody the hope to move the world from conflict to community.

The roadmap to survival is now clear: Political, ideological and economic domination of one group by another must give way to a new range of cultural and societal values to protect the common good of people who stand on common ground.

Notes

1 United Nations Population Fund, **The State of World Population 1993**
(Oxford: Nuffield Press). Current international migration levels are
described as an "uncontrollable tide of people", with women particularly
disadvantaged because immigration policies are biased towards men. There
are now 17 million refugees (in the conventional definition of a refugee as
one fleeing political persecution) and another 20 million fleeing violence,
drought and environmental destruction. The report points out that annual
remittances from international migrants to their families at home total $66
billion, second in value to oil exports in the global economy and larger than
all foreign development assistance from governments.

2 See **Human Development Report** (New York: Oxford University Press),
published annually by the United Nations Development Programme. The
1993 report states: "More than a billion of the world's people still languish
in absolute poverty, and the poorest fifth find that the richest fifth enjoy
more than 150 times their income. Women still earn only half as much as
men. ..." p.1.

3 **A Bargain for Humanity: Global Security By 2000** (Edmonton:
University of Alberta Press, 1993) treats this subject in detail.

4 The closing address at the 43rd Pugwash Conference (Stockholm, 1993),
"Reaching Out for the Impossible?" by Prof. Joseph Rotblat, President,
Pugwash Conferences on Science and World Affairs.

5 United Nations, "An Agenda for Peace: Preventive Diplomacy,
Peacemaking and Peace-Keeping", Report of the Secretary-General presented to the Security Council, UN Document DPI/1247, June 18, 1992. The
report makes recommendations to strengthen the UN's ability to identify
potential crises and areas of instability and to take collective action.

6 See the report of the Brandt Commission: Willy Brandt and Anthony
Sampson, eds., **North-South: A Program for Survival** (Cambridge: MIT
Press, 1981); the outcome of the commission headed by Inga Thorsson:
United Nations, Final Document, International Conference on the
Relationship between Disarmament and Development, UN Document
E.87,IX.8, 1987; the report of the commission headed by Olof Palme:
Independent Commission on Disarmament and Security Issues, **Common
Security: A Blueprint for Survival** (New York, Simon and Schuster, 1982);
the report of the commission headed by Gro Harlem Brundtland, **Our
Common Future** (New York: Oxford University Press, 1987); the report of
the commission headed by Julius Nyerere: **South Commission, the
Challenge to the South** (New York: Oxford University Press, 1990).

7 "United Nations Security Council Declaration", UN Document
S/PV.3046, January 31, 1992, p.143.

8 For a fuller discussion of the prospects for the Non-Proliferation Treaty, see Chapter 4 in this book and also William Epstein, "The Non-Proliferation Treaty and the Review Conferences: 1965 to the Present", **Encyclopedia of Arms Control and Disarmament** (New York: Charles Scribner & Sons, 1993).

9 Joseph Rotblat, Jack Steinberger and Bhalchandra Udgaonkar, eds., **A Nuclear-Weapon-Free World: Desirable? Feasible?** (Boulder: Westview Press, 1993).

10 Report of Working Group 1: 43rd Pugwash Conference on Science and World Affairs. Rapporteur: Regina Cowen Karp.

11 "Declaration Launching the Rajiv Gandhi Memorial Initiative for the Advancement of Human Civilization", New Delhi, May 2, 1993.

12 Ibid.

13 Stockholm International Peace Research Institute, **SIPRI Yearbook 1993** (New York: Oxford University Press, 1993), Chapter 9: "World Military Expenditure".

14 See Michael T. Klare, "The Next Great Arms Race", *Foreign Affairs*, Vol.72. No.3, pp.136-152.

15 Export of Military Goods from Canada 1992 (Ottawa: Export Controls Division, External Affairs and International Trade, 1993).

16 James P. Grant, **The State of the World's Children 1993**, published for UNICEF by Oxford University Press.

17 Ibid.

18 Dr. Mahbub ul Haq, address to NGO Committee on Disarmament Conference, "Disarmament, Peacebuilding and Global Security: Objectives for the Nineties". New York, April 21, 1993.

19 These four core principles have been adopted by Project Global 2000, a partnership of 20 international organizations, as the framework for a new global ethic (see Framework paper). Project Global 2000 is spearheaded by Global Education Associates, 475 Riverside Drive, Suite 1848, New York, New York, 10015, which has, for 20 years, published literature and conducted workshops on an equitable new world order.

20 Maurice Strong, Secretary-General, United Nations Conference on Environment and Development (Earth Summit), address to conference.

21 See, for example, Alexander King and Bertrand Schneider, **The First Global Revolution: A Report By the Club of Rome** (New York: Pantheon Books, 1991); Hans King, **Global Responsibility: In Search of a New World Ethic** (New York: Crossroad Publishing Company, 1991).

22 Plenary address by Ingvar Carlsson to 43rd Pugwash Conference, Stockholm, June 10, 1993.

23 Human Development Report 1993, Chapter 5, "People in Community Organizations".

CHAPTER 2

Reflections on Myths and Politics: The Not-So-New World Order

Carl G. Jacobsen

Abstract

Examples from the US, Europe and Asia make the case that ethnocentric and biased "histories" resting on self-serving myths and selective manipulation of news and information were defining parameters of the "Old World Order". The dominant apparent trends and early crises of the "New World Order" are then assessed: these include the questions of Communism or Bureautocracy — What died? and Russia Today — New or Old-born?; Yugoslav and Soviet Succession Wars; the problems of recognizing administrative borders drawn by dictators (often to split and weaken hostile groups while favouring others) as secessionist state borders; the problems of ethno- and exclusive nationalism. The compelling conclusion: today's defining parameters remain those of the past. Yet if the New World Order remains but a gleam, it is also true some of its promise can be realized, through newer structures and norms. These are addressed in the conclusion.

The New/Old World Order

The New World Order threatens to degenerate into something drearily familiar. It now looks quite as prone to self-serving and manipulated myth-preservation and myth-making, tribal ethnocentrism and the politics of fear and exclusion, as were older world orders [1]. If we cannot transcend the distorting bounds of our group or national cultures, then visions of a more just and less conflict-prone order will remain a mirage — the Holy Grail of our illusion, or delusion.

Parochial histories tell the tale — and illustrate the scope of the challenge. Today's predominant power is as susceptible to the foibles of arrogance and conceit as were and are others.

The American myth of invincibility lingers, dangerously, notwith-standing Vietnam, 1814 and other reverses — perhaps more so now that the Vietnam Syndrome has been expunged by the Gulf War, and the West's Cold War rival is prostrate. Celebrations of real victory can also distort. Glorification of Texas' "fight for independence", for example, stands in sharp contrast to Latin American views. Latin Americans see the story as the West saw Moscow's 1979 invasion of Afghanistan, with pretexts for war wilfully manipulated, to justify invasion and annexation [2].

America's 50th commemoration of Japan's 1941 attack on Pearl Harbor provided another classic example. The surprise nature of Japan's attack was "perfidious". Yet that was how Japan had attacked before, as against the Russians in 1904; if she was going to strike, there was every reason to expect surprise assault. Commentators also ignored the fact that the United States had established an oil embargo that promised to cripple Japanese industry, and presented an ultimatum and deadline for Japanese withdrawals from China that was physically impossible to meet. The view from Tokyo was and is different. Ironically, the United States itself launched most of its wars with surprise attack. The list runs from Indian Wars to more recent campaigns: the Bush Administration's 1989 attack on Panama; the Reagan Administration's strikes against Libya, invasion of Grenada, and war-by-proxy (and special forces) against Nicaragua; the Carter Administration's ill-fated hostage rescue mission against Iran; the Nixon Administration's secret wars against Cambodia and Laos; the Johnson Administration's escalation of the Vietnam War to North Vietnam, and invasion of the Dominican Republic.

But if the New World is prone to myth, the Old World is no less so. One typical example is the image of Richard the Third bequeathed to us through Shakespeare: a hunchback, ugly to behold, disliked by his people, a poor ruler, who murdered the princes who were rightful heirs. Yet a review of local and church records of his time shows a different Richard. He had no hunchback; he is described as handsome, well liked, widely admired and respected; and it appears that the princes may have outlived him — in the Tower of London [3].

The fault is not Shakespeare's. He merely passes on the history of his times. It was the history of Tudor propagandists, designed to justify and legitimate Henry VII's seizure of power after Richard's death.

The historiography of victors and successful usurpers of power finds no better example than Joseph Stalin's *Short Course History of the CPSU* (Communist Party of Soviet Union), which utterly distorted the cataclysmic events of 1917 and after [4]. It rewrote every stage of the Bolshevik Revolution, excised the name of Leon Trotsky — whose role was as crucial as Lenin's — and others, as well as any mention of Lenin's desperate, dying struggle against Stalinist dictatorship and chauvinism[5]. Stalin, a peripheral "grey blur" in the true history of 1917 (in the words of its foremost historian [6]), is here presented as its most influential figure.

When I first visited China, in 1971, the history museum was closed; a notice on the door explained that history was being re-examined. The disarming honesty of the announcement was novel; the underlying reality was not.

The self-servingly selective nature of national histories is evident in the myopia that bedevil Russo-Japanese relations. When Russia looks at Japan, she remembers Japan's surprise attack on Port Arthur, the fact that Japan's interventionary troops were the last to leave after the Revolution, the expansionary forays of Japan's armies in the late 1930s (finally defeated at Lake Khazan and Khalkin Gol), Japan's forward role in America's post-war security system, and Tokyo's later refusal to accept the southern Kurile boundary line that had been sanctioned by both the US and its own government of the time.

Japan remembers only early Russian challenges to its own designs for mainland expansion, Moscow's devastating attack on her Manchurian bastion in the waning days of World War II, the ending of Japanese rights in the southern Kuriles, and the threat of Soviet nuclear arms [7].

It is the same proclivity that allows Israelis and Palestinians, like Croats and Serbs, to remember only the other's evils — which are then seen to justify and legitimate those that they perpetrate [8].

Another aspect of national histories that makes them seem to come from different universes is illustrated in the following: French generals, seen in French texts as crucial to Washington's victory in the American Revolution, are absent or only incidental to US histories; Benedict Arnold, hero of British and Canadian texts, is *the* quintessential traitor in US accounts.

The point is not just that "my terrorist is your freedom fighter; my freedom fighter is your terrorist", though history's judgment on these matters can be capricious. Vidkun Quisling, Norway's Nazi collaborator, whose last name became a synonym for traitor, would clearly have emerged differently from a historiography of Nazi victory. Menachim Begin's terrorist past, including the 1946 carnage at the King David Hotel, appalled Israel's founders; yet a different context later allowed him to emerge as statesman, and Prime Minister. And there were and are many others.

The arrogant, racist-tinged myths that justified and drove colonial exploitation and expansion continue to reverberate in British, French, German and other societies. They are echoed in America's creed of *manifest destiny*, in Israel's *chosen people*, in Russia's self-image as guarantor of faith and fount of civilization (under Tsars and Commissars alike), in China's Middle Kingdom alter ego (again, no less so today than under older dynasties), and in Japan's notions of racial purity, and superiority [9]. The more absolutist (and hence racist) of these self-images all derive from scriptures, whose Churches and interpreters have historically, through policies of Crusades and exclusion, legitimized, exacerbated and rivalled the destructiveness of virulent nationalism.

The ideologies with which we sometimes cloak our prejudices, our instincts and fears, are equally deceptive. The self-proclaimed Communism of Stalin's and post-Stalin's USSR was in many ways the ultimate perversion, indeed antithesis, of that espoused by Karl Marx, and proved only that dictatorship can as easily adopt Communist as it can capitalist garb. Stalin's Marxism was shallow, if it existed at all. His *modus operandi*, governing style and system, was that of Ivan the Terrible — whose Russian nickname is more properly and more evocatively translated as Ivan the Awesome.

The same holds true of, for example, Mao Zedong. He also cannot be shown to have read the works of Marx, though he may have read some of Trotsky's. Still, if 5 percent of his ideology can be ascribed to Marxist influences, there is little doubt that 95% was rooted in Chinese culture, in the aspirations and dreams of the Taiping and other rebellions of the 19th century.

But if the Communism of our lazy theologies was false, then so was the capitalism. A Republican US President, Richard Nixon, introduced the first modicum of Medicare, though some of his countrymen had derided it as a Communist evil. Other administrations introduced female and universal suffrage, principles of elected and recallable officials and limited unemployment insurance schemes — other ideas initially dismissed as belonging to Marxism's subversive and nefarious realm. Even when capitalism was at its purest, in the days of John D. Rockefeller, his acquisition of Texas' oil fields owed as much and perhaps more to the quality of his hired guns as it did to that of his accountants [10].

And the Reaganomics creed that closed out the era of superpower duopoly was as much a perversion of its professed ideals as was Moscow's; with a tax system that favoured immediate wealth extraction (over wealth creation) and penalized both savings and longer-term investment, it licensed the feudal obscenity of dying-industry managers awarding themselves salaries more than a hundred times that of their employees, and million dollar bonuses that ultimately struck near-lethal blows at morale and competitiveness. It institutionalized greed *and* obsolescence; it was a caricature, and a perversion of capitalism, though some Marxists would see the perversion as its truest essence [11].

The *New* World Order

The proclamation of a new world order rested on the theses that Communism had died (and thus also the Cold War), that Soviet successor states had made final choices favouring democracy and capitalism, and that the Gulf War and UN intervention in the post-Yugoslav carnage signalled transition from peacekeeping to peacemaking and heralded a new era of co-operative rather than confrontational crisis containment and resolution. On closer scrutiny, however, all of these theses appear seriously flawed. Each derived from selective and politicized views of history; each bred precisely the type of partial, self-serving myths that defined older world orders. Rather than heralding the new, they again highlight the distance that must yet be travelled.

Failure of *Communism* — or bureautocracy?

The failure of Soviet and allied East European regimes is sometimes portrayed as the failure of Communism. The equation of Soviet and Communist is facile, and wrong. It also prevents the drawing of appropriate lessons.

What failed is not Karl Marx' Communism [12], which decreed the withering away of the state. He deemed the state's only purpose is to protect privilege; without privilege it has no purpose. What failed was the very opposite: a leviathan of a state, protecting a leviathan of privilege.

What failed is also not Lenin's Communism. Lenin founded the Party, and decreed its operating maxim of democratic centralism, a maxim which later, after his death, lost all pretence to democracy. He was indeed utterly ruthless in the fight against enemies of the state — Red Terror matched White Terror. But democratic centralism to him was not a recipe for the future; it was a means to thwart the Tsar's secret police, and to survive the bleak odds of civil war and foreign interventions [13]. He never governed as leader of the Party, but as Chairman of the Council of People's Commissars (or Ministers). The fateful 1922 decision to give Stalin the post of Party Secretary General, to control the flow of opportunists and new recruits, was made because more prominent Party members considered the job to be marginal; they chose ministerial and more "important" positions [14].

Lenin did not demand conformity. He took dissidents into his cabinet (notably Lev Kamenev and Gregory Zinoviev, who had leaked and thus betrayed the plans for the 1917 Bolshevik coup *cum* revolution); he encouraged vigorous internal debates, and placed no fetters on the extraordinary flood of experimentation in paintings, literature, poetry and the arts that marked the early years [15]. He acquiesced when outvoted — though he would work for another day, another vote. With the waning of civil war and the withdrawal of most (though not all) of the foreign armies that sustained it, he ended the stifling grip of War Communism and introduced NEP, the New Economic Policy that brought back the market and small-scale private enterprise [16]. He outlawed formal factions, but continued to insist on the free flow of inner-Party debate.

Only when impaired by a stroke, and looked after by Stalin-appointed doctors who limited his movements and intercepted his mail, did he realize that Stalin, by manipulating elections and rival egos, was turning the Party into an instrument of his personal will. Lenin spent his last years smuggling appeals to Trotsky and others (viz. his Last Testament), to act while there was still time, to thwart Stalinist dictatorship [17]. They dallied, and lost. Within little more than a decade, all members of Lenin's inner circle were dead, in exile, or in the *gulag*.

Stalin represented counter-revolution. Lenin's Party was internationalist, in vision and in membership, reflecting the tenets of Marxism, and Lenin's visceral disdain for chauvinism. Stalin's slogan, Socialism In One Country, spoke to a now different Party: Russian, Russified, and chauvinist. His form of government echoed that of Ivan "the Awesome". He crushed, then used the now subservient Church. The secret police became his personal watchdog and enforcer. Law was bent to his will, and his alone. The Red Army's leadership was isolated, and then liquidated; tsarist traditions, from epaulettes to ball-room dancing and Kutuzov and Suvorov medals, were re-introduced. Only duelling remained illegal! Stalin anointed himself Commander-in-Chief, and Generalissimo. Culture that did not glorify the regime became punishable by exile, prison or worse.

His successors abandoned the harsher aspects of Stalin's rule. Nikita Khrushchev opened the camps, and appealed for Soviet democracy, "Return to Socialist Legality" and "Leninist Norms". But his harshest denunciation of Stalin, his "crimes" and "megalomania" (in his Secret Speech to the 20th Party Congress, in February 1956) remained unpublished. His populism was reigned in. "Collective leadership" was asserted. The Party sought a new social compact, and to exorcize the demon of dictatorship. But though it had itself suffered perhaps more than any other societal group, or perhaps because of that very terror, it was now determined to protect the privilege of inherited power.

Freed from terror, the *apparat* found that it now controlled the levers of power. The Party had itself become the New Class, the establishment. As such, it was a conservative class, as are all ruling classes, concerned above all with the retention of power and the perpetuation of privilege, for its sons and daughters, and for their sons and daughters. Party officials became the new *boyars*, the noblemen of the day [18].

The parallel between post-Stalinist, neo-Stalinist rule and that of the later Tsars is quite extraordinary: autocracy — though striving for a benevolent facade; deadeningly extensive and intrusive bureaucracy; concentration of wealth and power; limited scope for private enterprise and initiative (at least prior to 1906); ubiquitous secret police; and exile, or worse, for cultural and other dissidents.

What failed was not Communism, and no Communist ever claimed that it was. Soviet officials proclaimed it the goal to which they aspired. Some did so genuinely, others not. Like General Pinochet of Chile, and other "democratic" dictators, they nurtured and gained nurture from foreign and domestic threats that justified pause on the road to progress. To put it another way: Stalin called himself a Communist because of the socialization process of the Revolution, much as Pinochet had to call himself a democrat, to accord with the aspirations of his culture and his backers, but Stalinism had as little to do with Karl Marx as Pinochet's bloody rule had to do with Plato. In the words of a British socialist: to blame Marx for Stalin is like blaming Jesus Christ for the Spanish Inquisition. (The Inquisition's end was surely greeted by some as the welcome death of Christianity!)

What failed was also not totalitarianism, though clearly some aspired to totalitarian power, enforced by overlapping levers of societal control, omnipresent police, informers, and neighbourhood committees — as in Pinochet's Chile. But the US Cold War claim that totalitarianism applied only to Moscow's dominions was so simplistic and ignorant, and so politicized its meaning, that it also distorted it. It was long evident in the anticommunism of Cold War *emigrés* (and later dramatized by the voters of both Eastern Europe and former Soviet lands) that totalitarian aspirations to mold minds or thought had failed miserably [19]. A totalitarian state cannot exist merely in the dreams of its masters, or the fears of its enemies. Although neo-Stalinist control was at times harshly authoritarian; it was not totalitarian.

But if it was not Communist and not totalitarian — except, perhaps, in aspiration — then what was it? Here I have introduced a new term, *bureautocracy,* because it embodies the essence of all-embracing bureaucracy and autocracy, and also because it facilitates the drawing of appropriate lessons. Bureaucracy, serving autocracy (Tsar/Politburo), legitimated by faith (Church/Communism), and bound by duty. The formula worked as well for Stalin as it had for the Tsars.

But by the late 1970s the context had changed; the Party's ideological Godfather, Mikhail Suslov, acknowledged that old formulas no longer worked. The superstructure was no longer appropriate. The base had changed. The country was no longer rural and illiterate; it was urban, educated, and no longer satisfied with the dogmas and homilies of the past. A middle class had emerged, with middle class aspirations, and demands. Marx' conditions for Capitalism in Russia — which he saw as the necessary precursor to Communism — were in fact being met. At the same time, the bureaucracy, able in the past to cope with evolutionary change and hide or circumvent failure, proved utterly unable to cope with the ever escalating pace and diversity of the high-tech revolution of the late 20th century. It imploded, in escapist corruption and self-serving greed.

Lenin's revolution, with its Communist ideal, failed not in 1991, but in 1924. Premature by definition, and so acknowledged by both Lenin and Trotsky who saw revolution in Germany as Communism's only sustaining hope, its failure followed the pattern of other revolutions that have sought fundamental socio-economic change. The desperation that fuels revolution is profoundly polarizing, compelling people to embrace visions that are necessarily utopian — for they must sustain them through the darkest hours — and expectations that no successor government can realize.

Revolutionary government cannot survive without compromise to its ideals. But if this course is precluded or aborted, the disillusioned will join reaction, counter-revolution in fact if not in name. Real socio-economic change must rest on cultural change and, as Mikhail Gorbachev so painfully learned, such change is always excruciatingly slow. The ideals of the French revolution are still not fully achieved. Those of the Paris Commune, such as women's equality and the right to recall elected officials, then dubbed Communist and subversive by the press barons of the West, are still being fought for. So also with the grander ideals of the *bolsheviki*; they will be fought for and quite likely hijacked and perverted again, whether violently or not, because they are also integral to the yearnings of much of humankind... In Moscow, the perversions of the system are repudiated, yet the ideals of the dreamers continue to resonate, and invite manipulation.

Yes, the Soviet *apparat* cloaked itself in the rhetoric of Communism. But the rhetoric was Orwellian Newsspeak. To talk of the death of Communism is to adopt that Orwellian Newsspeak. It is to be ignorant of the past, and of the future. To assert the death of Communism, with its concepts of truly equal opportunity and communal responsibility, is to encourage the very kind of rapacious (and narcissistic) capitalism that nurtured early Communist dreams, and that will inevitably revive them.

Soviet failure is not the failure of Communism. Rather, relative success and social peace in the West may ironically be due to the fact that capitalist societies could be and were forced to adopt more of Communism's demands for equal rights than was Moscow. Moscow failed because its ideals were betrayed, **not** because they were upheld [20].

There are many appropriately descriptive terms for what failed. One is neo-Stalinism; others, equally evocative, are state monopoly capitalism [21] and partocracy. The problem with these also, however, is that they suggest lessons that can too easily be dismissed as irrelevant to Western societies. The advantage of the term *bureautocracy* lies precisely in the fact that it, or its variants, may be seen to have wider applicability. The element of autocracy, as traditionally understood, may have been expunged from Western culture. Yet a stultifying, self-aggrandizing variant (power sclerosis?) might be seen as integral to the increasing bureaucratization of Western administrative structures. In the West as in the East, it is a phenomenon that alienates regions from the centre, people from government. Bureaucracies are the arteries of government; *bureautocracy* hardens them and clogs them.

Communism, like democracy (with which its ideal may equate), may at times and in places be perverted beyond all recognition, yet, as noted above, it will remain with us, because it also embodies some of our highest ideals — some see Jesus Christ as the first Communist, and Communism as the *sine qua non* of true Christianity [22]. Others have defined "Communism with a human face" as Social Democracy; and Socialism as "Capitalism with a human face". The ideals of our hearts may not be as different as we sometimes think.

Moscow: back to the future?

The 1991 "Revolution" in Moscow, the implosion of the *ancien regime* and phoenix-like proliferation of new, "democratic" states, appeared manifestly to confirm the New World Order launched and proclaimed by the Gulf War Coalition. Yet the new watchwords, redolent of Hope (at best), vainglory and hubris (at worst), mirrored politics and journalism, not history and reflection. History is not kind to too-rapid change. Revolutions beget counter-revolution.

The revolutionaries of 1917 sought to destroy an order they saw as unjust, exploitative and corrupt, as did those of 1991; both sought profound socio-economic change, universal rights and opportunities. The *Bolsheviki* were buoyed by the revolutionary wave that appeared to sweep Europe after World War I (the Bela Kun government in Hungary; the uprisings in Germany; mutinies in the French Army; the red flag waving over St. George's Square in Glasgow). In 1991 expectations of bountiful aid sustained visions of rapid transformation, but the hopes and illusions faded fast; by Summer 1992 sustaining visions were already frayed; opinion polls traced a rise in favour of law and order, and nationalist orthodoxies [23].

A different analogy, between the last Tsarist years and the first democratic governments of 1917 on the one hand and today's democrats on the other, is also notable. The lure of Istanbul and the Bosporus, promised by London and Paris at the outbreak of World War I, brought Tsarist offensives when Germany threatened break-throughs in the West; the offensives relieved the Allies, but doomed the Tsar. The successor Provisional governments acknowledged the need for peace, land redistribution and fair elections. But the Straits promise brought another offensive at Allied urging that turned into a rout and ultimately shredded regime support at home. In 1991 and later the offer was Western aid and investment, in return for adoption of Western economic prescriptions. By 1992 and '93 ever more reformers embraced regime opponents' refrain that this offer also was a mirage, because actual aid lagged far behind promises, most was tied to donors' needs, and the amount pledged plainly inadequate. The cost, adherence to an "alien" prescription ignorant of Russian condition and culture, was likely to worsen rather than improve the economic crisis [24].

Yet the sharper analogies, as well as some major differences, are between the early Bolshevik period and 1991-2. At the 1918 Brest-Litovsk peace treaty with Germany, Russia lost one-third of its population and one-fourth of its territory, including most of its iron and steel industries, the food-producing region of the Ukraine, Belorussia, Finland and the Baltic territories. Independence proclamations by Caucasian and Central Asian and other territories followed. Most were re-absorbed, in whole or in part, by 1926, but it was not until World War II that older Russian boundaries were re-established, minus Poland and Finland. The rush to independence by most Republics in late 1991 reflected similar centrifugal dynamics, again fed by the confluence of socio-economic crisis, the collapse of old, and uncertainty of new central power(s).

In 1918, beset by rapidly spreading civil war, foreign interventions in support of White armies in Ukraine and the Caucasus, the Baltics and

Siberia, and a collapsing economy, the Bolsheviks introduced War Communism, and harsh grain and other requisition policies. In 1992-3 also, the ideals of theory were soon buffeted by starker demands of reality and circumstance. Boris Yeltsin, as Gorbachev, failed to privatise most agricultural production — their "greatest failure", according to St. Petersburg Mayor Vitaly Sobchak — yet they had little choice; the reform economist and sociologist Tatyana Zaslavskaya's new Sociology Institute's first survey of peasant attitudes showed only one percent ready to accept the uncertain promise and insecurity of private ownership! By 1992 peasant collectives were again withholding produce and sometimes cutting output, in response to a new "scissors' crisis" that saw harvest price increases fall behind those of industrial goods and agricultural implements, whose deliveries also became ever more uncertain. Governments in Kiev and elsewhere again felt forced to impose and sometimes enforce increasing, state-priced requisition demands [25].

Another analogy affects personnel. In 1918 Party ranks were swelled by opportunists and careerists, for reasons of power and personal prospects, not ideals. So, in 1991, some "democratic" leaders, such as those of Uzbekistan, were erstwhile supporters of the August coup attempt, who embraced the new faith only after, and in response to the coup's failure. Also, in 1991 as in 1917, revolutionaries might proclaim socio-economic transformation, but the bureaucrats, administrators and managers needed to effect the new order were *perforce* trained by the old. In 1918 "old specialists" flooded into the Red Army, new Ministries and organizations. In 1992-3 also, and notwithstanding new names and the exclusion of those most prominently tainted by the old, the corridors of power and influence continued to be staffed by the *nomenklatura* of old. Bur(eaut)ocracies are uniquely trained and able to emasculate policy implementation. The Tsar's bur(eaut)ocracy became, largely, the Party's; the Party's, in turn, was also essentially reincarnated, and is today democracy's.

Under commissars and Tsars the Army was always part of, and never apart from the nation's leadership; the concept of military coup or regime is alien to its culture, and traditions [26]. A revolutionary context, however, as in 1917-18 and today, is by definition a time of flux, and uncertainty. Then, as now, the Army's conscript base and finance was ravaged; morale suffered under the onslaught of different loyalties; and some defected, to causes old and new. The best (arguably) followed

Marshal Alexsey Brusilov's advice, that while governments come and go, Russia remains; stay aloof from civil strife, but be ready to answer the call when your country needs you [27]. When Poland attacked, in 1920, they followed him into the ranks of the Red Army.

Colonel-General Boris Gromov, Moscow's last commander in Kabul, and perhaps most interesting of the increasingly prominent "Afghan cohort" (which includes also former Vice President Alexander Rutskoi) [28], may be today's Brusilov. The epitome of the professional soldier, like Brusilov, he resigned from the Army in early 1991, apparently foregoing Army leadership prospects and a Marshall's baton, to become Deputy Minister of the Interior, and what soldiers most dislike — a policeman. It was a measure of his concern. He reigned in, and reorganized the emergent network of *Omon* special forces security troops. Yet when his Minister joined the August plotters, surely assuming the network's activation, Gromov gave the contrary signal of no signal; this was not the exigency for which he had prepared. The Moscow Omon's defence of Russia's "White House" spared him guilt by association. By Fall, in a return to military prominence as unusual as his earlier departure, he was appointed Deputy Commander of the Army. In March 1992, echoing his Afghan finale, he directed the Army's withdrawal from Nagorno-Karabach. The next month he became the First Deputy Minister in Russia's new Ministry of Defence. He might have paraphrased Brusilov: stay aloof from civil strife where **Russia's** interests are not truly at stake! Conversely, the embrace of Russia's flag by the ex-Soviet army in Moldova, in response to Moldovan attacks on the dissident Russian population, a few weeks later, suggested that the Army may in fact now have identified today's Polish analogue: the defence of Russia's *diaspora* [29].

There are of course some major **differences** between 1917-18 and 1991-93. The first one, the one that drove Party reformers of the late 1970s and 1980s, was the changed nature of society. Earlier Soviet society mirrored that of Tsarist Russia — overwhelmingly peasant, poor and largely illiterate. It remained governable by the same, essential formula: authority, faith, discipline. The contemporary nation is fundamentally changed: urban, literate, highly educated, with a genuine middle class, and contemptuous of the homilies and dogmas of the past.

The second difference lies in the new reality of a far more interconnected world, in the global nature and impact of today's information and communications technology revolutions, and in the plug-in possibilities and potential that are inherent in the fact of an educated populace.

Third, the revolutionaries of today are not free from foreign threat. There are clearly neighbours that do have actual or potential designs on former Soviet lands. Yet these threats are obviously far less immediate and acute than those faced by the *Bolsheviki*.

Fourth, however: today's revolutionaries have neither the organizational discipline nor the focused faith of the early *Bolsheviki*. Most agree on the unacceptability of the past; few agree on the definition of the future. In lieu of vision, greed flourishes and undermines [30].

The comments above on the possibility that alien economic prescription(s) may be rejected, and of abiding military purpose and self-perception, point to the relevance of political and strategic culture. This is equally *apropos* when considering the applicability of foreign definitions of democracy. Russian advocates of foreign economic and political prescription have always ultimately lost out to more Slavophile sentiments and arguments. This is not to say that democracy is doomed to failure; rather, that definitions rooted in other political cultures are likely to be rejected. Russian political culture has been dominated by authoritarianism. But it also embodies its own notions of democracy, bred by its own historical experiences and aspirations. Today's context of circumstance and hope may be uniquely propitious. But if democracy is truly to evolve, then it must be defined and shaped by, and rest on these domestic roots.

The Gulf War

Against the background of Gorbachev's and Yeltsin's dismantling of the post-Stalinist Soviet regime and its imperial aspirations, the Moscow-supported and UN sanctioned Coalition war against Iraq did indeed appear, to many, to herald the arrival of a New World Order.

Yet the UN umbrella was more facade than substance: a promise for the future, perhaps, but not yet contemporary reality. The policies of both Washington and Moscow, as well as those of other participants, were true to older traditions and purpose [31].

Having denied Kuwait to Iraq, the failure of the major powers to deny others' equally brutal conquests, signalled their continuing refusal to abide by the universalist norms that are a *sine qua non* of true law. The fact that Iraq's occupation was in some ways the more defensible, at least of those in the Middle East, made the hypocrisy even more glaring. Historical atlases show nearly 5000 years of Kuwaiti authority answering to Basra, which answered to Baghdad [32].

The defining question and issue of the New World Order, and what decides whether it is indeed new or, rather, the resurrection of something all-too-old, is surely this: have we freed ourselves from myths of partiality, myths of selective purpose and temporal advantage? The Gulf War provided little evidence of real change. The next crisis provided even less.

The post-Yugoslav carnage: the media campaign; anti-Serbian "truth" — with caveats

The Croatian Relief Fund's TV and other media advertisements brought searing images of Croat victims of Serbian "aggression" into Western homes. Then came reports of ethnic cleansing and Serbian concentration camps. These were followed by the charge of systematic organized rape campaigns against Muslim women; the figure of 40-50,000 victims was and is generally accepted (some initial reports went as high as 250,000). Serbs became moral outcasts. Economic sanctions were imposed. A UN War Crimes Commission was constituted, with money and mandate focused on Serb atrocities, and Serb perpetrators. Editorials and op-ed articles in the *New York Times*, the *Washington Post* and other leading newspapers urged American intervention to save Bosnia from Serb dismemberment, and "Punish Serbs", bomb Serb forces and send more and heavier arms to the Muslims. The Clinton administration agreed, in early May 1993, though action was deferred for lack of consensus.

Serb leaders, followers and rogue elements had much to answer for. They had clearly been perpetrators. Yet they were also victims — not least of a manipulated media campaign that in its singleminded obsessiveness distorted the evidence, and made final judgment more difficult [33].

The persuasiveness of anti-Serb information and propaganda, and German insistence, drove Western support for the self-determination of Slovenes, Croats and Bosnian Muslims. The right to self-determination was not extended to Croatia's 600,000 Serbs. Little thought was given the fact that the Croatia thus recognized was the Croatia first given "independence" (and its current borders) by Hitler and Mussolini, with an *Ustasha* Nazi party clone, and a mini-Fuhrer, Ante Pavelic. It was convicted of genocide against Serbs and Jews, by the Nuremberg Tribunal.

Croatia's President, Franjo Tudjman, a Police General in the former Communist regime, denies the genocides of Serbs and Jews alike; his government and Party adopted the insignia, songs and legends of their *Ustasha* predecessors. To many Croats these were symbols of independence, and pride. To Croatia's Serb population they were starkly ominous, as was the suspension of police and judicial authorities in districts that voted against Tudjman in 1990 [34]. Tudjman's promulgation of a constitution that glaringly omitted Serbs from its list of recognized minorities, the publication of a *Black Book* (actually pale blue) that listed Serb family names in Western Slavonia, and the first ethnic cleansing, ordered by Croat commanders, sparked and fuelled the ensuing revolt by areas with larger Serb populations, such as the now "independent" state of Krajina [35].

In hindsight it is clear that the denial of self-determination to Croatia's Serbs was a tragic mistake. It was a reflection of the principle that established borders must be respected — never mind that Croatia's recognition denied that principle as it applied to Yugoslavia! To expect Serb populations to accept Croatian sovereignty was akin to expecting Warsaw Ghetto survivors to accept a German state with Nazi symbols — it made war inevitable [36].

The recognition of Bosnia, whose borders also reflected former Communist dictator Broz Tito's politics and purpose, and of its Serb Muslim minority as the legitimate inheritor of power, was also incendiary. Bosnia was historically Serb, as recognized by Nazi Germany when she annexed it to Croatia. Even after their wartime decimation, Orthodox (Christian) Serbs remained the larger ethnic group until the 1960s, when Tito first recognized the Muslims as ethnically distinct and organized the relocation of some Serbs to Serbia. Yet even today the non-Muslim Serb population, if one adds those who see themselves as Yugoslav or Montenegrin, rivals Muslim numbers, and dominates rural regions [see below] [37].

The Muslim-led government that claimed legitimacy furthermore rested on a temporal and highly uncertain alliance with Bosnia's third minority, the Croats. Croat support for Alija Izetbegovic's government was tactical, anti-Serb rather than pro-Muslim. By early 1993, as Western support for the Muslims and pressure on Bosnia's breakaway Serb state grew, and notwithstanding bloody Serb-Croat clashes in and around Krajina, there were instances of Serb-Croat military co-operation in the Fojnica-Kiseljak-Kresevo region of Central Bosnia; when Serb forces took and retook Sarajevo suburbs to the West and North-West they handed one, Stup, to the Croats [38]. In May, as fierce Croat-Muslim fighting flared in Mostar and elsewhere, Serb-Croat forces signed a formal ceasefire agreement.

Western media rarely reported such complexities, or their implications. The media generally accepted the Croat campaign's assertion that rebellions by Croatian or Bosnian Serbs were at the behest of the Milosevic government in Belgrade. There was little appreciation of the fact that many of the Serb rebels were opponents of that government too, or that many Croats, especially in the North-East, also voted overwhelmingly against Tudjman, and supported the secessionists, and/or union with Yugoslavia. Few reported on the Serbs who supported Bosnia's Izetbegovic government in the early days, until it reneged on the equally under-reported 18 March 1992 Lisbon agreement to protect constitutionally the tripartite nature of Bosnia's population and territory. This about-face was one of a number of occasions when the West's historical myopia and partisan morality encouraged maximalist Muslim expectations that ultimately served only to fuel and perpetuate war. One of today's ironies is that the government subsequently elected in secessionist Serb Bosnia in fact appears more representative and protective of ethnic diversity than the Sarajevo government [39].

There is a "Greater Serbia" spectre that sees the Serb populations of other republics/states as the outposts of imperial ambition, with the corollaries that their aspirations are extensions of Belgrade's, and/or that it is just to expect them to relocate to Serbia proper. Croats, indeed, remember that inter-war Yugoslavia became a fig leaf for Serb domination (partly in response to the legacy of World War I). Yet the Serb population constituted the majority of what is now Krajina long before Yugoslavia, and even longer before Croatia first became a state. Serb population pockets elsewhere in Croatia and Slovenia often had equally long or longer roots. Non-Muslim Serbs held title to 65% of Bosnia before the current conflict (Muslims were always more concentrated in urban areas); hence the Vance-Owen Plan, far from rewarding Serb aggression, in fact gives land to Bosnian Muslims and/or Croats that had never been theirs [37].

Serb paramilitary and private armies are assumed to reflect *Beograd* will, and their actions have at times been co-ordinated with those of the Yugoslav army, as in the final days of the siege of Vukovar. But there is ample evidence that many such units (now proliferating on all sides) have passionate nationalist agendas that would sustain them even if their supposed masters pulled back, while others are little more than bandit gangs. The infusion of mercenaries, from Iranian Revolutionary Guards to veterans of France's Foreign Legion, and British, German, Australian and other soldiers of fortune, highlighted the danger of anarchy.

The myopia and bias of the press is manifest. The *Washington Post*, France's *L'Observateur* and other leading newspapers have published pictures of paramilitary troops and forces with captions describing them as Serb, though their insignia clearly identify them as *Ustasha* [40]. A February 1993 *L'Express* cover story on *Yougoslavie — Crimes Sans Chatiment*, depicted a Serb paramilitary standing over "Croat" bodies after the fall of Vukovar; yet most were Serbs — as certified by the city's former Croat administrators [41].

When Muslim women's devastating charge of systematic rape hit the headlines, there was no mention of the fact that these pre-empted earlier Serb accusations. Muslim charges were accepted at face value, with no mention of the gynaecological evidence and psychiatric follow-up that accompanied the Serb case histories — Serb victim trauma, anger, shame and response closely resemble Western rape reaction patterns [42]. When the first "witness" to Muslim rapes, a young Serb captured and interrogated by Muslim troops, told of his unit's orders, it was splashed on every front page. Yet he also accused Canada's General Mackenzie of repeated rapes [43]. Editors cut this, but headlined the rest as fact. None asked whether the charge against Mackenzie, who secured Sarajevo airport for the UN, owed anything to his equally even-handed reports of Muslim atrocities. None asked whether the charge against Serbs might be similarly biased.

In April outrage focused on the Serb attack on Srebrenica; the scarcely covered Muslim offensive that took Srebrenica in May 1992, cleansed Serb villages in Eastern Bosnia and struck into Serbia proper, before the tides of battle changed, was forgotten, or ignored. There are countless such examples.

Ethnic cleansing was described as a Serb preserve. Yet, as of mid-February 1993, more than 50% of all Croat and Muslim refugees were in Serbia; this did not count Serb refugees (170,000 from Western Slavonia alone). As a result of sanctions and discriminatory aid policies, ignored by the Western press, they received only 5% of the aid provided to refugees in Croatia and Bosnia; the children and sick suffered disproportionately from shortages of medicines, diapers, dialysis machines, and a host of other essential articles [44].

UN agencies (and responsible media sources) acknowledged that atrocities were also committed by non-Serbs, yet Serbs were singled out as responsible for most. This was largely a matter of what was counted and what was not — and why. The detailed identification of Croat and Muslim camps prepared by the anti-Milosovic, opposition Serbian Council Information Center in Belgrade, with accompanying documentation of rape and other war crimes allegations, were excluded from UN reports and media coverage [45]. Some had not been visited by the UN because access was denied by Bosnian authorities; some, controlled by Bosnian Serb forces, were not visited because of UN mandate restrictions.

In February 1993 *New York Times Magazine* printed a typical article, on Milosevic's "stealing" of the January 1993 Serb Presidential election. It was written by the US campaign manager of Yugoslavia's moderate Serb-American Prime Minister Panic (who lost the election). Yet Western diplomats and other observers concluded that despite manifest irregularities, the election result and the second place showing of a right-wing party did reflect public opinion [46].

The diplomatic and other opinions were ignored in the article, as were the real reasons for Panic's defeat. One was Western sanctions. These did not constrict the now more homogeneous Serb army of the remaining state of Yugoslavia — its military industry was self-sufficient. But they devastated the lives of poorer Serbs, the old, the young and refugees. They caused a backlash of sharp resentment that clearly benefitted Milosevic. The second reason for Panic's defeat lay in his exchange of prisoners tried and convicted of Vukovar killings, for Croatian Serb prisoners many of whom were too young or old to have been combatants [47].

A State Department resignation protesting US inaction, and the letter signed by UN Ambassador Albright and twelve State officials that persuaded President Clinton to consider military action were presented in the *New York Times* as the considered opinion of area specialists. Yet only two had any area expertise at all. Most area specialists, who disagreed with both the analysis and the recommendation, in fact found the OpEd pages closed to them [48].

The *New York Times* embraced Senator Joe Biden's *bomb Serbs and arms-to-Muslims* call with scarcely a mention of its myopia. The targets, Serbian artillery, were less exposed than believed, and less relevant. All sides relied primarily on mortars, fired from ambulance floors (and therefore immediately mobile), and from locations protected by human shields (see below). The arms-to-Muslims advocacy ignored testimony that there was in fact no real weapons shortage; land and air deliveries were likely to lead to large-scale seepage to Croat or Serb forces; any lifting of the embargo would lead to an infusion of arms to all sides [49].

Newsweek's feature story on the Administration's early May decision to intervene (if the Allies would agree), followed the pattern [50]. The bloodied boy on the front cover was victim to the final Serb shelling of Srebrenica. Yet he should have left that city four days earlier, when 150 UN trucks were sent to evacuate children and refugees. Local Muslim commanders sent the trucks back empty, preferring to retain human shields. *Newsweek* made no note of this, or of the resultant moral conundrum. Three and a half of the four pages of pictures that introduce the text that follows were in fact of victims of Croat assault (from the flare-up of Croat-Muslim battle in Central Bosnia the week before); *Newsweek*'s captions did not note this, leaving readers to assume Serb blame.

Time magazine provided similar coverage [51]. The firing soldier in its cover photo of "Serb murders wounded man" in Brcko wears a uniform unlike any worn by Bosnian or Serb forces; a sign (Donn Zela) identifies the location as Slovenian; in fact, the picture was taken by a Reuters photographer more than a year earlier! And the *New York Times* also continued to demonstrate its susceptibility to ignorance, sloppiness, bias and jingoism, as when it headlined Karadzic's factual reporting of the results of the Bosnian Serb referendum as *flaunting* the United States [52].

Media manipulation as a prelude to intervention is nothing new. In the Persian Gulf, outrage at reports of babies thrown out of incubators so they could be shipped to Baghdad propelled the march to war. Only after the war did it become clear that the tale was Kuwaiti propaganda. The witness who testified so eloquently to Congress was the Ambassador's daughter; the incubators and babies had remained. Years earlier, the Tonkin Gulf resolution that authorized escalation of the Vietnam War, the Belgian "arms-severed" baby pictures that drove public support for British and American entry into World War I and the Hearst newspaper chain's depiction of the Maine sinking that led to the Spanish-American War were equally false. So also with other countries' PR campaigns on the threshold of war. In all these cases, however, it could be argued that the propaganda efforts, whether or not carried out directly by governments, did serve their purpose. Whether this campaign, funded largely by Croats and money that left Croatia after World War II, may be similarly described, is less certain.

Students of history and politics, politicians and commentators should perhaps all attend divorce court — before and after studying conflict in more formal ways. The lesson, that diametrically opposed yet equally logical versions of events can be construed from the same facts, when proceeding from different premises and values, needs constant reminder.

The lesson is not that we must not judge. It is that we best not judge so absolutely, for our knowledge is never absolute, our judgment never incontestable. To pretend otherwise is to embrace the banners of prejudice and war.

Soviet successor states: the larger uncertainty

The rush to recognize the independence of Baltic states (and others) after the failed Moscow coup of August 19 1991, appeared a moral imperative: the 1939 Hitler-Stalin pact was "illegal"; the ruthlessness of Sovietization, with mass deportations and Russian immigration, had been abhorrent. But what was being recognized? In the case of Lithuania, for example, was it the larger nation designed by Stalin, or was it the Lithuania of 1939 — smaller, and without Vilnius, today's capital? To Poles, Vilnius is Wilno, or Vilno, the city that gave birth to its greatest poets, to Marshall Josif Pilsudski and others — a **Polish** city! The *Belorussian* republic, now Belarus, would also be delighted to end the legacy of the 1939 pact; it also lost lands.

The horrors of Baltic Sovietization are undeniable. Yet in a sense the region's history reads like that of Palestine, where the horrors of one are matched by earlier horrors of the other [53]. For it is undeniable that Baltic independence from Russia (Latvia and Lithuania in 1917, Estonia in 1918) was also the result of foreign armies and arms — in this case German and British — and much horror. Lenin's Latvian Guard epitomized the fact that this region, with Finland (where German troops were also decisive in the ensuing struggle), was **Bolshevik** heartland, where their support was strongest. The rights of more recent Russian settlers in Estonia or Latvia are queried; historians remember Russian communities with older roots — expelled while German arms held sway [54].

Poles also remember Lvov (or Lviv) and Galicia, the heartland of Ukrainian independence movements, as **Polish**. Eastern Ukraine, with the Russians that make up nearly a quarter of Ukraine's population, and others who have been Russified, values its ties to Moscow. So does the Russian population of the Crimea — which Moscow or, rather, Khrushchev, gave to Sovietized Ukraine in 1955 as *quid pro quo* for loyalty and unity (and without even the fig leaf legality of Supreme Soviet approval). Does a de-Sovietized Ukraine have the same claim? Crimean Tartars, expelled by Stalin, but now returning, feel neither Ukrainian nor Russian.

All non-Slavic successor states have Russian, Ukrainian and White Russian minorities; in Kazakhstan they are the majority. All also contain other minorities, many with roots that go back centuries, and some that are truly aboriginal.

Each, including Russia, has felt alienated from the Centre; as in Quebec, that alienation spawned and nurtured dreams of Nationhood. All except Russia have long-established settler communities in their midst, like the English of Quebec, whose traditional privileges stoked fires of separatism. All, including Russia, also have their analogues of Quebec's aboriginal Cree and Mohawk Nations.

The Russians of Moldova, the Ossetians of Georgia, the Tartars of central Russia and a slew of other *nations*, most with ethnically distinct *Autonomous* Republics or Districts, declared independence in 1991. They were sometimes encouraged by those who wished to posit the same spectre to erstwhile Republics that these posited to the Centre. But that fact does not detract from the inherent moral question, and dilemma.

Today's democratic ideals are not new to these lands. They echo those of early Novgorod, before it fell to Moscow; of Cossacks; and the Soviets of 1905 and 1917. These democratic ideals generally transcend the question of individual rights; as evidenced also in the concept of the peasant *mir*, they tend to be communal, emphasizing the needs of the collective as well as those of the individual — duties as well as rights, for the State as for the citizen. It is also worth remembering, however, that such ideals have in the past always fallen victim to harsher reality, whether in Tsarist Russia, the Baltics of the '20s and '30s, or the USSR. The government that proclaimed Uzbekistan independent, in 1991, was the same that hailed the coup a week and a half earlier. Georgia's Gamsakhurdia government (since deposed, but long battling to regain power) embraced a racial exclusivity that echoed Nazism. Russia's *Pamyat* and Azerbaidzhan's religious zealots advocate latter-day *pogroms*. Lithuania's first democratic government conceded no minority rights [55].

Security borders: the need for a new prescription

The old prescription that borders are inviolate, a *sine qua non* of status quo power protection and power stability, led to *carte blanche* acceptance of Croatia's "established" borders — depriving 600,000 Serbs of their own right to independence from a polity they saw as hostile — and precipitated civil war. The same theology led to unquestioned acceptance of the borders of Lithuania, Ukraine, Azerbaijan, Tajikistan and others. Yet they contained others' lands, given by Stalin, for his purpose.

You cannot propagate democracy while condemning captive peoples. There are all-too-many borders that were delineated by dictators and authoritarian regimes, imposed by war or *fiat*, and sometimes specifically designed to contain ethnic mixes that would preclude viable independence; to recognize these is prescription for war, not peace.

You cannot embrace the right to independence of secessionist minded "democratically elected" governments and then stand back when, for example, Georgia's Gamsakhurdia declares minorities with roots that go back more than a millennium to have arrived too recently to deserve full citizenship.

You cannot accept the denial of civil rights to Baltic Russian populations because many settled there after Stalin's murderous pogroms against nationalists and Nazi collaborators. Many had ancestors who lived in these lands before World War I, who had been killed or exiled by German arms in 1917, and by British-supplied bayonets in the civil war that followed.

The point is not to disparage the yearnings of Croats, Lithuanians, Azeris or others. Some of these lands are like Palestine, where all can find earlier injustices to justify theirs. In Bosnia cultural prejudices are steeped in memories of more than a thousand years of slight and counter-slight, massacres and counter-massacres; when the past is unleashed, innocence falls victim. So also elsewhere.

There are some contexts where elementary notions of democracy demand either reciprocal border adjustments to produce more homogeneous populations, **or** truly effective political guarantees for minorities (see Spencer, Chapter 9). The former is particularly problematic in places such as Croatia and some Soviet successor states. The Austro-Hungarian and Russian empires were different in kind, leaving a legacy of ethnic mix that defy easy "withdrawal"; the roots are too deep, the numbers too large.

In older world orders the security of the state took precedence. If the New World Order is to be different, then precedence must shift to the security of groups and individuals, minorities of mind and circumstance. Democracy as majority rule does not suffice; democracy must be minority protective. Rights must be inclusive, not exclusive, and universal, not parochial.

At the other end of the scale the New World Order must also transcend the traditional bounds and prerogatives of the nation state. This demands a transcendent authority, a genuinely revitalized, more potent and more representative United Nations. This in turn demands expansion of the Security Council's permanent membership to Germany, Japan, India, Nigeria and Brazil, ending the exclusion of non-nuclear states and continents, and a weakening of the veto power. It also demands stand-by military potential, staff and logistics far beyond what is presently envisaged. It demands a qualifying and limiting of sovereignty for which few are ready, least of all the Great Powers. And there would always be the danger that the cure proved worse than the disease; the prospect of an omnipotent UN **bureautocracy** is not reassuring.

Whatever compromises evolve, people and nations will have to learn to see better the point of view of others. If, for example, national state histories come to incorporate more of the point of view of other nation states **as well as** those of their own and of minorities at home and abroad, then we shall have a different world — not a New World Order, for that is as dangerous as it is naive, but a more civilized, and tolerant world. Maybe the achieving is in the striving.

Postscript

Boris Yeltsin's unconstitutional dismissal of parliament in October 1993, which was an even sorrier precedent than his equally unconstitutional dismissal of Gorbachev two years earlier, spawned the instant myth of Democrat versus Reaction. The dismissed parliament was not Soviet; over 300 amendments had wrought fundamental change. Nor were his opponents *communist-fascists*. They had been elected as Yeltsin allies, and played crucial roles in opposing the *apparat's* coup attempt in August 1991. Parliamentary chairman Khazbulatov may have harboured Stalinist dreams, but they might equally have been Ghandian; he never had the power to demonstrate either. Vice-President Rutskoi, Acting President after Parliament's impeachment vote against Yeltsin, may have been rash in sending a mob to wrench control of TV stations, but he had legal authority. The first shots-to-kill were fired by Yeltsin-allied Interior Ministry troops inside the Ostankino TV complex. That and the assault on Parliament came after Khazbulatov and Rutskoi had agreed to early elections. They had sharply distanced themselves from their former ally. They thought Yeltsin's big-bang economic approach would lead to the latin americanization of Russia, and they feared his strong-presidency advocacy. Their fear was shared by many democrats. But in the end the distance that unleashed shots was reduced to six months; they demanded simultaneous elections for Parliament and President. Yeltsin insisted on parliamentary elections first with presidential six months later. For that, the precedent was set, blood spilled, opposition leaders jailed, parties and newspapers banned, **all** elected assemblies dismissed, and the Constitutional or Supreme Court disbanded. The promise of presidential elections was rescinded. Ironically, Yeltsin prevailed primarily due to popular and elite impatience with democracy's *sine qua non* of legislative bargaining and compromise, and because he co-opted core pillars of his opponent's constituencies, by assuaging the centre's economic concerns, and embracing the Army's

Russia First agenda [56]. The December parliamentary election campaign showed the fissures in Yeltsin's coalition; some hoisted extreme reform banners; others appealed directly to the constituencies and concerns of jailed leaders and parties, filling the political vacuum and setting the stage for renewed struggles.

Notes

1 C.G. Jacobsen, "On the search for a new world security order: 'the inviolability of borders'; prescription for peace — or war?", European Security, 1, No. 1, March 1992, pp.50-57.

2 Peter H. Smith, **Mexico, The Quest for a US Policy**, New York: Foreign Policy Association, 1980, pp.6-8.

3 Josephine Tey, **The Daughter of Time**, New York and Toronto: Penguin, 1989, pp.172-188.

4 **Istoriia Vsesoiuznoi Kommunisticheskoi Partii (Bolshevikov)**, Moscow: Gospolizdat, 1938.

5 Moshe Lewin, **Lenin's Last Struggle**, New York: Monthly Review Press, 1978.

6 N.N. Sukhanov, **The Russian Revolution 1917**, Oxford: OUP, 1955, p.2301.

7 C.G. Jacobsen, **Strategic Power: USA/USSR**, London & New York: Macmillan & St. Martin's Press, 1990, pp.346-351.

8 Edward W. Said, **The Question of Palestine**, New York: Times Books, 1980; R.A. Reiss, **Report Upon the Atrocities Committed by the Austro-Hungarian Army During the First Invasion of Serbia**, London: Simkin, 1915.

9 See, for example, *The Times'* (London) and *The New York Times'* coverage of the Paris Commune of 1870!

10 Paul A. Baran and Paul M. Sweezy, **Monopoly Capitalism**, New York: Monthly Review Press, 1966.

11 By 1992 US auto-executives' incomes (topped by Chrysler's Iaccocca, at $4.2 million) averaged five times that of their [more successful] Japanese counterparts, while US auto-workers received less than Japanese.

12 The main problem in discussing Communism derives from the ignorance of many of its critics of all but its most peripheral texts—such as **Communist Manifesto**; the problem is compounded by the fact that its adherents are also often ignorant of much of the literature. In part this may be explained by the very richness and diversity of the literature which, like that on democracy, transcends easy summary and simple definition. It may be explained by Marx' focus on German capitalism of the mid-19th century, which makes some of his writings appear outdated; by Rosa Luxemburg's

multilingual skills and correspondence — the bane of biographers and analysts; by Lenin's extraordinarily prolific, varied and multifaceted **oeuvre**, which in differing doses can sustain distinctly different legacies; and by the theologies of politicization, which have sometimes obscured the contributions of Trotsky, Gramsci and others. The major stumbling block, however, is the legacy of Stalin and the Cold War: in their embrace of dogma, neither Washington nor Moscow was interested in the nuance of theory or context; both preferred the simplicity of their respective catechisms of "quotations" and "selections" — and while those of different Soviet leaders were revised so as to reflect particular agendas, they remained partial, and superficial.

13 Lenin's correspondence with Rosa Luxembourg, who warned that the Party's organizational structure invited misuse. Note: at its apex democratic centralism is little different from the caucus discipline imposed in British-style Parliamentary systems. Where it differs—and what ultimately allowed the Stalinist perversion—is in its extension of that discipline to all Party members; and in the fact of a one-party state.

14 N.N. Sukhanov's "The Russian Revolution", and Moshe Lewin's "Lenin's Last Struggle", op. cit.

15 A Soviet joke had novelist Maxim Gorky turn to his companion, Lenin's urbane Commissar of Education Anatoli Lunacharsky, as they passed an *avant garde* exhibit: "I do not understand this modern art"; Lunacharsky concurred. Punchline: this was the last Soviet Commissar of Education who did not understand art!

16 The question of a socialist market constitutes the single most divisive issue of Marxism today. Opponents see it as an illusion, no more than temporary veneer for the inequities and law-of-the-jungle essence of the capitalist market. Adherents draw more positive lessons from elements of Scandinavian and Japanese market management; they fear that more regulated exchange mechanisms will inevitable degenerate into bureautocracy (see text, below).

17 Moshe Lewin, **Lenin's Last Struggle**, Monthly Review Press, 1978.

18 One joke had Brezhnev bring his mother to Moscow, where he shows off the opulence of his estates and luxury cars; but she leaves, for she fears the vengeance of the bolsheviki. Then there was the serum, to bring back the dead. Lenin is awakened, and offered power, gold and glory, but wants only a room with a desk, and back issues of Pravda. Later...tension builds when he does not emerge, yet who dares disturb him? ...finally, a hesitant, 'collective' knock, and later entry—but there is only a note: "returned to Switzerland; I must start anew!". In 1991 Lenin would have stood with the miners (with Trotsky—and Mao's spirit).

19 In its application to Nazi Germany, the term totalitarianism became synonymous with ultimate opprobrium. Yet the extreme politicization of its application — such as to Cambodia's Khmer Rouge only when **not** allies of Western will and purpose — has, unfortunately, twisted it into a mere barometer of prejudice, and political convenience.

20   These, of course, concerned the social agenda and the ability to stimulate growth — the essence of the Party's claim to legitimacy — not democracy as such. Failures of democracy alone do not spark systemic failure. One might note the $20 million plus cost of US Senatorial campaigns, which arguably limits access as effectively as did Party membership in the USSR; escalating costs and single-member constituencies in (other) Parliamentary systems may also allow special interests to thwart the will of the majority.

21   This, a consequence of bureautocracy, and perhaps the greatest single cause of failure, was also the ultimate irony: the market perversions and inevitable inequities of monopoly control epitomized *capitalist* evil(!); see for example Paul A. Baran and Paul M. Sweezy, **Monopoly Capital**, Penguin Books, 1968.

22   It is not the faith the Marxists decried; it was the fact of an often corrupt Church allied to government, manipulating faith to diffuse opposition, and perpetuate [its] privilege.

23   According to a September 1992 opinion poll, 80% felt they lived better before Gorbachev unleashed the first reforms, 67% favoured [past] socialism, and 50% had a positive view of Stalin (up from 29% in a September 1991 poll); from *Moskovskaya Pravda*, reprinted in *The Ottawa Citizen*, 26 September 1992.

24   "Rutskoi finds favour as Yeltsin's star fades", the [London] *Sunday Times*, 23 August 1992.

25   Sources in Kiev [not for quotation].

26   Russian history resounds to memories of peasant rebellions against the established order, to names like Stenka Razin and Pugachev. Yet the Army, as an institution, always remained loyal. There were mutinies, notably the 1925 Decembrists [Guards] revolt against the accession of Nicholas l; the Petrograd garrison's defection in 1917; and the Kronstadt [Fleet] revolt of 1921, which (as Lenin said) "lit up reality better than anything else", and led to Lenin's New Economic Policy. Yet the changes they wrought reflected the larger dynamics of which they were part; not the nature of their *metier* — they were **societal** agents, not military.

27   A. Levitskii, "General Brusilov", *Voennaia byl*, January 1968, p.19; see also David R. Jones, "The Youth of General A.A. Brusilov: the making of the unconventional, conventional professional", address to The Royal Military College, Kingston, March 1992 — and available from same.

28   For background on Gromov, the Afghantsy and Omon networks, see Sovinform Hypermedia on-disk release *Soviet Military Series #1; 1989-91: Transformation & Transition*, Carleton University Soviet National Security ORU, 1991.

29   See for example Stephen Foye, "Post-Soviet Russia: Politics and the New Russian Army", *RFL/RL Research Report*, 21 August 1992; *Voennaya Mysl* special issue, July 1992; and *Nezavisimaya Gazeta*, 19 August 1992; and C.G. Jacobsen, "Army and Society: Russia's Revolutionary Arbiter",

European Security, Fall 1993.

30 "Russia's New Code: Today, Anything Goes", *The New York Times*, 30 August 1992.

31 C.G. Jacobsen, "The Gulf: Washington's War; Moscow's War", Bulletin of Peace Proposals, PRIO/SAGE, London, Sept 1991, pp.249-255.

32 Geoffrey Barraclough, ed., **The Times Atlas of World History**, London: Times Books Limited, 1978.

33 C.G. Jacobsen, **War Crimes in the Balkans; media manipulation, historical amnesia and subjective morality**, Independent Committee on War Crimes in the Balkans, Ottawa, 17 May 1993. Contrast also John Zametica, "Squeezed off the map", *The Guardian*, 11 May 1993, and Vesna Pusic, "A Country by Any Other Name", *East European Politics and Societies*, Fall 1992.

34 Committee data indicates 80% of the Croat minority in Vukovar and Croatia's north-eastern districts (bordering on Serbia) voted against Tudjman in the 1990 elections that brought him to power.

35 The "Black Book"; **Tko Je Tko U Daruvaru**, Zagreb: Tiskara "Ognjen Prica" Daruvar, Jan. 1992; see also Mila Lucic, **L'Extermination des Serbes** '91, Novi Sad: Musee Historique de Voivodine, 1991.

36 See for example **The Uprooting: A Dossier of the Croatian Genocide Policy Against the Serbs**, Beograd: Valauto Intl & Beograf, 1992.

37 **Karta Nashchick Pobedela/Maps of Our Dividings: political atlas of yugoslav countries in the XX century**, Beograd: BMG (independent/Academy), 1991, provides historical population distribution maps of all former Yugoslav lands; re. Bosnia, specifically, see also **Territorial Distribution of Serbs in Bosnia and Herzegovina**, Beograd: [University] Faculty of Geography, 1992.

38 Radio intercepts. Larger-scale Croat-Muslim fighting erupted in late April 1993. For antecedents, see *New York Times*, 25 Oct. 1992.

39 Preliminary Committee finding; interviews with Serbska (the Bosnian Serb state government), muslim and opposition groups & citizens, March 1993—Committee archives. See also text below.

40 Committee archives.

41 Documents/certification available from the [opposition] Serbian Council Information Center, Belgrade, and Committee archives.

42 Rape and Sexual Abuse of Serb Women, Men and Children in Areas Controlled by Croatian and Moslem Formations in Bosnia and Herzegovina and Croatia, 1991-1993, Documentation on the Violation of Human Rights, Ethnic Cleansing and Violence by Croation and Moslem Armed Formations Against the Serb Population in Bosnia-Herzegovina, Belgrade: Serbian Council Information Center, 1993.

43 "Istraga Protiv Generala MacKenziea" et al; Committee archives.

44 For testimony/documentation, see Committee archives; also **Refugees in Serbia**, Beograd: Commissariat for Refugees, Feb. 1993.

45 Map of Settlements and Camps in Bosnia-Herzegovina and Croatia in which Systematic Rape and Sexual Harassment of Ethnic Serb Women, Men and Children was Performed, Documentation on the Violation of Human Rights.., op cit, pg 6. (this identifies and locates Croat-run camps, Muslim-run camps and "settlements in which systematic ethnic cleansing was performed").

46 This conclusion was shared by Western diplomats in Beograd and opposition politicians; interviews in Committee archives.

47 Testimony; Committee archives.

48 Raju Thomas, ed., Proceedings; Marquette University Conference on Yugoslav/post-Yugoslav Events (14-15 May 1993); forthcoming.

49 For elaboration on these points see General L. Mackenzie, "The Bosnian Quagmire", Interview with Kai Brand-Jacobsen, 8 May 1993; tape & transcript from I.C.W.C.B. archives.

50 Newsweek, 10 May 1993.

51 Time, 17 May 1993.

52 The New York Times, 16 May 1993.

53 The best coverage of the Israel/Palestine embroglio may be Edward W. Said's The Question of Palestine, New York: Times Books, 1980. Yugoslav history provides another, compelling example. As the horrors of Civil War unfolded, this author's fax machine periodically spewed forth Croat accounts of the bestiality of the Yugoslav army; conversely, Serbs were still haunted by the massacres inflicted on them by the Nazi-allied Croat Ustacha, during Word War II (which Nuremburg deemed "genocide" — estimates of dead range from 350.000 to 750.000), and by earlier massacres, under the aegis of the Austro-Hungarian army (see for example R.A. Reiss' Report Upon the Atrocities Committed by the Austro-Hungarian Army During the First Invasion of Serbia, London: Simkin, 1915). The bitter implacability of such long-nurtured, visceral hatreds clearly defy standard formulas designed to induce trust or guarantee security.

54 The best history of 1917 and immediate post-1917 reality is N.N. Sukhanov's "The Russian Revolution 1917", op cit.

55 The horror of Omon killings in January 1991 was (perhaps) in part fuelled by sanctioned or tolerated SS reunions in Vilnius the week before; after the Moscow coup Lithuania pardoned all former war criminals, ostensibly because they had been convicted in Soviet courts — and notwithstanding the fact that much of the evidence against them was provided by Western governments. See Sovinform Hypermedia release, Soviet Military Series #1; 1989-1991: Transformation & Transition, op cit; also Mikhail Gorbachev, The August Coup; The Truth and The Lessons, New York: HarperCollins, 1991, p.68; and New York Times, 8 November 1992 (for Yeltsin's appeal to the UN).

56 C.G. Jacobsen, "Arms and Society: Russia's Revolutionary Arbiter", Report to the Cooperative Security Competition Program, February 1994.

CHAPTER 3

A Military Policy for the Twenty-First Century

Leonard V. Johnson

The threats to Canada's security at the beginning of the next millennium will be situational threats arising from conditions in the global village. These conditions are already well established: soil erosion, deforestation, desertification, depletion of fresh water, overpopulation, poverty, disease, famine, debt and adverse terms of trade, to mention some. None of these conditions is amenable to military solutions. To the contrary, war and preparations for war can only squander the resources needed to ameliorate them.

On the other hand, these global situational threats cannot be met without military security. This can no longer be achieved by arming against other states but only in cooperation with them, however. The classical roles of national armed forces are being transformed from defence against military attack to service in multinational United Nations forces attempting to ameliorate the humanitarian and political consequences of the breakdown of civil order, whether through war, economic failure, or through revolution and political collapse. This trend is already apparent (see, for example, Chapter 6).

Rival nationalisms in multinational states, such as those which have torn Yugoslavia apart and which have appeared in the former Soviet republics, are likely to produce independence movements and civil wars as long as they exist. As states lose sovereign control of their affairs to global economic and financial forces they will be less and less able to protect the cultures of their constituent nations, thus weakening loyalties to the state among those who are threatened by changes over which they have no control. Anarchy and violence, not peace and a stable and prosperous international order, seem likely to characterize the world in which our children will live. Indeed, theirs may well be a world of perpetual conflict, a Hobbesian struggle for survival without boundaries or sanctuary and with no victors or feasible political or military solutions. Military intervention will take the form of protection and assistance to international authorities and non-governmental organizations attempting to feed the hungry and to restore political and economic order.

The material standards of the industrialized Western states are not accessible to the citizens of Latin America, Africa, most of Asia, and the micro-states scattered throughout the world's oceans. For that matter, they are not accessible to increasing numbers of the West's own citizens, people who have been marginalized by technological change, resource depletion, market trends, and failure to cope with new economic conditions in the world. Globalization of the world economy will benefit a few but it is unlikely to distribute wealth equitably or bring higher living standards to the majority of the world's people. To those societies with traditional and command economies lacking the ideology and infrastructure of capitalism, the present era may well be catastrophic, as those now being subjected to the decrees of the International Monetary Fund and World Bank are demonstrating.

In one of its dimensions, the global civil war now developing is a war between those who have too much and those who have too little — between those who have wealth and power and seek to maintain or increase it and those who are trapped in poverty and have nothing left to lose. Nor are the victims powerless: urban violence and terrorist bombings have demonstrated the vulnerability of even the most powerful states.

In this debt-ridden world, no state can afford the extravagance of military forces to meet remote or imaginary threats. The Cold War provided plausible threats that justified military-industrial establishments which soon acquired vested interests in preparedness and which safeguarded those interests behind a shield of prevarications and half-truths. Now that the threats have vanished, the justification they provided is no longer plausible. Canada, for example, can no longer afford to prepare to meet imaginary threats, such as Soviet lodgements in the Arctic or bomber attacks over the pole, or to prepare for distant, hypothetical threats invented to serve the needs of military and industrial establishments seeking justification.

New tasks are emerging which will continue to challenge the resourcefulness of the military and political leadership. The future promises to be different and more demanding than the past. It will be more demanding because new tasks are more difficult than the old and familiar, and because a very much higher standard of political and military judgment will be needed than were required during the static conditions of the Cold War. Hard choices must be made because Canada's military policy must not be held in thrall to political, economic and military vested interests.

What will be the military tasks in the future world, and what forces will be needed to meet them?

Let's start with what Canada will not be doing. Canada will not be part of a British Empire, as in 1914, when it was legally bound to imperial defence, nor will Canada rally to the side of Empire, when no longer part of it, as in 1939. There is no longer any such thing as imperial defence and there will be no more imperial wars involving Canada. The collapse of the Russian Empire in 1991 marked the end of the great empires that conquered, colonized and exploited so much of the world, and no great power can rebuild them. Without imperial rivalry, of which the Cold War was the most recent example, there can be no more world wars.

Britain, a member of the European Economic Community, will no longer be the balancing power in Europe, committed to preventing the domination of Europe by Germany, France or Russia. With the inevitable decline of the North Atlantic Treaty Organization, Britain will no longer have any special relationship with the United States, through which she sought to maintain the American commitment to European defence and her influence over American military policy while distancing herself from other Europeans. Canada and the United States will have no garrison forces in Europe or any commitments that justify preparation for another European war.

France and Germany, both democratic and embedded in the European Community, will not again make war on each other, as in 1870, 1914, and 1939. This will be so even if the Maastricht Treaty goes unratified and European union stagnates or reverses itself. Despite the resurgence of neo-fascism in Germany, it is by no means inevitable or even remotely likely that the conditions that led to the rise of Hitler will be repeated. What is needed is more European help toward the rehabilitation of the former German Democratic Republic, and especially the alleviation of economic and social distress there. Nothing is more dangerous to democracy than frustrated expectations arising from the promise that liberation from communism would improve the conditions of life. The West may have won the Cold War, but it has yet to win the peace.

Without the perception of a Soviet threat, the United States will have no justification for military intervention against the spread of Soviet influence, or to give security guarantees and military assistance to client states, such as Israel, South Korea and Pakistan. Although the United States is likely to remain the world's strongest military power, that power will not buy political and economic influence commensurate with the cost of maintaining it, nor will it protect its owner against the consequences of anarchy in the world economic and political order. There, and elsewhere, the protection of national territory and foreign interests, the historic task of armed forces, will diminish to coast guard functions against terrorists, drug runners and illegal immigrants fleeing hunger and the oppression of warlords with armed militias.

Without pressure from the United States to assume more of the burden of regional defence in the Western Pacific, Japan is unlikely to lift the constitutional restrictions on the employment of her armed forces outside of Japanese territory except, perhaps, in limited, non-combat support of the United Nations. Even if Russia and the other former Soviet Republics avoid the chaos that appears imminent, it is unlikely that they will become military threats to anyone but each other. China and India will be preoccupied with housing and feeding their masses. Who, in this beleaguered world, can afford to entertain dreams of conquest, and who will feel sufficiently threatened to continue to sacrifice scarce resources for unusable and unneeded military power? Surely the days of mass conscript armies and grand fleets are over.

What is not yet over is the vast flood of weapons that armed client states during the Cold War, the sales of which brought profits that helped to offset the costs of national military procurement in the producing states, primarily the five permanent members of the Security Council. Even though arms exports will diminish as national armed forces shrink and stop arming against each other, the M-16s and Kalashnikovs will continue to be lethal in the hands of private militias and armed bands seeking to profit from the breakdown of civil order.

Although it is not too late to stop the qualitative nuclear arms race among the five declared nuclear powers, it will continue to be relatively easy for even small states to acquire nuclear weapons and cruise missiles to deliver them. The technology of aircraft, jet engines, auto-pilots and guidance systems is within the reach of all but the poorest states, and there is no sure defence against them. Had the Scud missiles that landed in Tel Aviv been nuclear armed, the Gulf War would surely have become a nuclear war. Unless nuclear weapons are abolished under international supervision and verification, they will proliferate and nuclear deterrence will again be thought by some to be the ultimate guarantor of military security. As long as the five declared and several undeclared nuclear powers maintain their arsenals and their insistence that the weapons ensure their security, then who can blame others for following suit?

With the end of the Cold War and the restraint it imposed within client states, suppressed nationalisms have been unleashed and states are fragmenting into ethnic enclaves and mini-states with dissident minorities whose aims are national self-determination. As long as ethnocentrism is alive, it is unlikely that any multinational state will escape the centrifugal tensions of ethnic nationalism. Indeed, as central governments become less and less able to satisfy regional and provincial demands, power will tend to be diffused to clan, tribal and other traditional authorities contending for it.

Democracy — or at least the desire for democracy, however understood — has broken out almost everywhere, and democratic states do not make war on each other. The prospect of major interstate war is as low as it has ever been. There will be no war among the permanent members of the Security Council or the members of NATO, the Group of Seven or the OECD states. The Conference on Security and Cooperation in Europe, with its 52 members, is more problematical with respect to the Balkan states and some newly independent, former Soviet republics, but conflict among them is unlikely to ignite another world war, simply because they are not important enough to engage the great powers in wars against each other. Once the Cold War ended, the Angolas, Mozambiques, Somalias, Serbias, Croatias, El Salvadors and Nicaraguas of the world lost their temporary importance and gained the freedom to attempt to settle their internal disputes by their own means, including the use of arms provided by the cold warriors.

While democracies are not prone to make war on each other, democratic governments cannot easily impose sacrifices on electorates for the sake of distant and uncertain benefits. Unlike aboriginal North Americans, they do not weigh the consequences of their decisions on the seven generations to follow them, but only on the short-term effects on the electoral prospects of the governing party. Phasing out the private automobile would reduce fossil fuel consumption and all of its environmental and human costs, for example, including deaths and injuries exceeding those of most wars, but the consequences to all the economic activity dependent on the automobile would be unacceptable. Similarly, prohibition of the sale of alcohol and tobacco, if it were possible, would reduce health costs while depriving governments of major sources of tax revenues. Any massive effort to redistribute wealth would be bitterly resisted by the wealthy, who also, be it noted, are powerful enough to thwart measures that would reduce their privileged access to affluence. Even free elections are not a sufficient condition of democracy in the age of propaganda, political action committees, political lobbies and the mass media. It is not therefore, by itself, a sufficient condition of peace and justice.

In his 1992 report, "An Agenda for Peace," the Secretary-General of the United Nations identified four functions on which international peace and security will depend. In sequence, these are preventive diplomacy, peacemaking, peacekeeping, and post-conflict peacebuilding. These, it is important to note, are to occur within the existing Charter of the UN, i.e. between and among sovereign member states, not within them. Humanitarian or good-offices assistance within states or former states, as in Somalia, the former Yugoslavia, Nicaragua, El Salvador, Cambodia and Namibia seems more likely to command attention than keeping the peace between states, new instances of which are rare. Because conflict of any kind acquires a velocity of its own, the direction and speed of which are unpredictable, intervention carries with it unforeseeable risks and costs and no assurance of success in less than years and even decades. In any event, even if conflict could be contained by force, it cannot be resolved until its social, political and economic sources are dealt with.

What, in this context, might Canada's armed forces be doing? Coast guard tasks, such as surveillance and control of Canada's territory and approaches against small-scale intrusions, for one thing. Aid of the civil power against threats to the authority of government, as at Oka, Québec, in 1990, for another. Assistance to civil government in providing security when the task is beyond the resources of civil police, disaster relief, humanitarian assistance, search and rescue and opportune contingency tasks such as fire-fighting and environmental cleanup are others. All or most of these purely national domestic tasks could be handled by civilian agencies if they had the resources, but, as long as they do not and the Department of National Defence does, then they will continue to be performed by that department. On the other hand, unless there are military tasks that must be performed by military forces, there is no justification for maintaining standing military forces to do civilian work. Thus, the availability of the armed forces for these tasks depends ultimately on justification by some external military purpose.

Although North American Air Defence Command is finding new purpose in the interception of drug-running flights, none of these are via polar routes where the North Warning System can be involved. Without a credible bomber and cruise missile threat from Russia, the continuation and further development of which is unlikely in the extreme, it would appear that the North Warning System, the deployment operating bases in Northern Canada and the command, control and communications infrastructure of aerospace defence are redundant even as their modernization nears completion. This does not mean that they will soon be abandoned, but only that they seem unlikely to be modernized again. This issue will emerge when a replacement for the CF-18 is considered.

Canada's maritime forces are still structured and equipped to defend the supply routes to Europe against submarines in a protracted war. This also has lost its relevance. However, terminating the Canadian Patrol Frigate program — including its EH-101 helicopter replacement for the Sea King — would not be a simple equipment decision but a decision not to have surface maritime forces at all. Beyond Canadian waters, their future role will be to help to enforce UN sanctions against offending states and to prevent unauthorized intervention in conflicts.

Until Yugoslavia broke up, the future of Canada's land forces, i.e. army, appeared bleak. With withdrawal from Europe imminent and the small numbers of combat arms troops needed for peacekeeping, plans were made to reduce the armed forces by about 5,000 and most of the reductions were to come from the land forces. New commitments in

Croatia, Bosnia and Somalia during 1992 brought the infantry back into demand, however, and now there are too few of them to sustain the level of commitments (about 4,500), much less accept new ones. Withdrawal of Canadian troops from Cyprus and Germany will not change this permanently. Canada's military manpower will be severely constrained by its high cost, and so increases to the land forces are unlikely to occur.

The emergence of peacemaking has changed the apparent requirement from a few hundred lightly-equipped observers operating in a permissive environment to thousands of combat forces capable of defeating armed opposition. These demands cannot presently be met without the combat power, organization and logistics of the United States, which, if it is to be kept engaged, will require equitable burden-sharing from Canada and other states. The assumptions that fully-equipped and trained combat forces are the best peacekeepers and that Canada should provide its share of them need to be questioned, however. Above all, peacekeeping must not be permitted to become institutional justification for increasing or even maintaining Cold War levels of military spending, in Canada or anywhere else.

Once the qualitative and quantitative requirements of peacemaking are worked out in the laboratory of experience, it seems possible that collective security will be at least as demanding as collective defence. Military demands on Canada could well be comparable to those of NATO's demands on Canada in recent years, in which case it is doubtful if further substantial reductions will be made to military spending. Indeed, the so-called peace dividend may well be the opportunity to advance the cause of collective security, and thus to arrest the disintegration of civil order in the world. In so doing, the world's armed forces can find common purpose in the service of peace and security, cooperating to keep future generations safe from the scourge of war. The opportunity is too good to miss.

CHAPTER 4

A Nuclear Test Ban and the Problems of Nonproliferation

William Epstein

Contents

A nuclear test ban — The Non-Proliferation Treaty (NPT) — The NPT Review Conferences — The Test Ban Amendment initiative — The 1990 NPT Review Conference — The 1991 Test Ban — Amendment Conference — INF and START — Mass destruction weapon-free zones — Flaws in the nuclear proposals — Possible solutions — A test ban is the key — Recent favourable developments — An end to nuclear testing is now within reach

A nuclear test ban

No arms control and disarmament measure has been the subject of so much international concern and effort as a Comprehensive Nuclear Test Ban. The UN General Assembly has adopted some 70 resolutions on a nuclear test ban, far more than on any other disarmament issue. A test ban has been repeatedly described as a question of highest priority on the disarmament agenda and a litmus test of the nuclear powers' willingness to halt the nuclear arms race and pursue disarmament.

A nuclear test ban was always the number one issue for the non-nuclear states, particularly the neutral and nonaligned countries who were not covered by either an American or Soviet *nuclear umbrella*. Intensive efforts between 1958 and 1963 to achieve a comprehensive ban failed because of the inadequacy of verification techniques for underground tests. The United States, Britain, and the Soviet Union decided to sign the Partial Test Ban Treaty (PTBT) in Moscow on 5 August 1963, as a first step to a total ban. The Treaty banned tests in the atmosphere, under water and in outer space, but not underground.

Recognizing that all non-nuclear countries wanted a comprehensive ban, the three nations reaffirmed in both the preamble and operative part of the treaty that they sought "to achieve the discontinuance of all test explosions of nuclear weapons for all time," and were "determined to continue negotiations to this end."

The PTBT was the first international agreement of worldwide scope dealing specifically with nuclear weapons. It was hailed as a treaty of historic significance that would begin to curb the nuclear arms race and help to prevent the spread of nuclear weapons. But it has turned out to be more of a health and environmental measure than one of arms control. The United States and the Soviet Union proceeded to conduct underground tests at an even faster pace than the previous atmospheric tests. They have conducted more than 1,000 tests since 1963.

After the initialling of the agreed text of the PTBT on 26 July 1963, President John Kennedy, in a nationally televised address, drew the connection to nonproliferation: "This can be a step toward preventing the spread of nuclear weapons to nations not now possessing them ... This treaty can be an opening wedge in that campaign." The next step was widely understood to be a comprehensive ban. When the General Assembly approved the Partial Test Ban Treaty on 27 November 1963 and called on all states to become parties, it singled out and emphasized the provisions of the preamble and called for urgent negotiations to achieve the end of all nuclear tests.

The Non-Proliferation Treaty (NPT)

Efforts to achieve a comprehensive test ban were displaced between 1965 and 1968 by the Non-Proliferation Treaty (NPT) negotiations, which was the priority item for the nuclear powers. But the non-nuclear states made sure that a test ban played a prominent role in those negotiations as well. They put forward five disarmament measures: a comprehensive test ban, stopping production of fissile material for weapons, freezing and gradually reducing nuclear weapons stocks and delivery vehicles, non-use of nuclear weapons, and security guarantees by the nuclear powers to non-nuclear states. A comprehensive test ban was always at the top of the list, the one indispensable measure to end or at least restrain the nuclear arms race and to prevent the development of nuclear weapons by the nuclear powers as well as by the non-nuclear states.

During the NPT negotiations, the three participating nuclear powers — France and China were not present — were desperate to achieve agreement, and the non-nuclear states used their leverage to offset the inherently discriminatory nature of the treaty, which divided the world into a few nuclear-weapon *have* and many *have-not* states. The result was Article VI, by which the nuclear powers promise to negotiate first a halt to the nuclear arms race and then nuclear disarmament, as well as paragraph 10 of the Preamble emphasizing their determination to continue negotiations to achieve a comprehensive test ban.

All parties understood that the inclusion of that preambular paragraph signified that a test ban was the primary measure for achieving "the cessation of the nuclear arms race at an early date," provided for in Article VI. Ambassador Arthur Goldberg, US permanent representative to the NPT negotiations, told the General Assembly on 12 June 1968: "The language of this article indicates a practical order of priorities ... headed by cessation of the nuclear arms race at an early date 'and proceeding next to nuclear disarmament' and finally to general and complete disarmament."

Today the United States and Britain insist that nuclear disarmament, not a test ban, should have the highest priority. Although a comprehensive test ban cannot by itself stop the nuclear arms race, the qualitative race cannot be halted without a test ban. It is also clear that the pledge of the nuclear powers in Article VI to end their *vertical* proliferation of nuclear weapons was the most important obligation they undertook in exchange for the binding commitment of the non-nuclear states not to engage in *horizontal* proliferation.

The NPT review conferences

Prior to 1990, three review conferences were held — in 1975, 1980 and 1985 — to assess the operation of the NPT "with a view to assuring that the purpose of the preamble and the provisions of the treaty are being realized." At each of them, the non-nuclear states, especially the nonaligned nations, placed main emphasis on Article VI and on ending all testing, beginning with a moratorium on underground tests.

In 1975, a fragile consensus was achieved on a final declaration in which the nuclear powers in effect promised to try harder to meet the demands of the non-nuclear states. In 1980, no consensus was achieved. The nuclear powers would not agree to begin negotiations for a comprehensive test ban, and the review conference ended in failure without even a formal reaffirmation of support for the NPT. At this conference, Sigvard Eklund, Director General of the International Atomic Energy Agency (IAEA) stated:

> The nonproliferation regime can only survive on the tripod of the NPT, effective international safeguards, and a Comprehensive Test Ban Treaty. The vital third leg is still missing as it was five years ago.

It is still missing to this day, 1994.

In 1985, no consensus seemed likely at the end of the review. The nonaligned parties called for a vote on three resolutions: that the three participating nuclear powers resume negotiations immediately for a comprehensive test ban treaty; that testing be halted pending the conclusion of such a treaty; and that the testing, production and deployment of nuclear weapons be frozen. Fearing the resolutions would be adopted, the United States and its allies decided to agree to almost any reasonable compromise that would avert a vote.

The compromise was expressed in the final declaration as follows:

> The conference, except for certain states, deeply regretted that a comprehensive multilateral Nuclear Test Ban Treaty banning all nuclear tests by all states in all environments for all time had not been concluded so far and, therefore, called on the nuclear weapon states party to the Treaty to resume trilateral negotiations in 1985 and called on all the nuclear weapon states to participate in the urgent negotiation and conclusion of such a treaty as a matter of highest priority.

The declaration also noted that "certain states" considered deep and verifiable reductions in existing arsenals of nuclear weapons as having the highest priority. The "certain states" in both references were the United States and Britain.

The clear message from the non-nuclear states in the 1985 final document, and expressed on many occasions before and since, was that the nuclear parties must abide by their treaty obligations to halt and reverse the nuclear arms race if the NPT is to endure.

Despite all this, no comprehensive test ban negotiations — bilateral, trilateral, or multilateral — have taken place since talks were suspended in 1980. Although every American President from Eisenhower to Carter favoured a total test ban subject only to adequate verification, Ronald Reagan refused to renew the negotiations, and the US position has continued to harden against a comprehensive test ban. Non-nuclear states are becoming increasingly disillusioned by their failure to persuade the nuclear powers to live up to their treaty obligations, and this is eroding their confidence not only in the sincerity of the nuclear powers but also in the nonproliferation process itself.

The nuclear powers and industrial states, for their part, are growing more concerned about the proliferation of chemical weapons and sophisticated missiles among developing countries. The latter, however, are suspicious of what they regard as efforts to extend the nonproliferation process from the nuclear field to these additional areas. Having been let down by the nuclear powers' disregard of their NPT obligations, most are unwilling to put their faith in other nonproliferation regimes. This attitude was evident at the Paris Conference on chemical weapons in January 1989 and at a September 1989 government-industry conference of manufacturers of chemical agents in Australia. When the chemical weapons convention to eliminate all chemical weapons on a global basis was approved in 1992, it received the support of the neutral and nonaligned states since it applied to all states equally on a nondiscriminatory basis.

The Test Ban Amendment initiative

Frustrated by the refusal of the United States and Britain to begin negotiations for a comprehensive test ban (the Soviet Union had consistently expressed willingness to do so and had called for a test moratorium), in 1988 a group of nonaligned states led by Mexico decided to take action themselves. They took up an idea initiated by Parliamentarians for Global Action, a New York-based organization, in order to take advantage of the amendment provisions of the Partial Test Ban Treaty. On 5 August 1988, the 25th Anniversary of the signing of the PTBT, six parties to the Treaty — Indonesia, Mexico, Peru, Sri Lanka, Venezuela, and Yugoslavia — formally proposed to the three depositary governments (the Soviet Union, Britain and the United States) that a conference be convened to convert the Partial Test Ban Treaty into a Comprehensive Test Ban Treaty.

To the surprise of sceptics, the idea gained momentum in a series of General Assembly resolutions. By April 1989, more than the required one-third of the 118 parties had joined in the request, and the three depositary governments announced that they would abide by their treaty obligations and convene the conference in January 1991. Although only a majority of the current 121 parties, 61, must approve and ratify an amendment in order for it to enter into force, the three nuclear powers must be included in that majority and thus had a veto. The Soviet Union supported the amendment but the United States and Britain were opposed and have for years blocked all attempts to begin multilateral negotiations.

But the non-nuclear states believe that reason and public opinion are on their side and that the amendment initiative will eventually succeed. They do not regard the amendment conference as limited to a single session but as one that should continue for as many sessions as are required to achieve a consensus on a test ban. No votes will be taken until this occurs, so there will be no occasion for a veto.

Most of all, they rely on the linkage between a comprehensive test ban and the NPT to work to their advantage. The Partial Test Ban Treaty has a unique provision: once an amendment is ratified by the requisite majority, including the three depositaries, it becomes automatically binding on **all** parties. Argentina, Brazil, India, Israel, and Pakistan, which are considered to be near-nuclear powers, are all parties to the PTBT but not to the NPT. Hence they would all be bound by a comprehensive test ban amendment, which would be monitored by a detailed verification system. In this way, a comprehensive ban would curb both horizontal and vertical proliferation. The fact that the five hold-out countries would be bound by the comprehensive ban should provide a powerful incentive to the three nuclear parties to ratify the amendment.

Nearly all non-nuclear states, except the allies of the United States and Britain, are convinced that the nuclear arms race cannot be stopped unless all tests are stopped. They regard the 1990 Threshold

Test Ban Treaty and Peaceful Nuclear Explosions Treaty as mockeries because of the high thresholds at which the ban applies — 150 kilotons of explosive power — more than ten times the size of the Hiroshima bomb; moreover, these treaties would legitimate continued testing. The non-nuclear states also point out that even cutting the size of strategic arsenals by half would leave the superpowers with more than three times as many strategic weapons as they had when the NPT was signed in 1968.

For their part, US representatives have stated that if a comprehensive test ban is the price for preserving the NPT in 1995, the United States would abandon the Treaty. In December 1989, *Disarmament Times*, a UN-related publication, quoted Kathleen Bailey of the US Arms Control and Disarmament Agency:

> If the USA is forced to choose between its own national security and its nuclear testing program versus the survival of the NPT — which we would dearly like to see — the USA would choose maintenance of its own national security and therefore its own nuclear testing program.

The 1990 NPT Review Conference

Such was the backdrop for the fourth review conference of the Non-Proliferation Treaty (NPT), which was convened in Geneva during August-September 1990. Though the participants failed to agree on a final declaration or even a formal reaffirmation of support for the treaty, some of them considered the meeting a qualified success. It was the most interesting review to date because participants had their eyes fixed on 1995, when the first term of the NPT expires and a conference must be called to decide the treaty's future. Because the main decision at the future conference — how long to extend the NPT — will require a simple majority, the non-nuclear parties have acquired the kind of political leverage they have not possessed since the treaty was first negotiated.

The nonaligned and other non-nuclear states came to the 1990 review prepared to use their renewed leverage to once again press the case for a comprehensive test ban and nuclear disarmament. These demands were contained in a resolution listing many measures to halt and reverse the nuclear arms race, with top priority given to a comprehensive test ban and a moratorium on testing. Three other resolutions embodied the rest of the agenda. One focused on enhancing the International Atomic Energy Agency (IAEA) in its tasks of promoting peaceful uses of nuclear energy and safeguarding the nonproliferation regime. Another called for measures to strengthen the NPT to make possible a "significant extension of the treaty beyond 1995", including a total ban on nuclear testing.

Except for the measures regarding peaceful uses of nuclear energy and strengthened safeguards, the United States, Britain, and their allies found little to support in any of these proposals. Their statements mainly stressed recent arms control progress, which the nonaligned states claimed fell far short of compliance with the treaty. Although agreement with the nonaligned group seemed possible on many issues, it was clear that a confrontation was looming on disarmament.

The Soviet Union supported most of the aims of the non-nuclear states, including a comprehensive test ban and an immediate moratorium on nuclear testing as well as stronger security assurances to the non-nuclear states. On 25 September 1990, Soviet Foreign Minister Eduard Shevardnadze, in a statement to the United Nations General Assembly, supported a test ban in language stronger than had ever been used before by a senior statesman:

> As a matter of the utmost urgency, nuclear tests have to be stopped. If testing is stopped, we have a chance to survive; otherwise the world will perish. I have no doubt whatever about this. We need to tell people about this frankly, without taking refuge in all sorts of specious arguments.

Nevertheless, the Soviet Union maintained its traditional solidarity with the United States and Britain on matters relating to the NPT and insisted on the overriding importance of achieving consensus on a final declaration.

The main point of contention at the conference was in fact the comprehensive test ban initiative, with the United States and its allies on one side and the nonaligned states and some other non-nuclear states on the other. The Drafting Committee, under the chairmanship of Swedish Ambassador Carl-Magnus Hyltenius, produced a draft final

declaration containing some 135 paragraphs, about 115 of them representing consensus. Some 15 of the unresolved paragraphs dealt with
Article VI and preambular paragraphs 8-12 of the NPT, having to do
with disarmament and a test ban.

On the last day Ambassador Hyltenius entered into intensive private consultations in a smaller, balanced group of the most active participants in the conference. On one side were eight nonaligned countries — Indonesia, Iran, Mexico, Nigeria, Peru, Sri Lanka, Venezuela,
and Yugoslavia; on the other were the three nuclear parties and four of
their allies, Australia, Canada, New Zealand, and Poland, plus Sweden.
After hours of discussion, Hyltenius proposed a final compromise
which he urged the parties to accept without amendment:

> The [Review] Conference further recognized that the discontin-
> uance of nuclear testing would play a central role in the future
> of the NPT. The conference also stressed the significant impor-
> tance placed upon negotiations, multilateral and bilateral, dur-
> ing the next five years, to conclude a CTBT [Comprehensive
> Test Ban Treaty]. The Conference again calls for early action
> towards that objective, by the Conference on Disarmament at
> the beginning of its first session in 1991. The Conference urges
> that the ad hoc committee on a Nuclear Test Ban be given an
> appropriate mandate to pursue the objective of negotiations to
> conclude a comprehensive nuclear test ban treaty.

After a brief recess, the nonaligned participants agreed to accept the
text. But the United States insisted on adding the following paragraph:

> The conference notes the joint commitment of the United
> States and the Soviet Union to proceed with the step-by-step
> negotiations on further intermediate limitations on nuclear test-
> ing, leading to the ultimate objective of the complete cessation
> of nuclear testing as part of an effective disarmament process.

By insisting on this addition the United States was, in effect, rejecting
the chairman's compromise and making agreement on a final declaration impossible.

Opinions were divided on the failure to achieve consensus. Some thought it would do no harm, as in 1980. But others noted the special importance of this review because of its bearing on the 1995 extension conference. A number of the nonaligned delegations believe that their political leverage will increase as the 1995 conference approaches. In their view, the nuclear powers and their allies fervently wish to extend the NPT indefinitely or at least for many years, and will therefore have to negotiate with the large majority of nonaligned parties. For the first time there were serious private discussions of the possibility that, if the nuclear powers do not cooperate, the nonaligned parties would agree only to short extensions of two, three, or five years, with renewal depending on achievement of specified agreements on a fixed schedule.

In this connection, many stressed the importance they attach to serious multilateral negotiations beginning at the test ban amendment conference then scheduled for January 1991 and continuing until a comprehensive ban is achieved. UN Secretary-General Javier Perez de Cuellar added emphasis to the issue on 25 October 1990 in a statement at the General Assembly:

> The issue of nuclear weapons — and their continued testing — remains a divisive one, as the recent Fourth Review Conference on the Nuclear Non-Proliferation Treaty has shown ... It is of paramount importance that a viable regime for the nonprolifer-ation of nuclear weapons beyond 1995 is agreed upon by the international community ... I have repeatedly underlined the desirability of a comprehensive test ban treaty and I would urge that all sides seek to make progress on this sensitive and intractable question.

The 1991 Test Ban Amendment Conference

Though it was overshadowed by the countdown to war in the Persian Gulf, the Test Ban Amendment Conference convened in January 1991 at UN headquarters in New York. No one expected the two-week con-ference to produce a test ban. The real test was a vote on whether to continue the amendment work at a future date. That vote — 74 to 2 to reconvene, with 19 abstentions — left the conference's two adamant opponents, the United States and Britain, in not-so-splendid isolation. The Soviets supported the amendment proposal, but US and British

officials announced that they would veto it. They described the conference as a waste of time and money. However, seven Western nations that
were expected to abstain voted instead to reconvene the conference.

INF and START

In the INF Treaty of December 1987, the US and USSR banned all
their ground-launched nuclear missiles with a range of 500 to 5500
kilometres and, for the first time, eliminated an entire category of
nuclear weapons.

In the START Treaty of July 1991, they agreed, also for the first
time, to reduce their strategic (long range and intercontinental) nuclear
weapons from some 23,000 to between 16,000 and 18,000. This still
leaves an obscenely large number of strategic weapons, some five times
larger than their number at the time the nuclear Non-Proliferation
Treaty was signed in 1968. As recently noted by Robert McNamara,
who first implemented the policy of mutual nuclear deterrence, 200
such weapons, or even less, might be sufficient. Moreover, the Treaty
permits the two parties to continue to test, produce and deploy new or
modernized strategic weapons, and thus to continue the *qualitative*
nuclear arms race. In addition, the withdrawn warheads under both the
START and INF Treaties are not being dismantled or destroyed but are
being stockpiled.

Thus, while the two treaties are very important steps in the right
direction, they do not go far enough. It is essential that they should
mark only the beginning and not the end of the road to nuclear disarmament.

Mass-destruction weapon-free zones

As a result of the threat of use by Iraq in the Gulf War of nuclear,
chemical and biological weapons, and its actual use of SCUD missiles
with conventional warheads, the five permanent members of the
Security Council — the United States, Soviet Union, Britain, France
and China — decided that they must prevent the proliferation of mass-
destruction weapons. The Big Five are also the five nuclear powers and
the largest exporters of conventional arms.

They held their first meeting in Paris in July 1991 and laid out plans to stop the spread of these mass-destruction and conventional weapons on a global as well as on a regional basis. They also decided to support a universal United Nations arms transfer register, and to prevent the proliferation of mass-destruction weapons as a matter of urgency first of all in the Middle East.

On July 16, the summit meeting of the Group of Industrialized Nations (the G7) adopted a similar program, with greater emphasis on strengthening the NPT, which allows the five nuclear powers to retain their monopoly of these weapons. They also called for strengthening the export controls on nuclear materials and missiles under the guidelines laid down by the Nuclear Suppliers Group and the Missile Technology Control Regime.

The aims of the nuclear Big Five and the G7 are commendable. But the approach they adopted, based on stringent national and Group controls to prevent the export of critical materials and weapons by the supplier countries, is so flawed as to make their task almost impossible. While they recognize that their efforts can succeed only if they are supported by the importing countries and by the international community, they provide no incentives for obtaining such support.

Flaws in the new proposals

What the Big Five fail to take sufficiently into account is that the nuclear *have-not* countries are fed up with what they regard as discriminatory treatment by the *have* countries. If the nuclear powers consider that nuclear weapons are necessary for their security, non-nuclear countries who have serious security problems of their own believe that such weapons could also preserve or enhance their security. Some of these countries also regard chemical and biological weapons as "the poor man's atom bomb". We have seen that such countries as cannot import what they want from the main suppliers will follow the lead of countries that have found alternative or clandestine sources and have started making their own mass-destruction weapons.

Most non-nuclear countries are disillusioned with the working of the NPT, which all nuclear powers want to strengthen. The non-nuclear parties say they have lived up to their commitments not to acquire nuclear weapons, but that the nuclear powers have failed to live up to their promises to first halt and then reverse the nuclear arms race.

They regard the recent adherence of France and China to the NPT in 1992 as confirming their belief that all five nuclear powers want to preserve their nuclear monopoly.

Some leaders of the non-nuclear countries say that the day of discriminatory nonproliferation treaties is past, and that henceforth any ban on acquiring any type of weapons must apply universally to all countries or to none.

Possible solutions

There is hope, however, of finding a solution to the proliferation problem, but only if the Big Five should decide to work together with the importing countries to reach nondiscriminatory treaties that would ban all further proliferation by both the exporting and importing countries.

First, and most important, would be the establishment of a *non-acquisition* or *non-armament* regime by an agreement to freeze all existing arsenals of mass-destruction weapons at their present levels, together with a universal ban on testing and producing any new or *modernized* versions of these weapons. The countries now possessing them would have at the same time to undertake to continue negotiations to reduce and eliminate them. In this way all countries would be subject to the same restrictions without discrimination.

Second, would be for the five permanent members of the Security Council to enter into binding legal guarantees to come instantly to the defence of any country that agrees not to acquire mass-destruction weapons if that country becomes subject to attack or the clear threat of attack with such weapons. Such guarantees would be defined in treaties under Article 51 of the UN Charter ensuring the right of individual and collective self-defence, similar to the NATO and Warsaw Pact Treaties.

Third, would be to begin the process in regions where there are already successful arms control agreements, such as the nuclear free zones in Latin America and the South Pacific, and the reduction of armed forces in Europe. In each of these cases the zone agreements were initiated and negotiated by the states of the region themselves. Zones free of mass-destruction weapons cannot be imposed from the outside on any region of serious tensions, such as the Middle East or South Asia, by the Big Five or any other group. Only the countries of each zone can create such regimes. Legally binding security guarantees might make mass-destruction weapons free zones possible even in the Middle East and South Asia.

Fourth, would be to bear in mind that restricting exports by group efforts, such as the Nuclear Suppliers Group and the Missile Technology Control Regime have been only partially successful in the past. Partial success in preventing the spread of mass-destruction weapons is simply inadequate.

In the view of most military experts the problem of proliferation of the other two types of weapon of mass destruction — biological and chemical — is not nearly as important as that of nuclear weapons and their missiles. They view biological and chemical weapons as terror weapons rather than effective military weapons. Any country which initiates their use may win one battle but will almost certainly lose the war. In any case, the draft convention for the total destruction and elimination of all chemical weapons on a non-discriminatory basis, which was approved by the UN General Assembly in 1992, was opened for signature in Paris on 13 January 1993, and efforts are now underway to improve and strengthen the 1972 Biological Weapons Convention.

Accordingly, in order to create zones free of all mass-destruction weapons, it would seem to be necessary to concentrate first on preventing the proliferation of nuclear weapons and missiles.

A test ban is the key

The key to real progress towards ending the proliferation of nuclear weapons is to begin with a total ban on all testing. This would not only open the way to stopping the vertical and horizontal proliferation of nuclear weapons effectively but would also facilitate the efforts to end the proliferation of biological and chemical weapons, and also encourage hopes for the eventual elimination of all nuclear weapons.

The risk to the nuclear powers of ending their nuclear tests is far less than the risk of the NPT expiring. It is almost incredible that the nuclear powers seem to have failed to recognize this, and still act as though they can renew or extend the NPT indefinitely while continuing to test and proliferate their own nuclear weapons. If nuclear testing is not stopped, the NPT will be in jeopardy.

Recent favourable developments

As a result of the astonishing improvement in the world situation in the last few years, it is now possible to plan and work for an end to testing, the strengthening of the NPT, and also for the elimination of all mass-destruction weapons. The opportunities are better than ever before and should not be lost.

After the signing of the START Treaty in July 1991, and the failed coup in the USSR in August of the same year, far-reaching and dramatic unilateral actions were taken by the USA and the Soviet Union, and after the dissolution of the Soviet Union on Christmas Day 1991, by its successors, Russia and the states of the Commonwealth of Independent States.

In January 1993 the USA and Russia signed the START II Treaty in Moscow which provides for the reduction of their strategic nuclear weapons by the year 2003 to 3,500 for the USA and 3,000 for Russia. Some scholars have noted that this still leaves them with about two-thirds the number of strategic missiles and bombers they had in 1968 when the NPT was signed.

On 27 September 1991, President George Bush announced a unilateral US decision to withdraw and destroy all its ground-launched short range (tactical) nuclear weapons and all tactical nuclear weapons from its surface ships and submarines. In addition, the USA would remove from alert status all its strategic bombers and intercontinental ballistic missiles (ICBMs) due to be eliminated by the START Treaty, and also stop the development of the mobile MX missile and mobile single warhead ICBM.

On 5 October 1991, President Mikhail Gorbachev reciprocated by announcing similar unilateral actions. In addition, 1000 more Soviet strategic warheads than called for by the START Treaty would be eliminated and the Soviet Union would institute a one-year moratorium on nuclear testing.

On 23 May 1992, Belarus, Kazakhstan and Ukraine joined Russia and the United States in a Protocol to the START I Treaty whereby the three new states, which had unilaterally transferred all their tactical nuclear weapons to Russia, also agreed to transfer to Russia or to eliminate all strategic nuclear weapons from their territories and to join the NPT as non-nuclear parties.

On 16 June 1992, President George Bush and President Boris Yeltsin of Russia reached a Joint Understanding, which was confirmed by the above-mentioned treaty in January 1993, to reduce their strategic weapons by the year 2003 to 3500 and 3000 respectively, which levels are far below those fixed by the START I Treaty, but still amount to far more than can have any conceivable use or purpose.

As regards nuclear testing, the Soviet Union's 1991 announcement of a one-year unilateral moratorium on nuclear testing was followed by France's decision on 8 April 1992 to institute a unilateral suspension on testing, and her proposal to end all nuclear testing. On 2 October 1992, President Bush reluctantly accepted a US nine-month moratorium on nuclear testing, which had been included in legislation passed by the US Congress, and which also called for an end to all testing by 1996. Russia agreed to extend its moratorium, first until the middle of 1993, and later beyond.

In the meantime efforts are being pursued to begin negotiations to end all nuclear tests. A comprehensive test ban would clearly help to facilitate a lengthy extension of the NPT when its initial term in force expires in 1995 and a conference must be held to decide on its extension.

As noted, France and China also signed the NPT in 1991 and became parties to the Treaty in 1992. Thus all five of the declared nuclear powers had become parties to the NPT, bringing the total number of parties to more than 150.

On 3 November 1992, Bill Clinton, the candidate of the Democratic party, defeated George Bush in the elections and became the President of the United States in January 1993. Both he and the Democratic Congress are much more favourably inclined towards a total test ban than are ex-president Bush and the Republican party.

In addition, at the UN General Assembly, many more delegations than in previous years, including a number of the allies of the United States, were more insistent than ever before in their call for the beginning of negotiations for a CTBT and for the conclusion of the treaty by 1995 when the conference on the extension of the NPT will be held.

There were also repeated calls for a cessation of the production of nuclear weapons and for their destruction and elimination, as well as for legally binding assurances that the nuclear powers would not use or threaten to use nuclear weapons against non-nuclear states and would come to the aid and assistance of any non-nuclear state attacked or threatened with attack by nuclear weapons. While it is difficult to envisage that all these demands will be met before 1995, Article X of the NPT provides that the 1995 conference shall "decide whether the treaty shall continue in force indefinitely, or shall be extended for an additional fixed period or periods."

It is therefore reasonable to expect that, if the main demand for a comprehensive test ban is met by 1995, the NPT will be extended for a lengthy period of time. Such an extension or extensions could be linked to the achievement of the other demands of the non-nuclear states.

An end to nuclear testing is now within reach

President Clinton deserves high praise for his courage and wisdom in extending the moratorioum on nuclear testing on 3 July 1993 for at least 15 months, until 30 September 1994, and for deciding that the United States will not be the first to resume testing.

The next step is to begin the multilateral negotiations to achieve a comprehensive (meaning total) test ban treaty (CTBT) as agreed at the Vancouver summit meeting with Boris Yeltsin on 3 April 1993. In his weekly radio address on 3 July, President Clinton called on other nuclear powers to join the moratorium and negotiate a comprehensive test ban and thus "discourage other nations from developing their own nuclear arsenals". The Group of Seven summit meeting in Tokyo on 8 July called for the indefinite extension of the nuclear nonproliferation treaty in 1995 when its future will be decided.

After 12 years of adamant opposition by the United States under Presidents Reagan and Bush, on 10 August 1993 the Geneva Conference on Disarmament (CD) finally agreed, with United States' support, to undertake multilateral negotiations for a CTBT. While this was a breakthrough, the negotiations will not actually begin until January 1994.

The nuclear powers and their allies would like the CTBT to be negotiated in the CD. It has the advantage that all five declared nuclear powers — Britain, China, France, Russia and the United States are all members. But it has the disadvantage that all its decisions must be taken by consensus, that is, unanimously, which means they can be blocked or vetoed by any one of its 19 members.

It is most urgent to begin the negotiations as soon as possible in order to agree on a total test ban by March 1995 when the NPT's initial term of 25 years expires. For reasons never explained, current American legislation calls for an end to all testing only in September 1996. Some of the nonaligned parties to this treaty have warned that, unless a total test ban treaty is in place when they have to decide on how long to extend the NPT, they will agree only to a brief extension of two years or so, or perhaps adjourn the extension conference for two years, pending the completion of a CTBT. Since they constitute about two-thirds of the 158 parties to the NPT, and decisions on the treaty's extension can be taken by a simple majority (80) of the parties, the question of a total test ban may be decisive for the future of the NPT.

In 1988, a group of nonaligned countries, with the support of the United Nations, began the process of amending the 1963 PTBT to convert it into a CTBT. The amendment conference (see section above entitled: The 1991 Test Ban Amendment Conference) held its first session in January 1991, and will hold a second session in 1994. The PTBT has a unique provision: if an amendment is approved and ratified by a majority (61) of its parties, including Britain, Russia and the USA, it becomes automatically binding on all the 121 parties (see section above entitled: the Test Ban Amendment initiative). Thus Argentina, Brazil, India, Israel, Pakistan and Ukraine, all of which are parties to the test ban treaty but not to the NPT, would be barred from any nuclear testing.

On 10 August a special meeting of the parties to the PTBT, including the USA, Russia and the UK, also decided by consensus that negotiations for a CTBT could be pursued in both the CD and the Test Ban Amendment Conference and should be mutually reinforcing. The meeting also authorized the President of the Amendment Conference, Ali Alatas, the Foreign Minister of Indonesia, to continue consultaions with the parties to the 1963 PTBT, and with the CD and the five nuclear powers on the best way to proceed.

China and France are not parties to the test ban treaty and would therefore not be bound by any prohibition in the amended treaty. But both those nuclear powers did join the nonproliferation treaty in 1992. They surely would not want to undermine that treaty by continuing to test while the three other nuclear powers and all other parties to the NPT and the test ban treaty were prohibited from doing so.

Moreover, by adopting the amendment procedure to ban all nuclear testing, the nations of the world could avoid the lengthy and difficult process of negotiating an entirely new test ban treaty in the CD, and the equally long, slow process of obtaining the signatures and ratifications necessary for its entry into force.

The best solution would be to follow both tracks. The CD could immediately begin to negotiate the terms of new amendments to the PTBT in order to provide a system of verification and sanctions that are not provided for in the PTBT, to ensure that there are no clandestine tests. At the same time the Test Ban Amendment Conference could as a first step pursue its efforts — which are likely to be quicker and easier than in the CD — to ban all underground nuclear tests including those for so-called peaceful purposes that are now permitted under both the NPT and PTBT. The Amendment Conference could also insert a provision stating that the amended treaty could later be amended again to include a system of verification and sanctions, or that the treaty itself might be replaced by a new CTBT after the CD finishes its work.

Only the parallel co-operation of the two conferences could speed up the entire process of ending all nuclear testing so that it can be achieved before March 1995. That would ensure at least a lengthy extension of the NPT at the 1995 extension conference.

The outlook for a comprehensive test ban and for the continued extension and strengthening of the NPT is more favourable today than ever before.

CHAPTER 5

Creating Insecurity!

David Lorge Parnas

Introduction

The 45-year period that began at the end of World War II was characterised by two trends, an increasing feeling of insecurity and an increase in the level of armaments in the world. The arms were intended to make their owners feel more secure, but they had just the opposite effect. They led to a vicious cycle in which increased armaments led to a need for more armaments — the famous *arms race*. The excuse for this futile exercise was called the *Cold War*. This paper discusses the efforts of the arms industry to create the illusion that was the Cold War and to keep the arms race going. My life has paralleled the Cold War and I choose to explain the phenomenon by relating my perceptions of it.

I became aware of the world just about the time that World War II ended and the Cold War began. I watched, unquestioningly, as West Germans, evil enemies when I was born, were transformed into trusty allies, and the Russians, who had been our allies, became an evil empire intent on enslaving or destroying us. I accepted the assumption that the world was divided into two competing camps, ours with a system that provided happiness and efficiency, the other with a system that was cruel and inefficient. I was told that, in spite of the fact that our system was vastly superior, the race between the two systems was a close one. I accepted the statements that, because of this, we required the strongest possible military forces.

Having grown up with these assumptions, I thought it *good* to work for the military. I consulted for the military at a fraction of the fee that I received from other clients. Some of my best scientific work was done as an employee of the US Navy.

While accepting the need for strong military forces, I was troubled by the policy of nuclear deterrence. A defence that would destroy millions of innocent people, including many on *our side*, never made sense.

I never understood how we determined the number of nuclear weapons we needed; I never understood why we should keep the level so high or why it was important to keep improving them.

In March of 1983, President Reagan announced his Strategic Defense Initiative (SDI), a program often called *Star Wars*. He said, "I call upon the scientific community, who gave us nuclear weapons, to turn their great talents to the cause of mankind and world peace; to give us the means of rendering these nuclear weapons impotent and obsolete." Although I was much too involved with my own work to give this project serious thought, I liked those words and wished that they could be realised.

In May of 1985, I was asked by a representative of the Strategic Defense Initiative Organization (SDIO), the group within the Office of the US Secretary of Defense that was responsible for the *Star Wars* program, if I wanted to "save the world from nuclear conflagration". I was invited to serve on a $1000 per day advisory panel, the SDIO Panel on Computing in Support of Battle Management. The panel was to make recommendations about a research and development program to solve the computational problems inherent in space-based defence against ballistic missiles. We were told we could, and some panel members eventually did apply for contracts to study the problems that the panel would identify. It was a double-win situation: we would be well paid and could create additional funding for our own research areas.

I did not hesitate to serve on that panel. I was the intellectual leader of one of the US Navy's largest software engineering research projects. I was quite familiar with the computer aspects of weapon systems and found the work challenging. My research results were broadly applicable, that is, not limited to military applications. If my work could contribute to the elimination of nuclear weapons, why not?

Two months later, I resigned from that panel, convinced that the SDI was a fraud. It was clear to me that the advertised goals could not be met and that the engineers and scientists working on SDI knew that those goals could not be met. The money was being spent for other purposes. I felt that the technological limitations made the project dangerous and counterproductive. With my resignation letter, I supplied the SDIO with a set of eight papers that explained why I thought that fundamental limits on computer technology made it impossible to achieve the project's lofty goals. Those papers were eventually published by the *American Scientist*, and widely republished.

When my resignation became known to the public, I found myself thrust into the middle of the political debate over SDI. I was asked to debate the software issues at conferences and universities all over the USA, Canada, and Western Europe. As the debate over SDI unfolded, a series of incidents led me to question my fundamental assumptions about the Cold War and the role of scientists and engineers. Previously, I had assumed that those who made their living in the defence industry were seriously dedicated to keeping their country safe. I believed they would not participate in projects that were not consistent with that goal. The response of the scientific community to SDI showed me that my assumptions were false. I began to understand that I had been part of a much larger fraudulent enterprise. Below, I relate some incidents that opened my eyes and I use those stories to explain my current position.

Why SDI is a fraud

Although this paper is not primarily about SDI it is important that you understand why I concluded that SDI was a dangerous deceit.

My view of SDI was that of a computer scientist who had spent more than twenty years studying the construction of large software systems, with more than fourteen of those years involved in consulting and research on the use of computers in weapons. The usual view of SDI is that it comprises hundreds, perhaps thousands, of satellites, each containing sensors to track attacking missiles and weapons to destroy them. My experience led me to focus on the multitude of computers in the satellites and on the ground. The computers would perform critical functions, processing sensor data, controlling the communications among the satellites, identifying possible attacking rockets, discriminating between warheads and decoys, aiming the weapons, assessing the effectiveness of a weapon against a warhead, etc. Computers and computer software are the glue that holds weapon systems like SDI together. If the software does not work well, the system will be ineffective.

It is an indisputable fact that computer programs fail frequently, and are almost certain to fail when they are first used in situations where they have never been used before. We are unable to develop programs that work effectively the first time that they are put to use by real users. Instead, we deliver highly unreliable programs to selected user sites, having users that are prepared to live with frequent failures. The only way that we get trustworthy computer systems is to use them, let them fail, and fix them. There are fundamental reasons for the fragility of software technology; improved development methods can help, but the problems will not disappear.

SDI would be the most difficult software system ever attempted. As a computer system, it has an unprecedented combination of difficult properties. We cannot test it under realistic conditions and we cannot afford to let it fail the first time it is needed. Because one can never trust a software system that has never been used before, SDI will never be trusted.

Military planners must make *worst-case* assumptions. The owners of an untrustworthy system must plan as if it will not work. Their potential opponents must behave as if the system might work. The USA could not abandon their policy of *mutual assured destruction* (MAD) until it trusted the SDI shield. Other nuclear powers would feel forced to compensate for SDI by, among other things, building more weapons. The USA would see a growing *missile gap* and, not trusting the defensive system it had never used, could only respond by improving its own stock of missiles. Neither side would abandon MAD. Instead, the arms race would intensify.

Countries worried that the USA might use its nuclear sword and SDI shield to dominate them, would try to develop weapons to attack the vulnerable satellites and ground stations of SDI. The USA would then develop weapons to defend those resources. The arms race would have moved into space.

Technological evaluations make it clear that the attackers would have a fundamental advantage in this race. The Anti-Satellite weapons, jamming, simulation, countersimulation, and other tools available to confuse and defeat the system are far easier to build than SDI would be. SDI is like a fine watch, it is easier to break it than to make it.

Instead of the increased security promised by SDI supporters, we will have a world more heavily armed, and far more hazardous than ever before. We won't be, or feel, safer. *Au contraire!*

"It's OK to have 100,000 errors in the SDI software"

Shortly after I resigned, I received a telephone call from a US media network. I was told that the SDIO Chief Scientist had responded to my resignation by saying that the software was nothing to worry about. It could, he said, contain 100,000 errors and still work. The reporter asked me if his statement was correct. I was dumbfounded. It was true! If the 100,000 errors were *very carefully selected*, the incorrect program could work when used. However, it was also true that a single error in punctuation could cause complete failure, as it did on a Venus probe. I wondered whether the Chief Scientist was simply ignorant of the facts, or whether his words were carefully chosen to mislead the public.

The 90% distraction

When I first became involved in the SDI debate, I heard the argument that SDI could make lots of errors because it would be a three layer system. We were told that if each layer were only 90% effective, the whole system would be 99.9% effective. There are blatant errors in this argument. It assumed random processes and statistical independence where such assumptions were clearly not justified. Further, the 90% assumption was arbitrary. When I asked a high SDI official where the figure came from, he told me "We picked it for purposes of illustration". That 90% figure was accepted as fact by reporters and peace groups who never seemed to question it. Not one commentator asked where the number came from. Not one questioned the assumption that failures in the first layer have no effect on the later layers.

Some time later I heard another top SDI scientist give a talk on the subject at the Massachussetts Institute of Technology. Before giving the argument mentioned above, he paused, and said, "Now don't tell us that these arguments are not sound, we know that. We just think they sound good on television." He then continued to present that argument in his talk. At this point, I could have no doubt that there was a real attempt to mislead the public.

The Fletcher distraction

A few months after my resignation made the SDI software a public issue, the SDIO Panel on Computing in Support of Battle Management, which had renamed itself the *Eastport Group*, announced that all of the critics had been misled by an earlier report known as the *Fletcher Report*. They claimed that the report had described a highly centralised, tightly coordinated system. In such a system the failure of one component would bring the whole system to a halt. SDIO supporters claimed that a major breakthrough had been made. The system would be designed using *loose coordination* in which the various battle stations would provide each other with helpful information but could function independently. This, they claimed, made the software problem tractable.

Those who had read the Fletcher Report were astounded. That report, which was much more detailed and thoughtful than the Eastport Report, did not advocate a centralised design. In fact, it warned against systems with critical nodes and discussed the need for independence and degraded states of operation. By that time, ten contractors had turned in proposed designs as a result of Phase I contracts. None of them had advocated a centralised design. Furthermore, my report, and those of other critics, explicitly assumed a distributed, decentralised computing system. In fact, no computer expert had ever seriously proposed or assumed a centralised design. The issue was a red herring. It should be pointed out that the more decentralised one makes a system of this sort, the more difficult are the software problems.

The unpublished model(s)

The debate eventually moved to the pages of *Science* magazine. *Science* magazine is a highly respected journal normally used for communication between scientists. Its articles are usually scholarly and complete. *Science* ran several articles on the SDI software issue. One of these was based on the report of the SDIO's Eastport panel. *Science* informed its readers that the Eastport group had a model showing that failure to coordinate the battle stations would have only a small effect on the effectiveness of the system. Strangely enough, the model was not described. Dr. Herb Lin, then an MIT physicist, replied by listing some faults in the (unpublished) model but also did not describe the model. The committee members replied, asserting, without evidence, that Lin was wrong. Such a discussion, with assertions about an unstated mathematical model, are most unusual in the scientific literature.

I contacted Dr. Lin to find out what the committee's model was. He did not know. He had invented a model that had one data point in agreement with Eastport's figures. He told me that *Science* had refused to publish his model.

A few months later I was asked to serve on a Congressional Advisory Panel organised by the US Office of Technology Assessment (OTA). The panel also included one of the leading Eastport panelists. During these meetings, I asked Eastport to provide a description of the model. He avoided explaining the model by shrugging his shoulders and saying "There were three". To this day, not one of those models has been published.

This is not the way scientific discourse normally runs. When scientists discuss their conclusions with each other, they describe those models and allow their peers to examine them. The committee's use of an undocumented model, and their refusal to expose their reasoning to scrutiny, marked their report as propaganda, not a technical document. When *Science* magazine allowed this most unscientific exchange, it too was engaging in the debate on a political level.

In this, as well as many other incidents, I saw the press, both popular and scientific, publish nonsense. There was strong political pressure not to be one-sided. The fact is that when an issue is one-sided, any attempt to make it appear two-sided is misleading. The facts are quite simple and have been borne out by a carefully researched OTA study. Computer programs, even those much simpler than SDI, do not work until they have been used in battle. Successful military software has always evolved through a sequence of battles. SDI would have to work in its first real use. There would always be a significant probability that the system would fail completely when used. SDI scientists, meeting behind closed doors with other scientists, did not argue with those facts. Given the undisputed nature of these facts, any attempt to present the *other side* of that story must be seen as an attempt to mislead the public.

"It's easier to defend against well-planned attacks"

At one point I met, and worked with, a US congressman who was an avowed opponent of SDI. He asked me to help him formulate some questions that he would require the SDIO to answer. I therefore raised with the Panel the issue of survivability; how would the system work if key components were damaged? The usual answer to that question is that the system would be designed with redundant elements to make it robust. My question pointed out that redundancy was a defence against random failures and could be defeated by a coordinated attack designed to overcome the redundancy; it asked how SDIO was planning to deal with such carefully planned attacks on the system. The Congressman received an erudite, scientifically worded reply stating that it was easier to defend against planned, coordinated attacks than to defend against random attacks. This surprising and counterintuitive conclusion was supported by quoting a well-known theorem from communications theory. The theorem states that correcting for errors in noisy communications channels is easier if the noise is not random. From this, the SDIO, reasoning by analogy, concluded that compensation for attack-induced damage is easier if the attacks are not random.

There is a fundamental flaw in the argument. In the proof of the communications theorem it is assumed that the nonrandom characteristics of the noise are known in advance and used in designing the error-correction mechanism. The analogous assumption in the SDI situation is that the enemy's attack plans are known in advance and used to design the system. Of course, that would not be the case. SDI would be designed first, then the enemy would base its attack plans on the weaknesses it saw in that design. SDIO's official reply implicitly assumed that an enemy would tell them its attack plans in advance.

The author of the reply had either made an incredibly fundamental error, or he had cleverly worded a response that he hoped would delude someone who was not trained in science or engineering. The reply was so well-written, that I cannot believe that its author was stupid.

"There are no such things as bugs in software"

Somewhat later, I was called by a reporter for a reaction to a New York Times report. That report quoted a Professor at the California Institute of Technology, a world-famous technological institution, as saying that we did not need to worry about bugs in the SDI software. The reason given was that "there are no such things as bugs, there are only oversights". My reaction was to state that this would make a big change in my life. No longer would I have to debug programs, now I would de-oversight them. I know that scientist. He knows, as well as you and I, that replacing the word *bug* with *oversight* does not make the problem go away.

"It's just a system problem"

As the debate wore on a new red herring appeared. The head of MITRE Corporation (a major US arms contractor), who frequently presented himself as a critic of the program while accepting contracts from the program and its supporters, published an article in *Science*. He concluded that SDI was not a software problem, but a system problem. His argument was that the difficulty would be our inability to know what the software should do, not our inability to get it right. While I would argue that both problems are present, it is more important to note that renaming the problem does not make it go away. MITRE is considered to be a specialist in the integration of large computer-based systems. By calling the problem a systems integration problem, they could both belittle the software difficulties and justify their proposals to SDI for contracts to study the system integration issues.

"Congress might conclude that we can do nothing in this area"

As the OTA panel finished its discussions of the draft report, a physicist, who had presented himself to me as neutral on SDI, expressed concern about the report's strongly negative conclusions about software. Earlier he had admitted that he could not argue with the technical arguments or facts that were presented. Now he expressed concern, not about the truth of the conclusions, but their effect on the US Congress. He warned us that Congress might conclude that there was nothing that could be done to overcome the software difficulties.

The attitude of the military scientific establishment is that reporting technical difficulties in a Defence program is useful provided that one can use that report as an argument for increased funding. In a moment of candor at a computing conference, the SDIO officer in charge of computing told me that my resignation had been good for his project; it led to an increase in funding for the program that he managed. Shortly after that meeting, that *neutral* man became the chief scientist of SDIO. In that capacity, he commented on the report that he had helped to write. He said that it was too pessimistic, and that the

AEGIS system (a shipboard system intended to defend US ships against attacks from the air) showed that we could build reliable software. A few days after he made that statement, an AEGIS system on the USS Vincennes shot down an Iranian civilian airliner traveling on a published civilian trajectory. Subsequent investigations made it clear that the AEGIS software confused its operators. Even before this fatal failure, the AEGIS system was known in the industry to be a catastrophic software project; the first ship functioned so badly that its Captain declared the ship a casualty and turned back to port. It has never been proven effective against the threat that it was designed to handle. Many changes and corrections are still needed. AEGIS supports the arguments against SDI; it is just one more example of the fact that complex software systems must evolve in actual usage and may **never** become trustworthy.

"That's just what we tell the public"

Many responsible people were fully aware that the public was being misled. On one visit to Washington, I was asked to address some Senate staff members. As I began, the aide to a Republican Senator interjected, "Don't talk about making nuclear weapons impotent and obsolete, that is just what we tell the public." Not one of the staff members was embarrassed by the obvious hypocrisy in that statement. They thought it normal that the public would be told a story that none of the professionals believed.

"SDI is a faded Star"

In spite of the best efforts of its science fiction writers, SDIO could no longer defend the original claims before Congress. They began to propose less pretentious reasons for continuing the program. We began to hear that the system would be effective against accidental attacks or attacks from small countries like Libya. In fact, those plans were no more credible than the original one. As the weight of scientific evidence piled up, the SDIO decided that a low profile was the best way to proceed. We began to see news stories with headlines that suggested that SDI's budget had been cut. In fact, up to now, each year's budget has been bigger than that of the year before. Further, some of the work on nuclear weapons such as the *X-ray laser* is now funded through the Department of Energy directly instead of through SDIO. In recent years the budget has been more than $5,000,000,000 — an amount that is huge for a research budget. Nonetheless, most people have the impression that the project has been abandoned.

A recent newspaper story stated, "Many, including some of the program's erstwhile true believers, are having a good laugh over it". The *true believers* that I met, never believed in the official story. Privately, they scoffed at someone who quoted President Reagan's words. Now that he is out of office, they find it more effective to soft-pedal the approach. However, they continue to spend huge amounts of money on a project to extend the arms race into space and keep the funding coming to the defence research community. The original budgets and schedules were just another attempt to mislead the public. The schedules for this totally new weapon system were shorter than those for a new bomber. By Pentagon standards, SDIO is a success story, not a failure.

Was the fraud confined to SDI?

SDI represents an extreme case. It is a project so extremely silly that almost everyone involved knows it is not real. However, the same dishonest attitude pervades the defence establishment.

In the mid 1970s, there was a plan to station MX (*Peacekeeper*) missiles on moving trains in the desert. I was consulting for a company that was a major contractor in those plans. At lunch they showed me a *back-of-the-envelope* calculation that showed that the computation needed was not possible with the computers then available. Two hours later they asked me to work on a project to evaluate the feasibility of that program. When I asked if this was not the same project that they had shown infeasible with a simple argument earlier that day, they agreed. When I asked why they were doing the study, they replied, "They are going to pay us a million dollars to show it can't be done." There was no embarrassment or hesitation. They were proud that they understood how to play the game.

About a year later, I was consulting for another group and found them doing something in a way that would not possibly work. I said, "Eric, you know that is not the right way to do that." He replied, "The customer wants it that way." "Why don't you tell him it's wrong?"

asked I. "At XYZ corporation (not the real name) we don't tell our customers that they are wrong, we take their money."

Is this fraudulence just an American problem?

These incidents are American but one should not think that only Americans have these attitudes. Some time ago, I was part of a group of researchers who were approached by a Canadian Hi-Tech defence contractor for help on radar simulation. We got into a discussion on the effect of the proposed radar on Canadian security, as theirs was not obviously a good way to proceed. After a brief conversation about the advisability of the project, the discussion was stopped by the senior manager who said, "We know that this is not the right solution for Canada but this is where the money is so this is what we are working on."

In November of 1985, *Der Spiegel* published an interview with a German industrialist who headed a defence contracting firm. He was clearly a strong supporter of German participation of SDI, talking about how easy it would be to get money to support high technology research. However, when he was asked about the instability during deployment, he replied, "You don't understand; for me SDI is not a military project at all, ... if there ever were a decision to deploy, I would oppose it."

Many Canadians consider Canada to be above these problems and view Canada as a peaceful middle power that is not involved. This is not true; Canada's military industry is strong and closely linked with that of other countries. Manufacturers of cruise missiles and components have factories in Canada and the testing program for those missiles continues to go on over Canadian territory with the enthusiastic cooperation of the Canadian Forces. The planned developments for SDI were such that the battle would have been quite likely to take place over Canada. In my view, our government has taken no action to slow the arms race, or even to limit Canada's participation in it, except by limiting the total military budget.

Is this fraud a new problem?

We would be misleading ourselves if we thought that these incidents were something new. A few years ago I was reading a collection of speeches given by Albert Schweitzer on Radio Oslo, after winning the Nobel Peace Prize. They were broadcast in April of 1958, 30 years ago. Here are some excerpts that show how little the world has changed.

> Now the Soviet Union has proposed a disarmament plan which would provide a good basis for beginning new negotiations. It proposes that one begin by stopping all test explosions of nuclear weapons.

> How is this requirement seen? One should believe that it would be easy for all the negotiating nations to agree. None would have an impairment to its possession of nuclear weapons. And the disadvantage, not to be able to try out new nuclear weapons, would be the same for all.

> However, America and England find it difficult to go along with this proposal. Immediately after the proposal was put into discussion, they spoke out against it. Since then they have denied, in a lot of propaganda, that the radioactivity produced by these tests is so great that it is necessary to forego the tests. Material with this propaganda is continuously given to the American and European press by governmental atomic commissions and nuclear scientists who feel moved to express the same opinions.

He later gives a specific example, "In lyrical tones Edward Teller, the father of the dirty hydrogen bomb, in an American newspaper at the start of 1958, sang a hymn to the ideal Nuclear War that, one day, could be carried out with completely clean nuclear weapons. He demanded continuation of the nuclear tests in order to be able, by means of these tests, to develop this ideal nuclear bomb.

Two verses from Edward Teller's hymn to the ideal nuclear war:

> Further bomb tests will put us in a position to be able to fight the weapons of our opponents while the innocent stand nearby unharmed.

> The completely clean nuclear bomb will prevent unnecessary accidents in a nuclear war.

In these old quotations, I see the same attitude that I see now. Scientists are willing to make quite outrageous promises in order to continue to get support for the work they want to do. Think about where we might be today if Teller had not made those outrageous promises, if the tests had stopped, and neither the USA nor the USSR had developed the *Super* bombs we have today. Dr. Teller was a leading supporter of SDI. Many believe that he convinced President Reagan to go ahead with the program.

"The INF Treaty will result in a reduction in nuclear weapons"

The military industrial complex is working hard to create a false sense of progress in the minds of the public. Consider the Treaty on missiles of intermediate range, the *INF Treaty*. How often have we heard that this treaty was the first one to call for the actual destruction of nuclear weapons? In fact, no nuclear bomb was really destroyed. Before the relatively cheap missile hulls were destroyed, all warheads and guidance mechanisms were carefully removed and preserved for re-use. The treaty called for the elimination of a militarily and politically vulnerable class of weapons, but allows their replacement with equally dangerous weapons. During the period of destruction, three times as many weapons were scheduled for deployment as destruction. In addition, military leaders were calling for still more deployments to compensate for the loss of the INF weapons.

In fact, the arms merchants won. They were paid to build the missiles, are being paid to dismantle them, and will be paid to replace them and reuse the parts. What more could they want?

The best aspect of the INF treaty is the agreement for some very intrusive inspections. However, on balance the INF treaty probably contributed more to disarming the disarmament movement, than to disarming the superpowers.

What do these incidents show?

All of these incidents, and I could describe many more, show a consistent pattern. They show people who want the arms race to continue and who work hard to keep it going. SDI is, for some, a way to defeat the *freeze* movement, a movement of the 1980s to freeze production, testing and deployment of nuclear weapons. The INF Treaty is a way to get paid for building missiles, for destroying them and building new ones that get around the concept of reversing the arms race. It has quieted the peace groups and allowed the arms race to proceed. The more recent START treaties (Strategic Arms Reduction Treaties) will get rid of weapons with little military applicability, but allow the development and deployment of new weapons. Arms budgets are being reduced by reducing the number of people in the armed forces, but plans call for making the remaining soldiers more powerful and more mobile by continued development of weapon technology.

A vast array of well paid, highly motivated, highly skilled, people are working to keep the arms race going. There are, for example, *mission analysts*, who are paid to find flaws in our present defensive system and propose profitable ways to remove the flaws that they identify. Then there are people in *think tanks*, who were paid to write articles that tell us that we could not trust anything the Russians said, and today still warn of instabilities that the system they belong to is continuously creating. Aircraft manufacturers hire agencies to publish advertisements in popular magazines showing a map of Florida and Cuba with the caption "Take the worry out of being close". They suggest that Cuba is a danger to the USA and propose a protective device, a newer, more destructive, military aircraft. The industry works hard to keep the lucrative research and development contracts coming.

I could not find a real cause for conflict between East and West in the time of Soviet power. However, there clearly is a real *Cold War*. It is being fought between those who would like to see a safe, sane, and humane world, and those who want to see the arms race continue. There is an *evil empire*. Its inhabitants are a privileged few who profit, and profit well, from an industry that thrives on building hate and mistrust. I have repeatedly seen the inhabitants of this empire lie, mislead, and cheat to protect what they see as their rightful way of life. If someone, such as myself, leaves their empire and exposes it to public scrutiny he is branded a traitor. Anyone who exercises professional responsibility and reports on shady practices or systems that don't work is branded *unprofessional*. The resentment felt by the citizens of this empire toward those who depart for other places, is the same as the resentment that *nationalists* feel about emigrants. This evil empire knows no borders. It can be found in every land having the technological capability to make, and sell, modern weapons.

The last 45 years have made one thing crystal clear. Military technology will not bring us peace and security. We are less secure today than we were 45 years ago. The arms race can never be won and should not be continued.

Yet another Cold War

There is a second Cold War going on. This is a war between the major powers and the rest of the nations in the world. Even as the *superpowers* talked of arms reduction, they were careful to deny the rest of the world a seat at the table. When many nations, including Canada, because of the SDI program, expressed their concern about the violation of the 1972 ABM treaty, the US Secretary of State replied peevishly that the US needed no advice from its allies on the interpretation of a bilateral treaty between it and the USSR.

Some of the world's more thoughtful leaders have a refreshingly different outlook on upholding international agreements. For example, in January of 1988 in Stockholm the leaders of Argentina, India, Sweden, Greece, Mexico, and Tanzania stated: "All states have the responsibility to uphold the rule of law in international relations ... the rest of us, the non-nuclear-weapons states, have a legitimate interest in the abolition of these awesome weapons. We demand it. We owe it not only to ourselves, but also to future generations. The fate of weapons systems which can spread death and destruction regardless of national borders must not be left in the hands of only a few states."

The new detente between the two military superpowers, which we should all welcome, does not recognise this aspiration of the majority of humanity. The arms reductions recently negotiated by the USA and Russia under the START Treaties still leave the whole world in a nuclear tinderbox.

Although the leaders of both nations do have nice words about *The Rule of Law*, actions often fall far short of this. Both nations assume disproportionate control over international bodies that they have not supported consistently; for example, the arrears of US contributions to the UN have kept that body at the brink of financial disaster. The new financial dependency of Russia on American and other aid is not reassuring to those who fear US hegemony.

The dilemma of overweening power was anticipated in 1932 in correspondence between Albert Einstein and Sigmund Freud concerning of the League of Nations. Einstein had written to Freud to ask him how we could raise a generation of people who would not resort to force to resolve disputes, but would use the rule of law instead. Freud's reply, stated that law and force were not really different.

> That is the fundamental situation, the dominance of the stronger power; raw, or intellectually enhanced, force always dominates. We know that, in the course of evolution, things changed. There is a path that leads from force to law, but which path is it? I believe that there is only one path; it is based on the fact that the superior strength of one strong man can be countered by an alliance of many weaker ones. 'L'union fait la force.' Force can be overcome by unification, the power of allies represents Law in contrast to the force of individuals. Thus we see that Law, the power of a united community, is still force, ready to be used against any individual that opposes it, working with the same means, achieving the same purposes. The only real difference is that it is not the force of a single person that wins, but that of a group.

It should be clear to all that Freud is not talking about an alliance that is dominated by a single superpower, but an alliance of smaller countries.

Freud went on to state that there were two forces that would lead to change in the rule of law. "First, there would be the attempts of individuals to extract themselves from restrictions that were to apply to everyone, i.e. to retreat from the rule of law back towards the rule of force; second, the constant efforts of the suppressed, to get more power for themselves, to get those changes recognised in law, and so to work against inequalities and for universal equal rights." These words of Freud, more than half a century old, characterise the fundamental conflicts in today's society!

The conflict between the relatively wealthy nations of the North, and the poor peoples of the South, is but a special case of the conflict between the mighty and the weak of which Freud wrote. The arms race is keeping the heavily armed larger nations dominant over the middle and small powers. The scientists who participate in the arms race are part of the machinery that keeps the majority of the people of the world subject to the wishes of a very small minority.

"A nuclear war can never be won and should never be fought"

These famous words, which were used many times in the 1980s, for example by President Reagan himself, had the profound effect of brainwashing people because the majority who heard them and the press reacted as if it represented a change in US policy. The words were true only in the sense that none of the leaders in either the USA or the Soviet Union seriously thought that a nuclear war between their countries could be fought and won. Nevertheless they spent tremendous sums of money planning for the eventuality of war between them. The real purpose of all the US weapons was to assure the ability to dominate countries other than the USSR, as well as to curb possible Soviet excesses. If those weapons are ever used, it will not be against any state with many nuclear bombs, but against either non-nuclear or emerging nuclear powers. All the comments I ever read on that statement treated it as a positive development and not the cynical saying that it really was.

We continue to lose the real Cold Wars

In spite of the great fanfare about arms treaties, the arms race continues with little abatement but with changes in the patterns of supply and of confrontation. The military capabilities of small powers who pose little threat to a major power are exaggerated by the arms industry's public relations specialists, to justify continued development of weapons. The capabilities of weapon systems such as the PATRIOT air defence system, are misrepresented to justify further investments in a failed technology.

We are losing too because of lost opportunities. The scientists who are working on SDI could be fighting the war against pollution. The engineers who are developing the *third generation* nuclear weapons could be working on cleaner power sources and ways to reverse the greenhouse effect. The scientists looking at biological and chemical warfare could be working on improving the water supplies of people around the world. Science should be contributing to the betterment of humanity, not to building arms.

Seven rules for winning the real Cold Wars

The first rule is *know thine enemy.* Too many people believe that there is no enemy. They fail to recognise that those who profit from tension in the world, those who live by the arms race, are working cleverly, consistently, and tirelessly to keep it going. Those in small countries fail to recognise that their chief ally may be their greatest enemy. In the war that Freud warned us of, it is the great powers who are the enemy of the small. It is the small powers who should be allies.

The second rule is *the truth will make us free.* For more than 45 years we have been enslaved by a false conflict and blind to the real ones. The truth is inherently stronger than propaganda; if people are exposed to the truth, if we help them to understand, they too can be free. It is important that we educate, not harangue. Too often we assert rather than explain. Too often we take the shortcut of expressing our conclusions, but not providing our listeners with the basic data and way of thinking that we used to reach those conclusions. It is far more work to explain and educate than it is to shout and propagandise. It is more work, but it is the only thing that can succeed. It is here that socially responsible scientists can play a role. We must all work as educators, helping others to understand as we have come to understand.

The third rule is *expose the weaknesses of the present system.* Movements for change have succeeded in the past only after the populace recognised the old order as incompetent. Most people today believe that the arms race has made us safer. We are told that nuclear deterrence has kept us safe for 45 years so why change it? The most powerful argument in favour of the arms race is, "If it ain't broke, don't fix it". In fact, as former US President Eisenhower warned us it would, the system has run amok. Our danger increases daily, and the price we are paying is unacceptable. Only if we can expose the failure of the present system can we hope that the public will demand that it be replaced.

The fourth rule is *have a positive proposal.* Disarmament groups need to develop and promote a positive program. They are often perceived as negative, opposing something but having nothing to suggest instead. For example, it is not enough to be against NATO and similar alliances. A positive proposal is needed, for example, for another sort of alliance, a broader one whose force is devoted to enhancing the rule of law.

The fifth rule is *train your foot-soldiers*. Most peace groups consist of large numbers of concerned citizens who support a small number of eloquent researchers, speakers, and writers. We need to turn many of those supporters into adequate speakers and writers who have enough confidence to speak out on the issues that concern them.

The sixth rule is *focus on children*. On a recent trip to the USA I tuned in a show called *Focus on the Family*, a broadcast by a pro-arms group called the *Family Research Council*. This group, which included members of the Reagan administration, and was closely linked to the Bush administration, spoke worriedly of letters that children had written to President Reagan asking for an end to nuclear arms. They observed that "someone has been scaring those children". They noted that by scaring those children one could reverse the viewpoint of a nation in a single generation. They expressed the fear that children might actually believe that we did not need to have wars. It was to that end that Einstein wrote to Freud in 1932. There is hope here.

The final rule is *engage in dialogue*. People don't pay attention to us unless we are really paying attention to them. To engage them, we must forsake the one-way media (newspapers, radio, television, flyers, and books) and take to two-way media. I say that for two reasons. First the one-way media are controlled by industry. Second, the two-way media are more effective. People can watch a film or read a brochure without real involvement. They cannot engage in a conversation in a small group without active intellectual activity. If we are to educate, if we are to get people to do their own analysis and come to their own conclusions, we must follow the example of those religious groups that go door-to-door talking about the danger of hell in the next world. We can use their techniques to explain that we can turn this world into a hell. However, dialogue requires real two-way conversation. We must enter every discussion with the recognition that we may be wrong and that we too can learn.

Is the real Cold War over?

In the past few years thundering headlines have announced that *the Cold War is over*. Every day we read news reports that include phrases such as *the first post-cold-war summit*, and *post-cold-war military policies*, and even the first *post-cold-war crisis*. One has the impression that something has really changed.

Announcements from the *first post-cold-war* NATO summit meeting were quite misleading. We read that the old policy of *flexible response* was replaced by a policy of using nuclear weapons as a *last resort*. In fact, under the old policy nuclear weapons were reserved for use only when other weapons failed to do the job. Specially trained officers were in place to control these weapons and to make sure that they would not be used in any other situations. Although the words *last resort* were never used, everyone knew that these weapons would only be used in extreme circumstances. What has changed? Another announcement was that the large national units now in place in Europe would be replaced by more mobile international units. This was billed as a response to the new realities in post-cold-war Europe. Of course, the switch to more highly mobile integrated forces is something that NATO commanders have long wanted. This modernisation of the forces allows them to maintain, or even increase their strength, in spite of reductions in the number of troops stationed in Europe.

Military development continues as well. Although nuclear tests have been suspended, the USA still refuses to agree to a Comprehensive Test Ban Treaty (see Chapter 4). They continue to develop new missiles and Canada continues to allow their testing in our North. Roughly six billion dollars a year continues to be spent on SDI, now under the name BMD (Ballistic Missile Defense). Although the world clearly has a surfeit of weapons, even the poorest countries want more and countries with severe internal economic problems want to make and sell those weapons.

It is clear that things have changed. The Soviet Union and Yugoslavia have fallen apart. East Germany has disappeared in a second *Anschluss*. Economic conditions in many of Eastern European countries have gotten worse since state-directed economies have been replaced by chaos. In the countries that emerged from the Soviet Union large armies move about seemingly without clear political control. Ethnic hatred, economic frustration, and nationalism are growing rapidly. Millions of people are suffering the ravages of war in areas that were peaceful before 1989. None of these changes are causes for optimism.

In Canada the arms industry, still smarting from the failure to acquire contracts for nuclear powered submarines, is fighting hard to create jobs through the purchase of hugely expensive helicopters and air defence systems.

Not long after the *détente* between the Russians and the USA, former US Secretary of Defense, Dick Cheney, was asked what the mission of the United States military would be in five years. Cheney ticked off the following goals:

1) Dominant strategic and tactical nuclear force;
2) Military alliances around the world;
3) Forward deployment of US troops to guarantee those alliances without Japanese rearmament or German military expansion;
4) Control of the seas;
5) Capability to project force anywhere Americans are threatened;
6) Maintenance of our defense-related industrial base.

Does that sound like a *post-cold-war* policy or a policy designed to continue the arms race?

There is a great deal of effort to make us believe that the world has become a safer place. To those of us who want an end to the arms race nothing fundamental has changed. The Cold War, which never was a response to a military threat, goes on in spite of the fact that there is no military threat. As you read this, a large multi-national industry is working to make you less secure and doing so in the name of security; and, simultaneously, devastating wars are taking place in areas of the world remote from these industries.

Acknowledgement

Prof. David Thomson of Memorial University in Newfoundland provided useful comments on an earlier version of this paper.

CHAPTER 6

The Strengthening Role of the United Nations in Peacekeeping and Peacemaking

William Epstein

Contents

The current situation — Definitions and interpretations — The Security Council summit meeting — The outlook for the UN: Preventive diplomacy/Peacekeeping/Peacemaking/Peace-enforcement/Post-conflict peacebuilding/Safety of UN personnel — The role of regional organizations — The role of disarmament — The financial problem — Conclusion
Annex: United Nations Peacekeeping Operations

The current situation

As the Secretary-General of the United Nations, Javier Perez de Cuellar, said on his retirement at the end of 1991, the world is going through the greatest peaceful transformation in modern times:

> It is as if a political ice age had ended ... It is hard to realize now just how much the role of the United Nations has changed and expanded since the early 1980s ... International peacekeeping, for example, which earlier had largely become limited to the process of maintaining cease-fires, has gained new dimensions of peacemaking and peacebuilding.

He also pointed to other areas where:

> Operations of unprecedented versatility, nature and scope have been mounted ... even though the larger question of poverty in the majority of the human race is yet to be addressed with the same sense of urgency as is evoked by political crises.

Between 1948 and 1988, the UN established 13 peacekeeping operations and since 1988 the UN has undertaken 13 new operations. (See Annex.) The new ones involve not only peacekeeping for maintaining cease-fires but also peacemaking and peacebuilding, which are directly related to broader aspects of peacekeeping. These operations include several related to verification of arms control and disarmament, such as the supervision of the withdrawal and demobilization of armed forces, and the observance of security agreements and restrictions on the import of arms. Others provide for the supervision and monitoring of human rights and the provision of humanitarian aid, the protection of minorities and repatriation of refugees. Some also require the provision of civilian police and civilian experts, in addition to military personnel, to assist in the preparation and monitoring and even conducting of elections, and also in reconstruction and national reconciliation and in the organization and construction of democratic institutions for new national systems of government.

In the past year alone, the UN in effect has become the temporary governing authority in Cambodia (the UN Transitional Authority in Cambodia — UNTAC). It has also intervened in matters previously considered within domestic jurisdiction in the civil wars in El Salvador (the UN Observer Mission in El Salvador — ONUSAL) and in Yugoslavia (the UN Protection Force in Yugoslavia — UNPROFOR) and in Somalia (the UN Operation in Somalia — UNOSOM). It is also involved in peacemaking efforts in some of these operations and may also become involved in Nagorno-Karabakh.

An interesting new development has occurred in Somalia. In April 1992, the Security Council decided that in addition to some 50 unarmed military observers who will monitor the cease-fire between the two main contending parties, there will be some civilians to supervise the provision and distribution of humanitarian relief and assistance, and an armed military security force of some 500 infantrymen to provide security for all UN personnel, equipment and supplies and to escort the delivery of supplies to the distribution centres. A similar but larger operation was subsequently mounted in Bosnia-Herzegovina.

In addition to these expanded peacekeeping operations, the UN is also engaged in peace-enforcement by implementing the enforcement measures decreed by the Security Council in Iraq. These measures include the destruction of Iraq's nuclear, chemical and biological weapons capabilities and delivery missiles, the supervision of sanctions and humanitarian aid, and assuring the protection of minorities.

UN peacekeeping operations expanded from some 11,500 military and civilian personnel in January 1992 to some 80,000 in mid-1992, mainly due to the Cambodian, Somalia and Yugoslav operations. The cost rose from $421 million in 1991 to some $2.7 billion in 1992 (about two and a half times the regular UN budget), which has put a severe strain on UN resources. Arrears and delays in payment of dues and peacekeeping assessments by the Member States have so depleted the UN's financial resources that it is difficult for the UN to undertake new large-scale peacekeeping operations, such as in Bosnia-Herzegovina.

The turning point in the explosion of UN peacekeeping operations came at the summit meeting in Washington in December, 1987, with the signing of the Treaty between the United States and the Soviet Union on the Elimination of their Intermediate-Range and Shorter-Range Missiles (INF Treaty). This Treaty heralded a fundamental change in Soviet-American relations and unlocked the potential of the UN to implement the provisions of the UN Charter.

The end of the East-West Cold War freed the UN of its seeming paralysis and made possible its functioning in the way originally foreseen in the Charter. It also facilitated the success of the enforcement measures and the collective security operations in the Gulf War. As a result, the UN has been greatly strengthened and has acquired new confidence and credibility.

At the same time, the disintegration of the former Soviet Union and the collapse of the communist system have resulted in the resurgence of ethnic, religious and nationalistic forces that have led to tensions and conflict in the former USSR and Yugoslavia. Armed hostilities have broken out that threaten the peace and stability of Europe and have created fears of further nuclear proliferation and the possible outbreak of additional local or regional wars not only in Africa and the Middle East but also in what had previously been regarded as a stable Europe.

In addition, the Third World countries feel that their perilous economic situation and their growing needs are being marginalized. They fear that the increasing attention being paid to the requirements for peacekeeping and economic assistance to Eastern Europe and the Republics of the former Soviet Union will result in less attention being paid and fewer resources being made available for economic and social development and assistance to the Third World.

Thus, a paradoxical situation seems to have developed. On the one hand, the Member States demonstrate that there is a burgeoning need and desire to entrust the UN with increasingly lofty and complex tasks while, on the other hand, they are unable or reluctant to provide the resources to fulfil those mandates.

It seems almost incredible that the wealthier nations of the world balk at providing a few billion dollars, a relatively paltry sum when compared with the trillions of dollars they will spend on armaments during the decade of the 90s. The failure to provide these few billion dollars to the UN might cost them hundreds of billions of dollars during the decade if new threats to peace and to economic growth and development are not forestalled.

Far from looking forward with a sense of optimism to a new world order, the nations and peoples of the world, faced with even greater challenges than before, are living in a time of mixed hope and fear, of opportunity and danger.

Definitions and interpretations

Article I of the UN Charter, which sets out the Purposes of the United Nations, states in paragraph 1 the first and primary purpose:

1. To maintain international peace and security, and to that end to take effective collective measures for the prevention and removal of threats to the peace, and for the suppression of acts of aggression or other breaches of the peace, and to bring about by peaceful means, and in conformity with the principles of justice and international law, adjustment or settlement of international disputes or situations which might lead to a breach of the peace.

This primary purpose is often referred to as *keeping the peace* or as *peacekeeping*. Hence the term *peacekeeping* is regarded as a generic term covering all the activities and powers of the UN relating to international peace. The specific powers of the Security Council, the body responsible for maintaining world peace and security, are set out in Chapter V of the Charter describing its structure, functions and procedures; Chapter VI, dealing with the Pacific Settlement of Disputes; Chapter VII, dealing with Action with Respect to Threats to the Peace, Breaches of the Peace, and Acts of Aggression, commonly referred to as "enforcement measures" and Chapter VIII, dealing with Regional Arrangements.

As a result of the growing diversity of the tasks undertaken in the various operations decreed by the Security Council, and with the help of the General Assembly and the Secretary-General, various terms have taken on a specific technical meaning as a result of usage and practice that describes more precisely the exact nature of an operation. Thus the term *peacekeeping* (in its precise narrow sense) is now used or applied to a specific type of operation or action where military personnel (unarmed as military observers and only lightly armed as peacekeeping forces) are sent to one area of armed conflict, **with the consent of the contending parties,** to supervise and maintain a **cease-fire previously agreed to by the parties.** It is thus a sort of neutral buffer force intended to prevent the resumption of hostilities and to facilitate a peaceful solution of the conflict or dispute between the parties, either with or without the assistance of the UN.

There is nothing in either Chapter VI or VII of the Charter that specifically mentions or authorized this type of peacekeeping force, although Article 40 does authorize the Security Council to take "provisional measures". It was invented in 1956 at the time of the Suez war when the United Nations Emergency Force (UNEF) was created with the prior consent of the contending parties — the Israelis, the British, the French and the Egyptians — in order to supervise and maintain the cease-fire and the withdrawal of the respective armed forces.

The operation is often referred to, rather jokingly, as coming under Chapter 6 1/2 of the Charter. Because of the expanded nature of some of the later peacekeeping operations, it is sometimes said that they come under Chapter 6 3/4 of the Charter.

The term *peacemaking* is used to describe the process of the peaceful settlement of international disputes or the resolution of conflicts, and comes squarely under Chapter VI of the Charter. It includes all of the traditional peaceful political procedures and methods which may be undertaken by the parties, with or without the assistance of the UN, to achieve a solution of their dispute or problem. Peacemaking can be best negotiated either before the outbreak of armed conflict or after it is halted by a cease-fire. Peacemaking, like peacekeeping, can only be made or done with the consent of the parties.

Enforcement measures or actions are those undertaken or authorized by the Security Council under Chapter VII of the Charter to maintain or restore international peace and security in the case of any threat to the peace, breach of the peace or act of aggression. While peacekeeping and peacemaking measures and actions are made on the basis of *recommendations* of the Security Council and require the consent of the parties concerned, enforcement action or measures are taken by *decision* of the Security Council under Chapter VII and are binding upon the parties with or without their consent. Here, too, a variety of measures can be taken, including those listed in Articles 41 and 42 such as embargoes, various sanctions and military action by armed forces. Military enforcement actions have been authorized on only two occasions, in the Korean War in 1950 and in the Gulf War in 1990.

The term *peacebuilding* is of more recent vintage than both peacemaking and peacekeeping. It denotes a much broader and more fundamental process that covers all the areas of international relations and cooperation including the political, economic, social, legal and humanitarian concerns and related measures that are addressed in the Charter or as envisaged in its Preamble "to save succeeding generations from the scourge of war ... and ... to promote social progress and better standards of life in larger freedom". Thus, it is clear that peacebuilding includes peacemaking and peacekeeping in the latter's broader generic as well as narrower technical sense.

In recent years there has been growing recognition that many situations and developments, which at one time were regarded as being primarily the domestic or internal concern of states, had an international dimension and global impact. Not only global economic and social affairs, but also problems of poverty, population and pollution have an obvious transnational dimension and effect, as have human rights and humanitarian concerns, terrorism, narcotic drugs, AIDS and other diseases, the cross border flow of refugees and tides of immigrants. Action on these problems is now regarded as part of peacebuilding, with a potential role for both peacemaking and peacekeeping actions. There has therefore been some degree of overlap or blurring of the line between matters that are "essentially within the domestic jurisdiction"

(Article 2.7) and situations deemed likely "to impair the general welfare or friendly relations among nations" (Article 14) or "might lead to international friction or give rise to a dispute" (Article 34).

Whenever a disagreement has arisen about whether a situation is essentially domestic or international in nature, the matter has usually been resolved in favour of the international interest. There is continuing discussion and often disagreement due to different opinions on the limits of sovereignty and on whether national or international concerns should prevail. Each case that arises is settled on its own merits, but there is a growing trend towards an international solution. Most observers believe this trend will continue.

For many years there has been talk of enhancing the role of the UN in *preventive diplomacy* or in preventive peacekeeping or peacemaking. The basic concept is of pre-crisis management, that is, if the UN took early steps to avoid or manage a developing situation of tension or a growing problem, a worsening of the situation and a crisis could be prevented. While a number of suggestions have been put forward in the past, very little or nothing came of them, in large part because of the obstacles imposed by the Cold War.

However, with the new opportunities provided by the ending of the Cold War and the outcome of the Gulf War — which successfully repelled aggression — on the one hand, and with the danger posed on the other hand by the disintegrative tendencies that emerged in the aftermath of the Cold War, there has been a resultant mushrooming of peacekeeping demands made on the UN. This, in turn, has led to an upsurge of interest in encouraging and enhancing the role of the UN in preventive diplomacy. The heavy financial burdens of the new peacekeeping operations have also been a factor in stimulating interest in preventive diplomacy.

Steps are now underway to explore in depth the opportunities and possibilities for preventive diplomacy by the UN. For example, fact-finding commissions or representatives of the Secretary-General have been sent to several conflict areas such as Nagorno Karabakh, Moldavia and other countries of the former Soviet Union, with a view to preventing the outbreak of large-scale hostilities. So far they have been largely successful in preventing the outbreak of civil wars in those countries. Preventive diplomacy has been carried an important step further by the *preventive deployment* of a *UN presence in Macedonia* at the request of the Macedonian government in order to forestall any outbreak of hostilities there or invasion from Serbia. A battalion was sent to Macedonia from UNPROFOR (United Nations Protection Force) in Yugoslavia in 1992.

The Security Council summit meeting

It was in the light of this "time of momentous change" that the UN Security Council decided to hold for the first time a summit meeting of heads of state and government on January 31, 1992. The 15 members all agreed to a concluding statement by the then monthly President, Prime Minister John Major of the United Kingdom, which is summarized as follows.

The members of the Council noted that the ending of the Cold War had raised hopes for a safer, more equitable and more humane world and that rapid progress had been made towards democracy and achieving the purposes set out in the Charter. They also recognized that change had brought new risks for stability and security, and expected the UN to play "a central role" in facing the new challenges in the search for peace. They called for strengthening and improving the UN to increase its effectiveness, and noted that "the non-military sources of instability in the economic, social, humanitarian and ecological fields have become threats to peace and security". They called for the highest priority for the solution of these problems. They also reaffirmed their commitment to the collective security system of the Charter.

They invited the new Secretary-General, Boutros Boutros-Ghali, to prepare by July 1, 1992 recommendations to strengthen and make more efficient the capacity of the UN "for preventive diplomacy, for peacemaking and for peacekeeping". His recommendations could cover the role of the UN in "identifying potential crises and areas of instability as well as contributions to be made by regional organizations" in helping the work of the Council, and also the need for adequate resources, both material and financial. He could also consider how greater use might be made of his good offices and his other functions under the Charter.

The statement also expressed the commitment of members of the Council to take concrete steps to enhance the effectiveness of the UN in disarmament, arms control and non-proliferation. The members also stressed the need "to prevent the proliferation in all its aspects of all weapons of mass destruction" and to avoid excessive and destabilizing accumulations and transfers of arms. They said:

> The proliferation of all weapons of mass destruction constitutes a threat to international peace and security. The members of the Council commit themselves to working to prevent the spread of technology related to the research for or production of such weapons and to take appropriate action to that end.

They also stressed the importance of nuclear non-proliferation and the role of the Non-Proliferation Treaty and International Atomic Energy Agency safeguards, and as well as of effective export controls, and called for the completion in 1992 of the convention banning chemical weapons.

The statement concluded:

> The members of the Council agree that the world now has the best chance of achieving international peace and security since the foundation of the United Nations. They undertake to work in close cooperation with other United Nations Member States in their own efforts to achieve this, as well as to address urgently all the other problems, in particular those of economic and social development, requiring the collective response of the international community. They recognize that peace and prosperity are indivisible and that lasting peace and stability require effective international cooperation for the eradication of poverty and the promotion of a better life for all in larger freedom.

This is the first time that the Security Council had described international peace and security in its broadest sense, encompassing economic and social development, the humanitarian and ecological fields, the eradication of poverty and the promotion of a better life in larger freedom, all of which are necessary elements of peacebuilding.

The outlook for the UN

Because of the growing recognition that almost all problems that afflict the world are interlinked and are global in their scope, the conviction has grown that they can best be dealt with by global action. Indeed, in many cases only global solutions can be successful or effective. For this, the UN is ideally and uniquely competent and qualified. It is the only institution that has the authority, structure and machinery and includes all the nations of the Earth. It has not only the expertise and experience of the substantive staff but, above all, the operational capability.

It thus seems inevitable that the activities and role of the UN will continue to expand in the future. The only obvious limitations are its lack of financial resources and its dependence on the support of the major powers of the world for effective action. In this regard, there has been talk that in the post-Cold War era there is now an opportunity and need for the "middle powers" to resume the active and useful leadership role they had played in the early years of the UN.

The much-touted *new world order* has not been achieved and, if anything, seems to be receding further into the future. The UN Charter, however, provides the best prescription for its achievement. The prevalent talk of reforming the UN must be regarded as a long-term goal. What is needed urgently is a more effective implementation of the existing Charter.

Prior to the entry into force of the UN Charter, the waging of international war was not illegal under international law. Indeed, the large body of the international law of peace and war includes a large component on the laws of war. The UN Charter in effect declares now that the waging of international war is illegal, by banning "the threat or use of force against the territorial integrity or political independence of any state, or in any other manner inconsistent with the purposes of the United Nations," (Article 2.4). Only the Security Council has the power to use military force to maintain or restore international peace and security (Article 42). The "inherent right of individual or collective self-defence if an armed attack occurs" is preserved under Article 51 "until the Security Council has taken measures necessary to maintain international peace and security."

Now that the Security Council is able to function as foreseen in the Charter, as was demonstrated by the absence of any veto during and since the Gulf War, it is widely hoped that wars of aggression or unauthorized use of force by great or small powers will be deterred. And since the Security Council has now demonstrated that it is prepared to intervene in civil wars that may threaten international peace and security, it is also hoped that these too will diminish in number and ferocity or will at least be quickly contained. This hope is now being tested in Yugoslavia and Somalia.

The Stockholm Initiative on Global Security and Governance prepared a report in April, 1991 on "Common Responsibility in the 1990s" which dealt mainly with strengthening the UN across the broad spectrum of its responsibilities. It made 28 recommendations covering peace and security, development, environment, population, democracy and human rights, and global governance.

In August 1992 the UN Special Committee on Peacekeeping Operations in its report (A/47/253) to the General Assembly listed 33 ideas and suggestions for improving UN peacekeeping operations.

These reports were perhaps the most noteworthy in what had become a ferment of activity in the growth industry of efforts to improve, strengthen or reform the UN. While they contain a useful catalogue of proposals, their adoption and implementation will be selective and slow.

What is more likely is that the report of the Secretary-General that was submitted in June, 1992, as requested by the Security Council, will, to a large extent, encompass and delineate the nature and scope of the role of the UN for at least the remainder of this century. The report of the Secretary-General entitled "An Agenda for Peace" is dealt with below.

Preventive diplomacy

As regards preventive diplomacy, UN Secretaries-General, especially Dag Hammarskjold, have urged its use and, indeed, have used their good offices in a number of cases where *quiet diplomacy* has helped to defuse incipient disputes and crises. But, by the very nature of quiet diplomacy, they have received little or no publicity. A recent successful example, whose results could not be kept secret, was the release of the hostages held in Lebanon.

Article 99 of the Charter empowers the Secretary-General to bring to the attention of the Security Council "any matter which in his opinion may threaten the maintenance of international peace and security". But successive Secretaries-General have been very cautious in taking advantage of it because they did not have their own sources of intelligence or accurate information and some important members of the UN were unenthusiastic, both on the merits of the question and because of its cost, to provide the Secretaries-General with the necessary resources. It will be recalled in this connection that the proposal of the President of France in 1978, at the first UN Special Session on Disarmament, to establish an International Satellite Monitoring Agency did not succeed, despite widespread support, for the same reasons.

Nevertheless, various suggestions continue to be made to expand and improve the Secretary-General's sources of information by his undertaking of fact-finding missions on his own initiative, and also by making greater use of the 115 UN Development Program offices and the 67 UN Information Centres spread around the world.

In addition, the practice of greater consultation between the Secretary-General and members of the Security Council, and with various regional organizations and with the UN Specialized Agencies, could contribute to the acquisition of objective information by the Secretary-General and to the creation of a climate more conducive to effective preventive diplomacy.

There is certainly considerably more room for increased use of the good offices of the Secretary-General and there are greater possibilities for such use, either at the request of one or more parties to a situation or dispute or on his own initiative.

Apart from action initiated by the Secretary-General, there is, of course, great scope for earlier action to be taken by the Security Council, the General Assembly and other organs of the United Nations. To give just one example, Article 96 of the Charter authorizes the General Assembly and the Security Council to request an advisory opinion from the International Court of Justice on any legal question and the General Assembly may authorize other organs of the UN, including the Secretary-General and the Specialized Agencies, to request such opinions.

In the field of preventive diplomacy, as in other areas, much will depend on the willingness of the UN Members in the General Assembly to provide the necessary human and financial resources.

For some years, the Secretary-General and some delegations have suggested that the Security Council should authorize a peacekeeping operation at the request of a single state that fears it may be attacked, without requiring the consent of all the parties to a dispute or crisis. It has been argued that by sending a UN peacekeeping force to a single state that perceives itself under threat of armed attack, an attack may in fact be averted or deterred (as, for example, might have happened in the case of Kuwait). Such a "preventive peacekeeping" operation would go a step beyond preventive diplomacy and could play a decisive role in peacekeeping and, perhaps, also be an effective means of stimulating peacemaking efforts.

Despite what many observers regard as the inherent logic and appeal of this approach, it has turned out to be controversial. A number of important states, including Brazil, China, India, Russia and others have, in fact, voiced their reservations that such action could amount to an infringement of a state's sovereignty.

In June 1992 the Secretary-General submitted his report entitled "An Agenda for Peace" (available under DPI number 1247) to the Security Council in response to the request made by the summit meeting on 31 January 1992.

The specific comments and recommendations of the Secretary-General on Preventive Diplomacy are:

(a) Increased use of the many available confidence-building measures (CBMs). The regional organizations are requested to report to the UN on the further CBMs that might apply in their areas.

(b) The UN requires accurate information on economic and social trends as well as political developments that may lead to dangerous tensions. Increased resort to fact-finding is needed, whether initiated by the Secretary-General, by increased consultations with national governments, or by formal missions authorized by the Security Council or General Assembly.

(c) Strengthened arrangements for early warning systems regarding various threats to society require the close cooperation of the various specialized agencies and the functional offices of the UN. In addition, the Security Council could invite "a reinvigorated and restructured Economic and Social Council" to provide reports on those developments that might threaten international peace and security. Regional organizations could also play an important role in early warning.

(d) The "preventive deployment of an appropriate UN presence" could take place at the request of one government alone when a country feels threatened from either outside or inside the country. Such preventive deployment could include humanitarian assistance or assistance in maintaining security through military, police or civilian personnel.

(e) Consideration could be given to the establishment of demilitarized zones with the preventive deployment of UN personnel on both sides of a border with the agreement of both parties or on one side of the border at the request of one party.

The recommendations by the Secretary-General under (d) and (e) for "preventive deployment" of UN personnel at the request of one government alone or of one party to a dispute is still a matter of some disagreement among the UN members. It was therefore forward-looking on his part to have recommended it. If his recommendation is adopted as a normal practice by the Security Council, it could become an important element of preventive diplomacy.

Peacekeeping

As mentioned earlier, the main problems concerning peacekeeping arise out of the rapid increase in the number and scope of such operations and their financing.

Among the many ideas now being discussed and in some cases already being implemented, in connection with expanded or extended peacekeeping are:

- suggestions that Member States might consider entering into agreements with the UN to make military forces, assistance and facilities available to the Security Council solely for purposes of peacekeeping (as distinct from forces for enforcement action under Article 43), and that the forces need not be limited solely to military forces but could also include regular police forces and civilians;
- establishing training programmes for both civilians and military by the UN and by national governments, including the preparation of training manuals;

- institutionalizing arrangements and planning in the UN Secretariat and by national governments to ensure the most effective use of peacekeeping forces and the provision of adequate financing for them;
- planning arrangements for liaison and cooperation with regional and sub-regional organizations to develop the maximum coordination of efforts, including the establishment of regional training and operational centres.

The specific comments and recommendations of the Secretary-General in his report to the Security Council are the following:

(a) Because of the escalating cost of peacekeeping and the problems it creates, the General Assembly should encourage Member States to finance their peacekeeping contributions from defence rather than from foreign affairs budgets.

(b) Because of the evolving nature of peacekeeping operations, a new array of demands and problems regarding logistics, equipment, personnel and finance must be met. Member States should designate not only the number and kind of skilled military personnel they could make available, but also civilian political officers, human rights monitors, electoral officials, refugee and humanitarian aid specialists and police. This would require improved training of such peacekeeping personnel by national governments, Nongovernmental Organizations (NGOs) and the UN Secretariat. Pre-positioned stocks of basic peacekeeping equipment should be established so that they would be immediately available.

Peacemaking

As regards the question of peacemaking, Chapter VI of the Charter commends the various historic methods and procedures for the pacific settlement of disputes and conflict resolution. In this field the UN has been much less successful than it has in peacekeeping. It is, of course, much easier to persuade governments to halt armed hostilities than to agree to a peaceful resolution of their long-held and deeply-felt disputes, that usually are based on cultural, ethnic, language, racial, religious and nationalistic animosities. One need only recall examples, such as, the Arab-Israeli dispute, Cyprus, the Falkland (Malvinas) Islands, Kashmir, and South Africa, to mention just a few, that seem intractable.

In several of these cases UN peacekeeping operations have lasted for years with little progress towards peacemaking. Consideration is now being given to the possibility of withdrawing or ending the peacekeeping operation in Cyprus as a means of stimulating greater efforts by the parties to resolve their dispute.

Paradoxically, the very weakness of the UN which has no money and no forces and does not engage in trade and commerce, is the main source of its strength in peacemaking and peacekeeping. It gives the Organization and, in particular, the Secretary-General, a moral authority and credibility because they have no vested interest in anything but peace. Thus the neutrality and impartiality of the Secretary-General have been generally recognized and accepted.

Hence, it is possible that there will now be much greater opportunities for the Secretary-General to engage not only in preventive diplomacy but also in positive peacemaking initiatives. These opportunities will be enhanced by the determination of the new Secretary-General to achieve greater co-ordination of the efforts of the many Specialized Agencies that are a part of the UN system and of enlisting their active participation in UN peacemaking and peacekeeping.

In addition to the cooperation of the UN Specialized Agencies, as part of his policy of "decentralization" of peacebuilding, the Secretary-General has already begun to involve regional arrangements and agencies in UN peacemaking and peacekeeping efforts. He has also stated his intention to make use of Non-Governmental Organizations (NGOs), some of which have considerable experience in the field of humanitarian and other economic and social activities.

The specific recommendations made by the Secretary-General in his report to the Security Council are as follows:

(a) Continued use of the means envisaged in the Charter, such as mediation, negotiation and arbitration, by an individual selected by the Security Council, the General Assembly or the Secretary-General, or by the good offices of the Secretary-General himself. Both the Security Council and the General Assembly should take a more active role in efforts aimed at pre-empting or containing situations likely to threaten international peace and security.

(b) Greater use should be made of the International Court of Justice for the peaceful adjudication of disputes. The Secretary-General should be authorized to request advisory opinions of the Court. All states should accept, without reservation, the compulsory jurisdiction of the Court in the cases mentioned in the Statute of the Court.

(c) International assistance should be provided to ameliorate situations that contribute to a dispute, for example, assistance to displaced persons within a society. There are now no adequate mechanisms for mobilizing the resources needed for such assistance, but the Secretary-General is exploring with the UN agencies and programmes ways of improving the peaceful resolution of disputes.

Peace-enforcement

Enforcement action and measures by the Security Council under Chapter VII of the Charter have been used very sparingly in cases of a threat to the peace, breach of the peace or act of aggression. Among the reasons therefore, are the slow operation of the sanctions, doubts about their effectiveness, the difficulties of supervising their enforcement, and their sometimes negative impact on innocent neighbouring states and former trading partners of the delinquent state. As regards the use of military force, no forces have ever been made available to the Security Council as envisaged in Article 43 of the Charter, and there is an inherent reluctance on the part of most states to risk the lives of their military personnel except in cases where the vital interests of the states are directly involved.

In searching for some way of coping with the difficult problems involved, the Secretary-General has proposed the creation of a new category of UN forces which he calls "peace-enforcement units". Those units, composed of volunteers, would perform tasks that fall somewhere in between those for which military forces are needed to maintain or restore peace in the case of armed acts of war and those for which peacekeeping forces are used to supervise or monitor a cease-fire.

The specific recommendations of the Secretary-General are as follows:

(a) When the Security Council imposes sanctions, it should devise a set of measures for addressing the special economic problems that may result for some states and thus encourage their cooperation with the Council's decisions.

(b) When all peaceful means for maintaining or restoring international peace and security have failed and the Council decides on the use of military force, the special agreements foreseen in Chapter VII of the Charter, whereby states would make armed forces available to the Security Council on a permanent basis, should be implemented. The ready availability of such armed forces on call would, in itself, be a means of deterring breaches of the peace. Accordingly, the Security Council should begin negotiations with the support of the Military Staff Committee to implement Article 43 of the Charter.

(c) Since the forces envisaged under Article 43 are not likely to be available for some time to come, the Security Council should consider the use of peace-enforcement units as a new category of UN forces. Such units should be available on call and would consist of volunteers. Their task would exceed the mission of peacekeeping forces, as they would be required to restore and maintain cease-fires that had been agreed but not complied with. These peace-enforcement units would be more heavily armed than peacekeeping forces. They would not be the same as either the military forces that may be eventually constituted under Article 43 to deal with acts of aggression, or as the forces used for peacekeeping operations. (Already some observers are beginning to describe them as forces under Chapter 6 3/4 or 6 7/8 of the Charter.)

Here, too, if the innovative proposal of the Secretary-General is implemented in practice by the Security Council, it would significantly improve the usefulness and effectiveness of peacekeeping operations in the maintenance of cease-fires.

Post-conflict peacebuilding

Although the Security Council had not specifically requested the Secretary-General to report on the broad subject of peacebuilding, in his report "An Agenda for Peace", he deals with this subject, not in terms of a general program for action, but only in regard to what would be necessary in a post-conflict situation. His comments and suggestions in this regard are:

(a) Peacebuilding, in the sense of constructing a new environment of peace, is the counterpart of preventive diplomacy, which seeks to avoid the breakdown of peace. Once peace-making and peacekeeping have been successful, sustained cooperative efforts to deal with the underlying economic, social, cultural and humanitarian problems are necessary to put peace on a durable foundation to prevent the recurrence of a crisis.

(b) In addition to the customary removal of land mines and restoration of transport, the UN must provide new technical assistance for transforming deficient national structures and strengthening new democratic institutions. This would involve the recognition that social peace is as important as strategic or political peace.

Safety of UN personnel

The Secretary-General, who is always concerned about the safety of personnel on UN operations, had the following to say on that subject in his report.

It is necessary to ensure the safety of UN personnel even though duty in areas of danger can never be risk-free. The Security Council should consider what action should be taken towards those who put UN personnel in danger. It should consider in advance collective measures that could be taken, possibly including those under Chapter VII, when the UN operation is systematically frustrated and hostilities occur.

The role of regional organizations

The United Nations and its family of 16 Specialized Agencies are universal in membership and global in scope. The term *regional organizations* is used to denote those permanent international organizations that are neither universal nor global, but rather regional in geographical scope or with a limited defined membership and purpose set out in a formal treaty or a similar legally binding instrument.

As mentioned earlier, except for the exercise of the inherent right of individual or collective self-defense in case of an armed attack, only the UN Security Council is empowered to take or authorize the use of armed forces to maintain or restore international peace and security. Chapter VIII of the Charter, however, permits "regional arrangements or agencies" (referred to here as *regional organizations*) to deal with matters relating to international peace and security. The Security Council must encourage the peaceful settlement of local disputes through or by such regional agencies either on the initiative of the states concerned or by reference from the Security Council and, where appropriate, utilize such regional arrangements for enforcement action, but only under its authority. For their part, the regional agencies must keep the Security Council fully informed of their activities for the maintenance of international peace and security.

This role of the regional agencies has been exercised only infrequently in the past, mainly because they were not yet organized or ready to undertake such activities. With the growing strain on the UN caused by the remarkable expansion of the Security Council activities, however, there has been increasing talk of the need and the desirability of making fuller use of such regional organizations in peacemaking and peacekeeping. Indeed, the Security Council invited the Secretary-General to deal with the contribution of such organizations in his report.

It is clear that for conflict avoidance and resolution, for preventive diplomacy and for peacemaking in general, the regional organizations have a definite role to play because of their geographic, historical, ethnic, cultural or religious knowledge of and experience with the problems and countries of the region. But, because of their very close association with those countries, they have often acquired special interests or attitudes of their own which may give rise to questions regarding their objectivity and which might detract from their usefulness in the peace process. Nevertheless, in many cases they will be able to play a useful role and the UN will no doubt wish to consult and work more closely in the future with the regional organizations to make the best use of whatever functions or services they can render.

In Yugoslavia, the 12-member European Community, and in Nagorno-Karabakh, the 52-member Conference on Security and Cooperation in Europe (CSCE) have undertaken efforts, mainly of a political nature, to help or encourage the peace process. In Somalia, the Secretary-General has enlisted the support of the Organization of African Unity (OAU), the League of Arab States (LAS) and the Organization of the Islamic Conference (OIC); and in Western Sahara, of the OAU. Previously the Secretary-General has maintained close contacts with the Organization of American States (OAS) on problems in Latin America and with various groups of Central American states with regard to problems there.

When it comes to peacekeeping operations, however, none of the regional organizations has the structure, the specialized experience, and, above all, the operational capabilities, to play an effective role in actual operations. It is possible that NATO might be able to do so in the future in Europe, if it undergoes some restructuring of its membership and of its original purpose. In fact, on June 4, 1992, at a ministerial meeting in Oslo, NATO agreed in principle to undertake peacekeeping operations in Europe or former territories of the Soviet Union, "under the responsibility of the CSCE". Such activities however, it was stated by NATO's Secretary-General, could only be undertaken by request of all members of the CSCE (52, at the time of writing) and would have to be agreed by all members of NATO. It is also possible that, if the unification process of the European Community is successful, and if it establishes a coherent military force and doctrine, it too could readily acquire the necessary operational capabilities for peacekeeping through the development and utilization of the forces assigned to the Western European Union (WEU). This would seem to be even more likely for the CSCE, after the far-reaching new decisions taken at its meeting in Helsinki in July 1992. As for the other regions of the world, with the possible exception of the Commonwealth of Independent States (CIS), none of them seems likely to acquire the necessary operational capabilities in the immediate future.

The UN, however, could cooperate with the regional organizations and national governments in helping to organize and train national forces for peacekeeping that could be made available for future peace-keeping operations of either or both the UN and the regional organization concerned. The creation of such forces, could certainly help the UN with the burden it now bears because of its shortage of financial and material resources and of trained personnel. The existence of such forces could also relieve the UN of its very difficult tasks of deciding the priorities of the competing demands that are made on it. But the final responsibility and decision remain vested in the Security Council for both peacekeeping and peace-enforcement.

In his report, the Secretary-General supports greater cooperation with regional organizations. He notes that they possess a potential that should be used in preventive diplomacy, peacemaking, peacekeeping and post-conflict peacebuilding. Regional action, as a process of decentralization, delegation and cooperation with the UN efforts, could lighten the burden of the Security Council and also add to a deeper sense of participation, consensus and democratization in international affairs. He also adds that NGOs, academic institutions, parliamentarians, business and professional committees, the media and the public at large must all be involved if the UN is to be strengthened.

The role of disarmament

Another noteworthy development in recent years is the increasing use in UN peacekeeping operations of arms control and disarmament measures. On a few rare occasions in the past, an arms embargo has been used as an enforcement measure under Chapter VII of the Charter, and recently it has been used extensively and intrusively by the Security Council for the disarming of Iraq's mass-destruction weapon capabilities as an integral part of the cease-fire arrangements that ended the Gulf War.

But, apart from enforcement measures, arms control and disarmament measures of various kinds have come to be used as necessary peacemaking and peacebuilding aspects of UN peacekeeping operations. Such measures of one kind or another have been and are being used in the peacekeeping operations in Afghanistan, Angola, Cambodia, Central America, El Salvador, the Golan Heights, Iran-Iraq and Yugoslavia. With the peacekeeping activities of the UN taking on greater importance, so too will the arms control and disarmament elements of the peacebuilding process, as the inter-relationship of disarmament and international security, both globally and regionally, becomes more clearly recognized and accepted.

Confidence- and security-building measures have long been recognized as measures of arms control and disarmament. They have gained in importance after the signature in 1975 of the Helsinki Declaration on Security and Cooperation in Europe. Other disarmament measures including withdrawal of armed forces and the surrender or reduction of their arms, embargoes and other limitations on the export or import of weapons, the avoidance of excessive build-ups and imbalances in the development or acquisition of conventional arms, and the prevention of the proliferation of all mass-destruction weapons (nuclear, chemical, biological and their delivery vehicles) and their ultimate elimination, are all considered important measures for preventive diplomacy, peacemaking, peacekeeping and peacebuilding.

Effective verification of the various disarmament measures is, of course, an essential element of the disarmament process and an indispensable ingredient of confidence building. As verification of the enforced disarming of Iraq has demonstrated, it is a very difficult and complex task. In order to ensure that it is effectively undertaken in UN peacekeeping operations, it may be necessary for the UN to co-operate with regional organizations and national governments to build up a trained group or corps of technical experts and specialists on inspection and verification.

There is a definite inter-relationship and linkage among preventive diplomacy and action, peacemaking, peacekeeping, peacebuilding and disarmament on both a global and regional dimension. Progress in any of these areas creates a synergistic interaction with the others. As peace and international security are strengthened, far-reaching measures of disarmament become more feasible, as does even the abolition and elimination of all nuclear and other mass-destruction weapons. So, too, does the reduction of all conventional weapons and forces to levels needed only for the maintenance of internal domestic peace and for making military forces available to the United Nations as required for enforcement measures and for peacekeeping.

The financial problem

The question of adequate financing for the manifold activities of the UN, whether for the regular budget or for peacekeeping operations, has been a major problem for successive Secretaries-General. By 1992 it had become particularly acute.

The UN regular budget in 1992 totalled $1.03 billion. The budgets of UN agencies, such as UNICEF, the UN Development Programme, and the World Food Programme, which are raised by voluntary contributions, cost some additional billions of dollars. As mentioned previously the budget for peacekeeping operations rose dramatically from $421 million in 1991 to some $2.7 billion in 1992, although the latter sum is still only of the same order as the cost of a single B-2 (Stealth) bomber (now $2.2 billion). Unpaid assessments at April 30, 1992, amounted to $1,093.4 million for the regular budget and $805.3 million for peacekeeping operations, not counting four of the newest peacekeeping operations for which assessments had not yet been approved by the General Assembly.

Continuing efforts and appeals to the Member States for prompt payment of their over-due assessments have not been very successful and other means therefore had to be found for raising the required funds. From time to time it was necessary to resort to short-term borrowing from other internal UN funds or to obtaining advance payments against future assessments from a few members.

In the mid-1960s, faced with another acute financial crisis, the General Assembly on one occasion approved the issuance of bonds to raise the necessary funds. The General Assembly, however, has consistently rejected requests by the Secretary-General to borrow commercially. Several Specialized Agencies of the UN, however, have in the last few years been authorized to resort to commercial borrowing.

The time has come to seek once more some innovative ways of raising the necessary funds to enable the UN to fulfil its growing and, indeed, indispensable responsibilities. Among the various options that might be considered is once again to issue bonds or to resort to commercial short-term borrowing. Perhaps the UN should seek voluntary contributions from Member States, private foundations and corporations, as is done by several of the UN's own agencies and programmes, either for current costs or for establishing a special revolving capital fund or some permanent trust or reserve fund.

In his report to the Security Council, the Secretary-General made the following observations and recommendations on the question of UN financing:

(a) Adoption of a set of listed measures to deal with cash flow problems, including charging interest on overdue assessments, increasing the Working Capital Fund to a level of 25% of the regular UN budget (i.e. to $250 million now), establishing a temporary Peacekeeping Reserve Fund of $50 million for starting up peacekeeping operations, and authorizing the Secretary-General to borrow commercially.

(b) Creating a Humanitarian Revolving Fund for emergency situations. (This proposal has been implemented.)

(c) Establishment of a UN Peace Endowment Fund with an initial target of $1 billion, with contributions from governments, the private sector and individuals. Other potential sources of funds include a levy on arms sales and air travel, borrowing from the World Bank and the IMF, and tax exemption for donations to the UN.

(d) While the above proposals are being debated, there should be established immediately a revolving peacekeeping reserve fund of $50 million. The General Assembly should appropriate one-third of the estimated cost of any peacekeeping operation decided on by the Security Council, and the Secretary-General should be authorized, in exceptional cases, to place contracts without competitive bidding.

The Secretary-General has asked a select group of qualified eminent persons to examine the whole question of UN financing and to report to him. He will present their advice, with his comments, to the General Assembly.

Conclusion

Any talk of a new era in international affairs or of a new rededication to the purposes and principles of the Charter will remain empty if the Organization cannot fulfil its urgent responsibilities. It would be unconscionable if the UN were deprived by a shortage of funds of the opportunity to take advantage of the favourable international climate and, thus, were prevented from achieving its goals.

On the other hand, if the necessary funds are provided, the nations and peoples of the world could look to the future with greater confidence. It would be possible for the UN to undertake a new and expanded programme of positive peacebuilding activities.

Since all people want peace, and democracies do not as a rule resort to war to settle their disputes, the UN could decide to pay greater attention to helping nations to build democratic institutions and systems of government and thus greatly enhance the prospects for peace and justice.

It will, however, also be necessary to devote close attention and exercise extreme care to make sure that the military-political Cold War is not succeeded by an economic Cold War in the industrial North, or by a North-South confrontation, due to not-so-benign neglect.

In order to promote the achievement of the UN's goals, it is more important to implement the existing provisions of the Charter than to go through the long and difficult process of attempting to amend it. It must be remembered that in practice the constitution of the world organization has been interpreted on the basis of the "growing tree" doctrine and that many reforms and innovations have been introduced through practice and a liberal interpretation of the provisions of the Charter. There is, however, increasing discussion and some expectation that the year 1995, the 50th anniversary of the UN, may provide an opportunity for convening a conference for the review of the UN Charter and of all of the Organization's activities.

For the immediate future, however, and probably for most of the decade of the '90s, it would seem that the easiest and most effective way to maintain and promote international peace and security is to strengthen the UN in all its peacebuilding activities and to ensure that it has adequate resources to meet all the peacekeeping tasks it is called upon to perform.

Earlier in this Chapter I said that the UN Charter provides the best prescription for achieving a new world order. Whether the ideal world order is ever achieved is highly problematical. But, given the strong support of its Member States and adequate resources, there are good reasons for hoping that a new and better era of international affairs can be achieved by the end of the century.

The Secretary-General's Agenda for Peace will require lengthy consideration and debate by the Security Council, the General Assembly, the Specialized Agencies, the Member States and regional organizations. Its implementation will probably take place in a piecemeal fashion. It seems clear that his report will provide the blueprint for strengthening the role and effectiveness of the UN for the rest of this century.

Annex

United Nations Peacekeeping Operations
1948 - 1992

1948-present	UNTSO
	United Nations Truce Supervision Organization (Israel and its neighbouring four Arab states)
1949-present	UNMOGIP
	United Nations Military Observer Group in India and Pakistan
1956-67	UNEF I
	First United Nations Emergency Force (Sinai Peninsula)
1958	UNOGIL
	United Nations Observation Group in Lebanon
1960-64	ONUC
	United Nations Operation in the Congo
1962-63	UNTEA/UNSF
	United Nations Temporary Executive Authority and United Nations Security Force in West New Guinea (West Irian)
1963-64	UNYOM
	United Nations Yemen Observation Mission
1964-present	UNFICYP
	United Nations Peacekeeping Force in Cyprus
1965-66	DOMREP
	Representative of the Secretary-General in the Dominican Republic

1965-66	UNIPOM	
	United Nations India-Pakistan Observation Mission	
1973-79	UNEF II	
	Second United Nations Emergency Force (Sinai Peninsula)	
1974-present	UNDOF	
	United Nations Disengagement Observer Force (Golan Heights)	
1978-present	UNIFIL	
	United Nations Interim Force in Lebanon	
1988-90	UNGOMAP	
	United Nations Good Offices Mission in Afghanistan and Pakistan	
1988-91	UNIIMOG	
	United Nations Iran-Iraq Military Observer Group	
1988-91	UNAVEM I	
	United Nations Angola Verification Mission	
1989-90	UNTAG	
	United Nations Transition Assistance Group in Namibia	
1989-92	ONUCA	
	United Nations Observer Group in Central America	
1991-present	UNIKOM	
	United Nations Iraq-Kuwait Observation Mission	
1991-present	UNAVEM II	
	United Nations Angola Verification Mission	
1991-present	ONUSAL	
	United Nations Observer Mission in El Salvador	
1991-present	UNAMIC	
	United Nations Advance Mission in Cambodia (UNAMIC is absorbed in the UNTAC)	
1991-present	MINURSO	
	United Nations Mission for the Referendum in Western Sahara	
1992-present	UNTAC	
	United Nations Transitional Authority in Cambodia	
1992-present	ONUMOZ	
	United Nations Operation in Mozambique	

1992-present	UNPROFOR
	United Nations Protection Force (Yugoslavia)
1992-present	UNOSOM
	United Nations Operation in Somalia
1993-present	United Nations Operation in Somalia II
1993-present	UNOMUR
	United Nations Observer Mission Uganda-Rwanda
1993-present	UNOMIG
	United Nations Observer Mission in Georgia
Established 1993	UNOMIL
	United Nations Observer Mission in Liberia
Established 1993	UNMIH
	United Nations Mission in Haiti
Established 1993	UNAMIR
	United Nations Assistance Mission for Rwanda

Part II
TOWARD A SUSTAINABLE SOCIETY

CHAPTER 7

Why Control Population?

Digby J. McLaren

Abstract. Because of the continuing acceleration in number of births, in resource use and in many aspects of environmental rundown, the planet's carrying capacity has long been exceeded and any immediate prospect of sustainability has faded. Nearly half the population of the world is below breeding age and, although growth rates are falling in some regions, they are constant in others. Family planning has only been effective in limited areas of the world. Any prospect of demographic transition to lower fertility for most is still far from realization. Future scenarios depend on how quickly education of women, family planning, including contraception, and improved health support programs can be introduced. The costs of such activities would be about one percent of current global military expenditures.

The Academies' Declaration

Before the United Nations Conference on the Environment and Development (UNCED) took place in Rio in 1992, the Royal Society of London and the US National Academy of Sciences issued a joint declaration on "Population Growth, Resource Consumption, and a Sustainable World". The Declaration warned that the world population was growing at almost 100 million a year and that if present trends continue, science and technology may not be able to prevent either irreversible degradation of the environment or growing poverty for much of the world. They suggested that with continued growth, the population, which at that time was about 5.4 billion (5,400 million) might reach 10 billion by 2050, and would continue to grow if global fertility rates do not stabilize very soon at replacement level (2.1 children per woman). The Declaration gave some facts on environmental changes in this century, and deplored unrestrained resource consumption in the developed world that might produce irreversible damage and already threatens the living standards of those who live in developing countries. The two Academies recognize the huge economic disparity between North and South, and the growth of poverty and starvation, and advocate family planning on a global scale. They called for international action and proposed to invite Academies from other countries to a scientific conference in 1993 to examine issues in detail. This conference, the *Population Summit of the World's Scientific Academies*, was held in New Delhi in October 1993.

Different futures, some opinions

The Declaration makes a good starting point for discussion on population growth, and resultant changes already apparent. Although a somewhat restrained statement, the two Academies nevertheless call for action and recognize certain important issues currently being debated. They accept explicitly that population growth and unrestrained use of resources are the prime movers in increasing human poverty and environmental degradation, although there is a substantial body of opinion that questions these assumptions.

This paper will review some of the controversies and possible priorities for action. Although we live at a unique moment of history and are faced with an uncertain future, there is a disparity of opinion regarding the causes of our present situation and the measures that might be taken to slow and, if need be, reverse current trends. One may summarize briefly the extremes of three opinions on what is going on. The first is held by the *economic optimists* who consider that people are our greatest asset and that technology is capable of sustaining and improving the lot of humankind indefinitely, as well as "managing" the ecosystem. The second holds that humankind must question the accelerating use of resources and technology and attempt to return to a life in balance with the ecosphere. The third opinion holds that all life on the planet has been in balance with its physical surroundings since it began and adjusts to the ever-changing environment. The rapid human-induced changes we observe today may soon be balanced by equally rapid adjustments within the ecosystem, with results that might be highly unfavourable to our species. Such an opinion would recognize the physical reality of the situation, based upon empirical observation, and act accordingly.

Whereas the first two opinions are firmly opposed, each, nevertheless, represents a reductionist approach to problems, which leads to piecemeal solutions. The third, on the other hand, demands a more holistic approach and would integrate solutions into a general theory that allowed prediction and modelling, of which Lovelock's Gaia theory (1976) might be an example, although not necessarily the only one.

Ecosphere is used in this paper whenever relevant in preference to the much misunderstood concept *environment*. The term ecosphere ascribes equal importance to the atmosphere, hydrosphere and lithosphere, together with all forms of life (biota) that exist within them, and can be divided into regional and local ecosystems, each a three-dimensional sector including air, water and/or land and the organisms that populate them (Stan Rowe, personal communication). The ecosphere is literally our home that we affect through our activities and our numbers. The terms *North* and *South* are used interchangeably in this paper for developed and developing regions or countries.

The accelerations currently observable, and referred to in this paper, including population, resource use, waste production,— extinctions, deforestation, and many others, effectively prevent the spread of Utopian economic systems by which all humankind might live in a sustainable environment indefinitely into the future. In fact, the problems we currently face must be solved in a very short time — perhaps 15 or 20 years at the most — if we are to influence the changes that must be made to our present system.

Dynamics of growth

We know how fast the population of the world is growing today and it is possible to project the effects of current trends forward in time, not necessarily to predict the future but to point out what the world's population would be if present trends continue under varying future conditions, and what the impact would be. Many scenarios have been suggested, but there is no dispute that currently the numbers are growing relentlessly and will do so for the next 20 or 30 years. The age effect, as the result of past growth, will ensure the expected acceleration in numbers (Arizpe et al., 1991). This may be summed up by the remark that "half the people in the world haven't started having children — they are children" (Gillespie, 1992).

What happens next? If growth continues indefinitely, various unpleasant futures may be predicted. Even if the demographic transition (discussed below) eventually lowers growth rates due to falling fertility in balance with increasing education and prosperity, projections for the next 20 or 30 years are relatively reliable and indicate 8 or more billion. Subsequent projections will depend on assumptions of fertility change although the momentum of growth within young populations will continue a long time. The growth of population is, indeed, a fact, and demographers agree on the reality of the figures cited by the two Academies. Opinions differ, however, on possible futures and how uncertainties will increase. Forecasting the behaviour of population over a longer term becomes increasingly uncertain, and the possibilities of disruption in the patterns of growth projections become increasingly probable. Current projections of possible futures remain approximately the same to about 2010-20 and then diverge increasingly according to a variety of assumptions (Lee, 1991, and Figure 1).

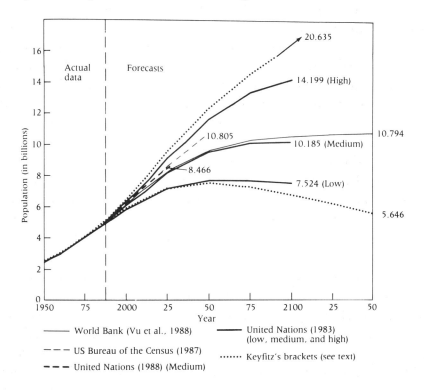

Fig. 1 World population projections, from R.D. Lee
(in Davis and Bernstam, 1991)

A major difficulty in demographic modelling is the effectiveness of the much discussed demographic transition. This proves to be a difficult concept to pin down. Rate of population growth or decline depends on the balance between mortality and fertility. High mortality and high fertility lead to a low rate of increase — the norm in the more distant past. More recently, decrease in mortality and increase in fertility have led to rapid population increase, the current condition in much of the world. The third balance, found today in most developed countries, is low mortality and low fertility leading to reduction in birth rate down to or below replacement level. This last development was brought about by the demographic transition, which took over 100 years, and there is discussion and doubt as to whether this represents a universal law and how quickly it might take place.

Demographers are not unanimous in accepting the transition as a law. Some require it if we are to emerge from the current crisis in runaway growth. On the other hand Abernethy (1991) has stated that recent research suggests that the fertility reduction predicted by demographic transition theory may not materialize. Demographic transition seems to occur when the population of a country or region becomes more highly educated, urbanized and developed economically. The ultimate cause appears to be a manifestation of the Industrial Revolution combined with advances in hygiene, leading to increased consumption of goods and services, although the timing and magnitude of the transition is highly irregular (Davis, 1991). In the developed world, the early-transition countries, reduction in fertility began before 1950 and sometimes happened very quickly. A Canadian example may be cited from Quebec, where after World War II, a variety of social factors led to a rapid emancipation of women and a change from having the highest birth-rate in the Western World to the lowest in less than one generation.

In the developing world there is a great variety of population growth rates. Horiuchi (1992) has given a summary of the post-War years of global changes. Annual rates, expressed as a percentage of population, rose from 1.79% to 2.06% in the 1950s and 60s. In 1975-80 they decreased to 1.73% and have remained constant since then — with no further decrease. Sub-Sahara Africa and some South Asia countries are *pre-transition*, but fertility declines have started, although they have a long way to go before falling to replacement level or below. The built-in inertia to changing the growth rate is illustrated by the fact that currently 48% of Sub-Saharan Africans are aged below 15, and in order to stabilize the population they would have to have one-child families for the next 30 years. Latin America and Asia, with 37% of the population below 15, would require 25 years of one-child families to stabilize (Gillespie, 1992). No one is suggesting that these scenarios are feasible but the facts show why it will take a long time for the present developing population surge to work itself out. The so-called *late-transition* countries - East and Southeast Asia, including China and India, and Latin America, began reduction in growth rate after World War II, but the decline stalled some 12 years ago. No one can predict when it may resume. Whether the global growth rate continues to fall or remains constant makes a very large difference to the future. If growth had continued to fall at the 1970s rate, the world population would have reached stability or zero growth at 6.7 billion in 2030. If growth, however, continues at its present rate, the population will increase to 10.7 billion in 2030. This represents a huge discrepancy, and, because the demographic transition is not understood, the degree of future uncertainty is also unknown and possibly menacing (Horiuchi, 1992).

The stand-off

The major controversy between two schools of thought, regarding cause and effect between population and resource availability, also extends into the idea of carrying capacity of the planet and possible limits to growth of all kinds — physical and economic. The advocates of the two opposing views might be characterized as technological optimists, who believe that new technology will allow continued economic growth indefinitely (Ausuble, 1992), versus the technological sceptics who consider that growth in population and resource use will reduce possibilities of sustainability and that we should plan accordingly (Arizpe et. al., 1991). Their opinions are astonishingly far apart and range from statements such as: "there is no correlation between people and environmental change" (Whitmore, 1990), to Keyfitz's listing of many manifestations of further environmental degradation and extinction of plants and animals to be expected within the next 30 years and the remark "every one of the unmeasured negative elements... is related to population" (Keyfitz, 1991c).

The significance of *carrying capacity* depends upon differing points of view. The notion is congenial to natural scientists and an irritation to the social scientists (Keyfitz, 1991b). To the former it is the maximum population of a given species that can be supported indefinitely in any particular region and the term has been applied globally to the human species. The economic viewpoint, in contrast, points out that any limitations to output of goods and services merely reduces unnecessarily the capacity to produce. This argument fails, however, when the environment is brought into consideration. Most economists ignore population growth and consumption limitations because they ignore the ecosystem. They think in terms of an infinite world (Keyfitz, 1991b). Because of population growth, however, most inhabited regions are overpopulated in terms of stress on local ecosystems, far beyond sustainability. As long as all accelerations continue, sustainability is a vain hope. The authors of both "Limits to Growth" (Meadows et. al., 1972) and its recently published successor "Beyond the Limits" (Meadows et. al., 1991) have been accused of making predictions which either have not proved to be correct or are improbable. In fact, the authors make it abundantly clear that they were projecting current empirically observed trends into the future and examining the effects of varying postulated conditions on such trends. This proved to be a significant and useful exercise. Davis (1991) gives a full and fair account of the controversy and finally concedes that the *limits* have essentially been shown to be right.

The controversy is also at the centre of the carrying capacity discussion, with assurances from one side in the argument, that the world can support a much larger population, as opposed to warnings on the other side of approaching catastrophe. Standard economic theory has depended upon a closed system of circular flow of exchange values, to which the environment and the reservoir of resources are externalities. The future looked bright because no heed was paid to uncosted materials such as water, air, forests, animals and plants, without which the ecosystem would cease to exist and, inevitably, we too. Economics as a science must now become concerned with a materially closed system, the ecosystem, of which we are a component part, and which we cannot manage. Today's economic model, within the ecosystem, must describe the use of energy and materials as a one-way throughput of matter-energy derived from a reservoir of diminishing finite resources and discharging waste as emissions, effluents and solids requiring disposal in a manner that does not increase environmental pollution, and the costs of which must be assessed and paid for (Daly and Cobb, 1989). We are trapped within a finite and therefore diminishing resource system while the world still talks of growth.

The problem of costs and costing human induced environmental change has recently surfaced in examining policy options in slowing climate change. Nordhaus (1992) rightly acknowledges that costs of protective measures might be staggeringly large, but makes the familiar error of assuming that physical changes in the ecosystem and economic costs in a human value system may legitimately be included in a single model. They are in fact in entirely different dimensions of reality. Costing ecosystem values is equivalent to costing one's own blood supply — without it you don't exist, and it is, therefore, invaluable. Nordhaus's suggestions constitute a good example of the dilemma posed by Pascal's wager (Orr, 1992), in which he would advocate betting on an optimistic outcome that will, however, lead to disaster (or eternal damnation, in Pascal's terms!) if he should prove to be wrong.

Population and the ecosphere

Sustainable development is a catch-phrase that defies accurate definition but is taken to imply that we can continue economic growth and look after the environment at the same time — we can have our cake and eat it. Sustainability should certainly be one of our goals, but until the present accelerations, including population, that are observable all over the planet are slowed and reversed, there can be no talk of sustainability (Rees, 1990). Mention has been made of the differences of opinion concerning the effects of population and resource use on environmental rundown. Keyfitz (1991a) recently wrote a paper with the title "Population Growth Can Prevent the Development that Would Slow Population Growth" — in other words, the causes prevent the cures. I have named this the Keyfitz Block effect and find that it is recognizable worldwide (McLaren, 1993a).

We are the recipients of brave talk of how we may "manage" the environment and how humankind must assume the "stewardship" of the threatened areas of the world and its life. Reality is very different. In

North and South we find that the Keyfitz Block is inexorably writing the rules. A few examples are offered: (1) If present trends continue Brazilian forests will be cleared within the next 30 years. The importance of forests in the ecosystem can scarcely be exaggerated because of their role in photosynthesis, acting as a CO_2 sink, and in climate modulation. In addition, the tropical forests support a huge diversity of plant and animal species in many specialized habitats (Myers, 1984, Ehrlich & Wilson, 1991). The pressures forcing deforestation are formidable. Today there are about one and a half billion people with no feasible energy alternative who are cutting firewood faster than it can grow, and, through no fault of their own, constitute a major block to ending deforestation. (2) The disparity in economic well-being, and quality of life between North and the South continues to accelerate. Over 1.2 billion people now live below the poverty line, and most of these, although not all, are in the South. Atmospheric pollution and climate warming are inevitably linked to energy use, which is, currently, largely from fossil fuels in the North. But if the whole world were to use resources at today's rate in the North, current reserves of oil would last 2 years and coal less than 100 years. Disparity and pollution are also linked to social and political problems, particularly the contrast in rate of resource use between the North and South. Governments in, for example, the United States and Canada, while recognizing that emission reduction is necessary, are, nevertheless, reluctant to incur major economic costs. (Abelson, 1991, and Canadian Council of Ministers of the Environment, 1990). (3) Pereira (1991), in discussing population and starvation in the world remarks "there is no economic or logistic prospect of feeding the increasing millions in the tropics and sub-tropics from the costly and energy-intensive food production of the higher latitudes". We must expect increasing numbers to leave the family farms as these will only offer subsistence while the family plots remain large enough to yield a surplus for sale to pay for essential inputs, and can therefore no longer be divided, in spite of increasing numbers.

Many other effects flow from population growth and impact on the ecosphere. Some effects may be reversible, such as increasing greenhouse gas release or the continued production of CFCs and related compounds that reduce the stratospheric ozone shield. Some are not reversible, for example, the extinction of animals and plants is now proceeding at 1000 times the normal rate. Others that are non-reversible in the medium term include: global lowering of water tables that will not recover in a human lifetime, and soil degradation, poisoning and loss owing to detrimental agricultural practices. In addition, many social and economic problems that affect the environment are caused directly or indirectly by population growth: increase in pollution by transport systems; mass migration; mass tourism; mass urbanization — half the global population by 2000; increasing resource overuse and waste production in the developed world, and resource depletion in the developing world as a result of poverty and starvation; world security gravely threatened by increasing social and military instability; threat of nuclear instability arising from availability of existing bombs and weapons-grade materials as well as vulnerability of power stations and waste disposal sites.

Finally it should be emphasized that problems arising from population growth are not limited to the developing countries of the South, but the North also is grossly overpopulated because of its current consumption of 85% of world resources and production of an equivalent proportion of pollution and waste of all kinds. A baby born in the North will use up to 30 times the resources of all kinds and produce an equivalent amount of waste as a poor inhabitant of Bangladesh. At a conservative estimate, population figures for countries in the North should be increased by a factor of 10 when considering their impact on the ecosphere, relative to countries in the South. While these generalizations remain true, the scene is changing rapidly. Pollution is fast increasing in the South owing to growing consumption by the affluent, industrialization, and the accelerating horrors of runaway city growth, exacerbated by failing peasant agricultural systems.

What to do about growth?

It will be extremely difficult to bring about global acceptance of the reality of population growth and its consequences and to define and take the necessary measures to alleviate the problem. Yet, because accelerations are involved, every day that passes increases the difficulty of initiating effective action and the cost of doing so. It must be emphasized, however, that measures taken to slow other accelerations, identified earlier, will not become effective until the growth in population and the related North-South discrepancy have begun to slow and reverse. The immediate results of such actions would be entirely beneficial, socially, economically and morally.

Immediate actions must be taken now to begin lowering the birth rate globally and do not require justification by further data gathering, research or discussion. Although the statistics are alarming and the acceleration seems insurmountable, reduction in fertility without increasing the mortality rate is probably one of the easier problems to solve that currently face humankind. We know enough to act now, and the effects will be immediately apparent. The resulting pay-back will far exceed the costs of taking action. Suggested actions should include: (1) immediate plans to encourage an awareness among men and women of the importance of family planning, combined with an assault against those who would deny humane and effective measures to assist women to gain control of their own reproductive capacity and these must include those who subscribe to the current teachings of some religious sects. (2) Simultaneously, social development must improve the education and status of women, as well as pre- and post-natal health care for mother and child. (3) A third condition would call for environmentally sustainable economic development _ which would be aided by reduction in birth rate (Shenstone, 1993).

Family planning demands improved social and economic measures as noted above, but central to their success is knowledge and availability, for both sexes, of contraception techniques. Many methods are in use and there is great need for broad-based research and for educational materials and information on all aspects of family health. The ultimate goals of family planning may be summarized as finally to reduce the need for fertility control; improve maternal and child health care through birth spacing; and eliminate the need for illegal abortion. These goals must be linked to an integrated development strategy combining men and women in family planning with income generation, small scale agriculture, water and sanitation improvements, leading to better quality of life while reducing births (Jacobson, 1988, and Djerassi, 1992).

A puzzling feature associated with family planning is the evident reluctance, among decision makers and some religious leaders, to discuss openly the needs for research in contraception and the expressed recognition of the dangers of population growth. The failure of the Rio Conference (UNCED) to emphasize the population issue continued the process of largely ignoring the single most destructive force ever to threaten human well-being and the ecosphere. It should be said that the official position taken by Canada at the Conference also made little attempt to raise the population issue. Even when growth is recognized, however, many officials cannot face the reality of the kind of measures that must be adopted, or even the language that must now be used. For instance, UNCED's Agenda 21, Chapter 5 (1992) talks of demographic dynamics without using the apparently proscribed terms birth control, contraception and even family planning as such, and there is no mention of contraception research and applications in any terminology. This Byzantine and repetitious document, while on the side of the angels in recommending better conditions for women, may be typified by one quote: "ensure that women and men have the same right to decide freely and responsibly on the number and spacing of their children, to have access to the information, education and means, as appropriate, to enable them to exercise this right in keeping with their freedom, dignity and personally held values taking into account ethical and cultural considerations". In gambling jargon, this is known as "hedging your bets". Fortunately, there are regions of the world where the demographic transition is being brought about by family planning programs. These are the late-transition countries, China, India, East and Southeast Asia and Latin America. Changes are taking place at varying rates but the efficacy of birth-control is established.

The cost

The efficiency of birth-control in economic terms is well demonstrated by a Mexican example. Between 1972 and 1984 $165 million was spent to provide 800,000 women with contraceptive supplies, thereby averting 3.6 million births and 363,000 abortions, and saving $1.4 billion that would have been spent on maternal and infant care. Developing countries that encourage family planning may be the first to experience rapid and widespread social and economic advances (Jacobson, 1988).

In spite of the fact that the cost of measures to reduce fertility rates without raising mortality will be repaid many times over, there is still concern for the immediate costs that must be born in advance of the benefits. Perhaps the most serious immediate deficiency is the relatively small amount expended on reproductive research and contraceptive technologies, and forms a serious block to quick improvement. It can take 15 years or more for a new contraceptive to move from laboratory to the market. Worldwide expenditures on reproductive technologies peaked in 1973 at $280 million and have since declined in Europe and North America. Reduced funding and an inhospitable political climate are delaying the development and introduction of contraceptive technology just as demand, awareness and need are multiplying for old and new methods. Over the last two decades $10 billion has been spent on family planning in developing countries. The current budget is about $2.5 billion per year. The Population Crisis Committee, Washington, estimates that to reach population stabilization by the end of the next century, global expenditures of only $7 billion a year are needed over the next decade. Developing countries need to make larger contributions to family planning. In 1986 the Third World spent more than 4 times as much on weaponry and upkeep of military forces as it did on health care — $150 billion compared to $38 billion, while the whole world spent one trillion on military needs. US reduction in funding for international population assistance between 1985 and 1987 and withdrawal of funding for the UN Fund for Population Activities (UNFPA) meant that more then 340 million couples in 65 countries were affected (Jacobson, 1988).

Sadik (1991) of UNFPA points out that immediate adjustments to growth rate will have effect in the longer range predictions for 2025. A realistic goal is to extend family planning services to 1.5 billion people in the next 10 years. The number of couples using family planning will rise by 50% from 381 million in 1991 to 567 million in 2000. The overall cost will be about $9 billion a year by the end of the century — double today's expenditure, but far smaller than the cost of failure. For example, India has calculated that averting 106 million births since 1979 represents a saving of $742 billion. The gains to the environment and development prospects generally are far higher.

Finally Agenda 21, Chapter 5, suggests "implementing integrated environment and development programs at the local level taking into account demographic trends and factors". The authors suggest funding from 1993-2000 at $7 billion annually, but make no attempt to suggest what effect the program will have on population growth. They outline certain areas of research that, in the guarded language of the proposal, include improving "appropriate policy instruments"; but there is no indication of what this means.

The general consensus appears to be that the world must double the amount currently spent from all sources on family planning in the broadest sense of that term, and that this will mean a global expenditure of something in the order of $7 to $10 billion a year, or about one percent of current expenditure on armaments and armies. This is a small amount indeed, especially when it is realized that expenditures on fertility reduction are repaid many times over in cash terms as well as reducing environmental stress and increasing quality of life.

The moral dilemma

We live at a crisis point in history and we are largely unaware of it. If an unseen intelligent being from somewhere else in our galaxy were to visit the planet, perhaps the most incomprehensible phenomenon it would observe would be that the planet's apparently wise and competent dominant beings are totally ignorant of the life-support system they are condemned to live within. They are, furthermore, blissfully unaware that their uncontrolled reproductive capacity is growing to the extent that it is rapidly destroying this system, while fighting among themselves to preserve their freedom to do so. The problem of having too many babies born is evidently mixed up in some people's minds with morality. Some would say that it is immoral to interfere with a women's childbearing capacity; on the other hand others might suggest that it is immoral to bring unwanted babies into the world to die in infancy or at best to live short and desperate lives in poverty and hunger. Morality is a relative concept that has varied throughout history and varies today from place to place or between adherents of differing beliefs. Commonly, though, a moral act however defined is concerned with humanity alone. Is this always desirable or right?

Today we are becoming conscious that we are damaging our physical and biological surroundings, our home or ecosphere, and that such damage may be looked upon as an evil act. Awareness of this might lead to a new morality that encompasses both humanity and the well-being of all life within the ecosphere. We also find that there is a harsh reality lying behind this apparently simple suggestion. A code of ethics that is seen to be humane and just, in a human framework, may result in increased stress on the ecosystem; only humane actions that also benefit the ecosphere may be considered ethically acceptable. Such a principle bears on our population problems. Undoubtedly continued increase in world population will produce more and more environmental degradation and will further reduce the planetary carrying capacity. This must, therefore, be looked on as an immoral act on the part of our race (McLaren, 1993b). Pimentel (1987) has suggested that the world might support 10-15 billion humans at or near poverty or one billion with a relatively high standard of living.

The most urgent actions we can take, therefore, are those that reduce the number of human beings. This is not a cut and dried matter of simple choice, however. Consider the horror of bringing children into the world only to die or live a life in misery. To such children, the cause of death is being born. So that in some cases at least, not having children may be looked on as humane from a human as well as an ecosystem point of view; we might consider such actions as enlightened self-interest.

China reduced its birth rate from 34 per thousand in 1970 to 18 in 1979. This was achieved by a birth control program whose implementation arouses serious reservations. The Chinese experiment is discussed by V. and B. Bullough (1983) who express deep regret that coercion was used in the program. Nevertheless, the horrors of children dying of starvation in the overpopulated and poorer parts of China over many years far outweigh the drastic powers of persuasion used to reduce births. They comment that they can offer no viable alternatives. Such a comment from brave and concerned people has summarized for us our future — in which most problems we shall face will require a choice between two evils.

In conclusion, we must return to the three opinions that were discussed at the beginning of this paper and that now become options. The speed at which changes are currently happening would appear to deny the possibility of a suggested technological economic Utopia (Option 1), which is essentially a declaration of ignorance of the fact that we live within a life-support system over which we have little control. Restoring balance with the ecosphere (Option 2), although desirable, assumes a relatively passive relationship within which reactive measures may be taken as problems are perceived, but with little attempt to synthesize or examine cause and effect. A holistic approach

(Option 3) differs from Option 2 in that there can be no we/they relationship within the ecosystem of which we are a coherent component. We must recognize the enormity of the offence we are committing in our blind misuse of power to achieve a temporary dominance that is directed to exploitation and killing within the framework of the system. We must redirect our group intellect towards changing current behaviour patterns to patterns based on a holistic general theory of cause and effect derived from empirical evidence furnished by the physical, biological and social sciences. And we must recognize that the subject of this paper, population, is unconsciously the overall driving force for humankind's attack on the ecosphere and, by the impetus of its growth, is preventing an immediate and urgently needed end to destruction of our own life-support system.

References

Abelson, P.H. 1991. "National energy strategy", *Science* 251 1405.

Abernethy, V. 1991. Comment: The "One World" thesis as an obstacle to environmental preservation, see K. Davis and M.S. Bernstam, pp.323-328.

Arizpe, L., Constantza, R. and Lutz, W. 1992. "Population and natural resource use" in J.C.I. Dooge et al. (eds.)., **An Agenda of Science for Environment and Development into the 21st Century** (Cambridge University Press) pp.61-78.

Ausubel, J.H. 1991. "Does climate still matter?", Commentary, *Nature* 350 649-52.

Bullough, V. and Bullough, B. "Population control vs. freedom in China", *Free Inquiry*. Winter 1983/84, pp.12-15.

Canadian Council of Ministers of the Environment. National action strategy on global warming. CCME, November, 1990.

Daly, H.E. and Cobb, J.B.,Jr. 1989. **For the Common Good** (Beacon Press, Boston).

Davis, K. and Bernstam, M.S. (eds.) 1991. **Resources, Environment and Population: present knowledge, future options** (The Population Council, New York, and Oxford University Press, New York and Oxford).

Davis, K. 1991. "Population and resources: Fact and interpretation", see K. Davis and M.S. Bernstam pp.1-24.

Djerassi, C. 1992. "The need for birth control: why and what kind?", *Engineering and Science* (California Institute of Technology) 55(3) 21-24.

Ehrlich, P.R. and Wilson, E.O. 1991. "Biodiversity studies: science and policy", *Science* 253 758-762.

Gillespie, R., 1992. "Discussion in the demographic transition and the techno-logical transition", *Engineering and Science* (California Institute of Technology) 55(3) 25.

Horiuchi, S. 1992. "Stagnation in the decline of the world population growth rate during the 1980s", *Science* 257 761-76.

Jacobson, J. 1988. "Planning the global family" in L.R. Brown et al. **State of the World** (Norton, New York) pp.151-169.

Keyfitz, N. 1981. "The limits of population forecasting", *Population and Development Review* 7, No.4 (December) pp.579-93.

Keyfitz, N. 1991a. "Population growth can prevent the development that would slow population growth" in. J.T. Mathews (ed.) **Preserving the Global Environment** (The American Assembly, and World Resources Institute. Norton, New York and London) pp.39-77.

_____1991b. "Population and development within the Ecosphere: one view of the literature", *Population Index* 57(1) 5-22.

_____1991c. "Toward a theory of population - development interaction", see K. Davis and M.S. Bernstam pp.295-314.

Lee, R.D. "Long-run global population forecasts: a critical appraisal", see K. Davis and M.S. Bernstam pp.44-71.

Lovelock, J.E. 1976. **A New Look at Life on Earth** (Oxford University Press, Oxford and New York).

McLaren, D.J. 1993a. "Aspects of reality: survival and the myth of sustainability", UNESCO: Third International Forum, **Towards Eco-Ethics: Alternative Visions of Culture, Science, Technology and Nature**, Belem, Brazil, April 1992. In press.

_____1993b. "Humankind - the agent and victim of global change in the geosphere-biosphere system" in **Planet Earth - Problems and Prospects** (McGill/Queen's University Press, in press).

Meadows, D.H., Meadows, D.L., Randers, J. and Behrens, W.W.III. 1972. **The Limits to Growth** (Universe Books, New York).

Meadows, D.H., Meadows, D.L., and Randers, J. 1992. **Beyond the Limits: envisioning a sustainable future** (Chelsea Green/Earthscan).

Myers, N. 1991. "Tropical deforestation: the latest situation", Viewpoint, *Bioscience* 41(5) 282.

Nordhaus, W.D. 1992. "An optimal transition path for controlling greenhouse gases", *Science* 258 1315-1319.

Orr, D.W. 1992. "Pascals's wager and economics in a hotter time", Editorial, *The Ecologist* 22(3) 42-43.

Pereira, H.C. 1991. "Birth rights", *Science and Public Affairs,* November, pp.20-23.

Pimentel, D. 1987. "Technology and natural resources", in D.J. McLaren and B..J. Skinner (eds.) **Resources and World Development** (John Wiley & Son Ltd., Dahlem Konferenzen) pp.679-95.

Rees, W.E. 1990. "The ecology of sustainable development", *The Ecologist* 20(1) 19-23.

The Royal Society and US National Acadeny of Sciences. 1992. "Population growth, resource consumption, and a sustainable world", a Statement, February.

Sadik, N. 1991. "The state of world population", United Nations Population Fund (New York) pp.1-48.

Shenstone, M. 1992. "Population growth", Proceedings: International Summer Institute on Environmental Degradation, Population Displacement and Global Security, Whistler, BC, August. (Centre for Sustainable Regional Development, University of Victoria, in press).

United Nations Conference on Environment & Development. 1992. "Demographic dynamics and sustainability", Chapter 5, Agenda 21 (UNCED, Switzerland).

United Nations Secretariat. 1983. "Long-range global population projections, as assessed in 1980", *Population Bulletin of the United Nations* No.14 pp.17-30.

United Nations Secretariat. 1988. "Population growth and structure in the less developed regions of the world according to the 1988 United Nations assessment", a paper presented at the United Nations Expert Group Meeting on Consequences of Rapid Population Growth in Developing Countries, New York (August).

United States Bureau of the Census. 1978. "World Population Profile". US Government Printing Office, Washington, DC.

Vu, My T., Bos, Eduard and Bulatao, Rodlofo. 1988. *Africa Region Population Projections (1988-9 edition)*, working papers of the Population and Human Resources Department of the World Bank (October), WPS 114. Working papers for the other regions were also used.

Whitmore, T.M. et al. 1990. "Long-term population change" in B.L. Turner II, et al. (eds.) **The Earth Transformed by Human Action: Global and Regional Changes in the Biosphere over the Past 300 Years** (Cambridge University Press, with Clark University, New York) pp.25-39.

World Commission on Environment and Development, chaired by G. Harlem Brundtland. 1987. **Our Common Future** (Oxford University Press, Oxford and New York) pp.1-383.

CHAPTER 8

Security for Future Generations: Investing in Maternal and Child Health Programs

Colette Frances

There are risks associated with writing about the perilous state of the children of poverty. One can become emotionally inundated by the magnitude and scope of their suffering, or so distanced by objectivity that the absolute truth of it is lost. Wading through endless documents that frankly illustrate the atrocities committed upon the world's poorest children, or tables and charts that rob them of their humanity by turning them into statistics, is by no means a pleasant task. However, this assignment was undertaken to prevent a further tragedy.

Children are traditionally the powerless ones in society. They have no voice, no vote, no credibility as an information source. The purpose of this chapter is to provide an opportunity to hear the voices of those children who live in some of the most difficult circumstances on our planet and to delineate the scope of child welfare issues as they integrate with global security. Although it is recognized that over one million children in Canada live below the poverty level, this chapter must focus primarily on the poorest of the poor. It is also hoped that we can learn to see beyond the statistics, cost-effectiveness analyses and budgetary measures to the truth which underlies this issue.

Children are the most vulnerable yet the most precious resource we have. The way in which we treat them is indicative of the shameful state of our society as a whole. They are not our future, they are their own, and they deserve the best that we can give them simply because ... they are.

Introduction

Obstacles come to light while addressing issues affecting the state of the world's children: the situation is neither static nor isolated. Problems that existed a decade ago have been intensified or shifted to encompass a larger scope. There is no *one* problem which can be singularly focused on and many of the difficulties that children have to deal with are impacted by several factors. The collective action of the components of cyclical poverty tend to produce an effect greater than the outcome of all the components acting separately. This synergistic effect can be seen as detrimental and overwhelming or it can be seen as a vehicle for positive change.

At its worst, the synergism inherent in cyclical poverty can cripple positive change and disempower any who try to implement those changes. Child health measures, such as universal vaccination programs, often falter when the sheer magnitude of the task is faced. Although initiatives that reduce the incidence of targeted diseases are accomplished, children still suffer poverty, malnutrition, little or no resistance to influenza or pneumonia, and are highly susceptible to water-borne diseases where there is inadequate sanitation. Sometimes it can seem that efforts are futile, or that there are far too many difficulties to tackle all at once.

Conversely, with so many factors so closely related, measures to alleviate one aspect often positively affect others. As an example, when efforts were made to commence vaccination programs, mechanisms for communication and distribution had to be instigated where often there had been no previous concerted effort at any kind of health care delivery system. These efforts called on cooperation from governments, schools, religious groups, radio stations, musicians, community groups, women's groups, nongovernmental organizations and others.

Where vaccination efforts have been successful as shown in Figure 1, the network in place for their delivery can be used for other health care related issues. Local workers have been trained in many countries and there are now avenues for dissemination of information on family planning, nutrition, oral rehydration therapy, basic health care, literacy and other community-based projects. Community success paves the way for future efforts at improving the quality of life where possible.

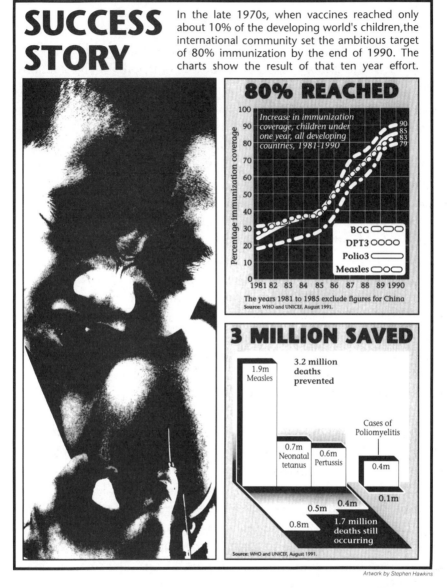

Fig. 1: Success of vaccination efforts 1981-1991 [1: pp.11-12]

Contributing factors

We know that one quarter of the world's people live in abject poverty. More than one billion people live and die with preventable malnutrition, illiteracy and disease [1: pp.11-12]. The majority of these people are children and 97% of all child deaths occur in poor countries [2: p.41]. Cumulative statistics show that in the last decade approximately 25 million children died from three vaccine-preventable diseases: measles, whooping cough and tetanus. That is more than the *entire under-five population* of Canada, the United States and Western Europe combined [2: p.41]. Currently, over a quarter of a million children continue to die each and every week — in 1991 some 14 million died [1: p.5] — that is approximately one child every two seconds. If you are a reader of average speed, then 12 children have died since you started reading this paragraph. The greatest tragedy is that their deaths could have been prevented. The good news is that 3.5 million children were saved due to the successes of immunization, oral rehydration therapy and other child health services [3: p.5].

The single most important factor in prevention programs is to break the cycle of poverty. When a child is born into poverty, the cycle is already in place and many choices and possibilities have been eliminated from that child's life. One underlying factor is a lack of security, both personal and political. Children need to feel that they are cared for within a family that has the opportunity and means to properly provide for them. Poverty absolutely prevents this.

Families must have avenues to meet their basic needs for food, shelter, clothing, clean water, sanitation, basic health care and education. If they cannot do this alone then the community they live in and the governments of their countries must provide leadership, doing what is in their power to supply the necessary means. In turn, the emerging global community must also take a share of the responsibility to enable individual nations to provide for their people. Poverty is without doubt both a personal and a global issue.

Pregnancy and early care

When a pregnant woman does not have optimal health due to malnutrition and/or inadequate health care, or where there are other implications from excessive stress, age, or a lack of autonomy in childbearing decisions, both her health and the health of her baby are at risk. She is more likely to suffer life-threatening complications and to deliver an under-weight premature baby whose health is already compromised and whose future is uncertain.

In 1992 half a million women in poor countries died of causes related to pregnancy and child birth. Most of these deaths could have been prevented through improved prenatal care, better child spacing and family planning, or through better access to birth control and legal safe abortions. One third of all maternal deaths were due to complications arising from illegal abortions [1: pp.11-12].

A child born into poverty is more likely to suffer from repeated infections, recovering more slowly and incompletely from each subsequent illness. The situation is aggravated by malnutrition and opportunistic infections. Even if primary education is available, the hungry child cannot learn or concentrate on tasks. Many children in poor countries who are able to start school drop out by grade two or three; only half of all poor children complete primary school [1: pp.11-12]. Uneducated, their prospects for finding useful employment become minimal. Three out of ten adults are illiterate, and the statistics are worse for women — six out of ten [3: p.5].

The overall result of the recurring pattern of poverty for poor nations serves to more firmly entrench their position of dependency and inability to compete for their share of the world's resources. They suffer from high child mortality rates, high birth rates, high levels of illiteracy, and a growing, permanently disabled population unable to meet their genetic or human potential. Impoverished families tragically lose hope for a better future, suffer disempowerment and are trapped in a perpetuating repetition of having more high-risk babies.

If a mother has access to good health care, the child may be born in a *baby-friendly hospital* where breastfeeding is encouraged, rather than following the disastrous and increasing trend toward bottle-feeding. In poor communities bottle-fed babies are 15 times more likely to die from diarrhoeal disease and four times more likely to die of pneumonia than babies who are breastfed exclusively [1: p.44]. The World Health Organization estimates that the lives of over one million children could be saved every year if babies were breastfed for the first four to six months of life [1: p.44].

In recognition of this need WHO and UNICEF have undertaken a campaign to encourage hospitals to adopt a new code of practice that promotes breastfeeding in maternity units [1: p.44]. This campaign must confront multinationals who advertise bottle-feeding as more modern and sophisticated, and the distribution of free formula samples in maternity units. Increasing urbanization and greater numbers of working mothers also contribute to the growing trend toward bottle-feeding. It is interesting to note that only in the last 10 years has breast-feeding once again become socially acceptable in North America. But babies born in stricken areas cannot wait until breastfeeding comes back into fashion.

Family planning and maternal health

Reducing birth and infant mortality rates has both personal and social implications. Apropos to informed childbearing decisions is the confidence that children born will indeed survive. The crux of family planning is the availability of mechanisms to women that facilitate personal autonomy, education for informed choices, access to appropriate prevention measures and safe legal abortions.

The dissemination of current information on reproductive health management strategies, aimed at educating women in family planning and child spacing, has met with some success. Many local women's groups have taken a leadership role in their communities, providing necessary support and education to meet family planning goals. Though advocacy programs provide modern solutions, they must also be sensitive to cultural parameters thus fostering acceptance. Respect for women's traditional knowledge and midwifery skills encourages the utilization of appropriate traditional methods. Women's indigenous knowledge becomes even more relevant where importation restrictions and laws impede modern birth-control methods.

Reproductive health care and women's needs are factors in the comprehensive issue of child health and development. It must be recognized that they cannot be separated. The absence of a concerted international campaign to meet women's health needs, as part of the current thrust to meet the needs of children, is witnessed in the statistical projections for the next decade. Based on the rising incidence of illegal abortions, reproductive tract infections, AIDS, and the need for

increased family planning, by the end of the 1990s death from reproductive causes will exceed two million women a year [4: p.97].

This issue cannot be ignored nor can it be stigmatized as *just a
women's issue*. Clearly, women's health, wellbeing and empowerment
must comprise a broadening of the global population issue, particularly
with respect to family planning decisions, and due recognition of its
importance will significantly affect both family and global economics.

Family planning can drastically affect the quality of women's lives
and the lives of those that they must care for. Ensuring widely spaced
births can reduce the number of maternal and infant deaths while
improving the nutritional status of planned children and the mother
herself. Planned pregnancies will reduce both the number of illegal
abortions performed and the number of women who die from complications often associated with them. Women must be allowed and
encouraged to have fewer babies. Overall, the quality of child care in
terms of time, energy, and money available to invest in children will be
better because parents will simply have more to give. Women's lives will
also improve because they will have more autonomy, better health, and
more time to devote to personal development, education and vocation-
al training. Their energy can then be expended toward earning
incomes, community enhancement, and even rest and leisure. If the
health and wellbeing of a woman improves, then the health and wellbeing of her family and her community improves [1: pp.58-9].

The importance of education

Child and maternal health improvement initiatives are only one component of a nation's strategy for bettering the lives of its people and promoting its own future. A fundamental investment in the education of its
citizens is urgently required. Many poor countries have been criticized
for not providing a basic education for all, while spending disproportionate amounts on higher education for the privileged few, and much
larger sums still on military equipment.

Without a doubt (and whether we like it or not) we live in a highly
technological communication-oriented global society. Everyone
deserves the right to glean the necessary components to enhance the
quality of their life and to choose to participate fully within such a society. For individuals, this pursuit of personal autonomy involves taking

the first step towards literacy. Within nations, the attainment of a decent standard of living and future economic security requires a literate and educated populace. If this requirement is not met, participation in the technological global economy is unattainable.

The combination of new technologies, community-based strategies and falling costs has contributed significantly to the feasibility of providing a basic education to the majority in poor countries. Colombia and Bangladesh have shown that a basic, relevant education can be provided at a cost of about US $20.00 per child, per year [5: p.6].

There have been many studies in recent years relating education to the enhancement of a nation's well being. Results have shown that an investment in the education of girls realizes dividends for future families. Education can raise self-esteem and give greater confidence to try new ways of doing things. It is associated with the acceptance of family planning and the ability to earn higher incomes. This in turn improves child and maternal health, reduces child deaths, reduces family size, improves child nutrition, increases use of social services (including child health and welfare programs), and most importantly, ensures the literacy of succeeding generations [1: p.6].

Child labour

We know that poverty-induced cycles of malnourishment and illness, lack of basic health care and potable water, illiteracy and inadequate sanitation, do not encompass the total scenario affecting the world's children. They are also profoundly affected by the adults who care for them. Between 50 and 150 million children are bound by adults to a lifetime of manual labour in unsafe and unhealthy conditions, starting as young as six years of age [2: p.100]. Children are found in the mines of Peru, in the shoe factories of Italy, on construction sites in Egypt, and in glassworks in India; making carpets in Morocco, laboring on sugarcane plantations in Brazil, sorting rubbish in Mexico City, or potting seedlings in Sri Lanka. Defence for Children International estimates are much higher — 150 million child labourers in Asia alone — and every child labourer means an adult out of work and a child not in school [2: p.100].

There are several components involved in child labour traffic which need to be addressed separately to do justice to the issue. Some components are internally driven while others are generated beyond a country's borders.

Children are smaller, require less working space, are quicker, more agile, complain less, do not demand anything from employers, can be fed less, and are more easily exploited than adults. In most cases they are all too willing to do the work because the food or money their labour brings is needed for their family to survive. Sadly, there are usually younger children at home to take the place of a child killed or injured on the job.

Factories and businesses contribute to a nation's Gross National Product and as expected are profit-driven. In many cases, factories would not be as profitable without the hiring of children. Poor countries would lose their foreign business if they could no longer offer manufacturers and retailers such incredibly low labour costs — ultimately affecting the ability of a country to compete in the growing global economy. Those of us who reside in rich nations need to become socially aware consumers, actively seeking out and supporting community-based initiatives that do not exploit children. Ignorance of the chain of production is no longer an acceptable excuse.

We may be morally outraged that child labour continues to exist in the 1990s, that there is a perceived need for it, and an economic niche that it fills. Even though many countries have legislation against it, the fact remains that child labour still exists, and will continue to exist until strong measures are enforced to dismantle this crippling thief of childhood [2: pp.87-102].

Street children

The plight of children in war-torn homelands or poverty-stricken nations is only a part of the overall struggle of families to provide the basic necessities of survival for today and hope for improvement in the future. Due to circumstances beyond their control, children often end up on the street to fend for themselves. In 1990 their number was estimated at 30 million and climbing [3: p.5].

In industrialized nations street children are the so-called *throwaways* who are escaping dysfunctional or abusive homes. In developing countries undergoing structural failure, and those war-ravaged nations where social safety nets no longer exist, they are refugees, orphans, or simply abandoned. These are the children most at risk, whose chances of survival are minimal. Even where programs or agencies do exist to promote literacy or primary health care, street children often do not access them. They are truly the invisible ones.

The political impact of a *first call for children*

Optimists believe that the tide is finally turning in the struggle for a fair deal for all people. A growing international movement is gaining momentum as it seeks to redress the inadequacies and failures of previous political and economic systems to meet children's needs. James P. Grant, Executive Director of UNICEF, describes this new movement which emphasizes a *first call for children* as having such power and initial success that it is unprecedented in UNICEF'S 40-year history [1: p.5]. Most notable landmarks are the 1989 International Convention on the Rights of the Child, which has been ratified by over 100 nations to date, and the 1990 World Summit for Children, attended by representatives from 159 countries (of whom more than 70 were heads of state) [1: p.7].

The principal of a first call for children recognizes that the young are vulnerable, having only one chance to grow and develop optimally; should that one opportunity be impaired they may well be physically, emotionally or mentally disabled for the rest of their lives. As such, it is essential that children be protected and given first call in the allocation of resources no matter what the circumstances are within families, nations, or international arenas. **Protection accorded to children must be the last element of social protection sacrificed rather than the first,** as has often been the case.

Children bear the brunt of the hardships confronted by their countries whether it is: the debt crisis and internal structural adjustment faced by Latin America and Africa; political reorganization in Central and Eastern Europe and Russia; or the outbreak of wars in the Gulf, Africa and Europe. A direct correlation exists between debilitating international debt loads and increasing child malnutrition and mortality rates in several countries in Latin America and sub-Saharan Africa [1: p.16]. *The forty least-developed countries have slashed health care spending by 50% and education by 25% during the past few years to help pay their debts* [2: p.58]. This travesty of sacrificing the poor world's children to repay debts to wealthy nations **must not** be allowed to continue.

While a complete discussion of the debt crisis in developing countries is undertaken by Morris Miller in Chapter 10, a few comments are necessary here. World Bank Debt Tables state that the total indebtedness of the developing world to international financial institutions and industrial world banks is US $1,300 billion, with yearly capital and interest repayments at approximately US $150 billion [1: p.43]. For many developing countries, inability to make interest repayments compounds the debt such that the unpaid amount is continually added to the total debt and interest recalculated accordingly. The net effect is a burgeoning debt load which has hopelessly surpassed the point at which it can be repaid. It has been suggested by international agencies that the debt restructuring programs proposed to date do not fully address the magnitude of this problem, and that especially in Africa the debt must be absolved [6: p.6]. In consideration of the magnitude and urgency of this problem, and most importantly, in light of the devastation to social programs that are a direct result of the debt crisis, an immediate resolution is imperative.

Restructuring

At the World Summit for Children, world leaders promised to implement several courses of action to fulfill the principle of a *first call for children.* The basic goals include: a reduction of child death rates by at least one third; a halving of maternal mortality rates; a halving of severe and moderate malnutrition; 90% immunization coverage; a 95% decline in deaths from measles; an end to polio and tetanus; clean water and safe sanitation for all families; a basic education for all children and completion of primary school for at least 80%; the availability of family planning services to all; the end of the apartheid of gender; and observance by all nations of the Convention on the Rights of the Child [1: p.5].

The total cost to finance these goals is estimated by UNICEF at US $25 billion a year throughout the 1990s [5: p.1]. It must be understood that global cost estimates are limited by the variety of circumstances found within individual countries and therefore the approaches necessary to achieve these goals will substantially differ. A cost breakdown of the social programs outlined in this chapter is presented in Table 1 [7: p.43; 8: p.240]. By necessity, items are presented in groupings which encompass the main thrust of the initiative and costs are given within a range of values.

To visualize the value of $25 billion, or to relate the amount in such a way that it becomes comprehensible, the following are presented: it is about what the USA and former USSR spent in 1989 on strategic nuclear weapons [7: p.43]; it is much less than Europeans spend on wine or Americans on beer in a year [5: p.2]; and it is only three times what Canadians spent in 1990 on recreation and amusement alone [9: p.5].

The primary method to fund improvement measures does not require generation of new dollars or increases in public spending but involves a reallocation of budgets within both poor and rich nations. This is not as simple as it sounds. Any changes should build upon a mandate to address poverty as a high-priority issue by all governments and to embody the principles of a *first call for children* in subsequent policies and procedures.

Table 1

Estimated annual costs for specific programs to alleviate basic human suffering

Item	Cost (US $ billions)
1. Safe drinking water and adequate sanitation	8-10
2. Maternal health and family planning education	5-6
3. Literacy programs	5-6
4. Nutrition: supplemental feeding programs	2-3
5. Community health measures, including staffing of permanent local units, immunization for all children, refrigeration for vaccines, mobile outreach units, public health information	1.8-3.4
Total annual expenditures	21-29

Governments of developing countries should increase the proportion of expenditures that are allocated to direct methods of meeting priority human needs, while decreasing support to high cost services for the privileged and for military spending. The United Nations Development Programme (UNDP) suggests that 20% of a government's spending be allocated to helping its poor [5: p.19]. This is a challenge considering that the majority of the developing world spends over a third of their budgets on repayment of debt and financing the military [5: p.20]. The internal and external pressures that have contributed to such spending patterns are not easily overcome, nor is it possible to generate more income from export commodities when world prices are not fairly set and markets do not operate to mutual advantage.

Supplementation of funding to help meet humanitarian goals in developing nations lies within the aid packages already supplied by the industrial nations. A restructuring of aid expenditures so as to target 20% of development aid to meet these basic needs would generate about US $8 billion per year [5: p.20]. Strong measures must be undertaken to ensure that these funds are spent as designated.

Alternatively, the required US $25 billion could be realized through a direct reduction in military spending. UNICEF suggests that US $13 to $14 billion a year would be generated if developing nations were to reduce arms expenditures by 10%, while the remaining $11 to $12 billion could come from less than a 2% reduction in military spending by the rest of the world [5: p.49].

The principle of assessing the ability of world governments to solve world problems by a reduction in military spending has been studied extensively by peace groups in recent years. For example, the US $25 billion per year required to fulfill the promises of the World Summit for Children is approximately 2.5 percent of global yearly military expenditures of $1 trillion, or about one week's worth of world military spending [10: p.20].

If it seems unrealistic to suggest a 10% reduction in military spending by poor countries and a 2% reduction by rich countries, then the problem is that of perception of needs for excessive military spending in the first place! The poverty that we manifest globally in our outer world is only a mirror for the poverty of spirit that plagues our inner world. Any government that believes it must spend hundreds of billions of dollars annually in a manifestation of military power will likely find it difficult set priorities for humanitarian endeavours.

Military expenditures comprise an important portion of the GNP of some rich nations, and many poor countries are increasing military spending to the detriment of social programs. In view of the fact that militarization often serves to fuel hostilities, ultimately undermining human development, looking to reallocate military budgets is only logical. In all conscience can there be any argument against demilitarization or any further delays in its implementation?

Assessment and achievement of improvements in quality of life have also been addressed by the UNDP in their Human Development Report [6]. It discusses the role of economic growth, free and open global markets and a new Global Development Compact. The UNDP stresses the importance of opening up global markets and initiating more equitable financial markets, such that developing countries receive massive investments in human capital and technological development. Ideally, this will enable them to compete on a more equal footing. The Compact puts people first in national policies and cooperative international development efforts, thus ensuring sustainable human development in a peaceful world.

Conclusion

We are living in a dynamic age of globalization where changes in one area have the potential to profoundly influence another. We have an understanding of the nature and scope of the problems that are the daily reality for millions of children and their families around the globe, and there are numerous organizations and governments that have made commitments to alleviate their suffering. Though economic solutions to rectify these problems are not simple, we do know how to achieve them. Improvement strategies require a clear identification of objectives in terms of human development, the sources of funding to achieve these goals, and a serious commitment by the world's leaders to implement programs. All that remains is to find the personal and political will to do so.

Therefore it is critical that we not be trapped into thinking that the aforementioned budget reallocations, changes in spending priorities and patterns and minor decreases in military spending be seen as anything other than band-aid half-measures — or less even than that. None of these remedies attempts to delve into the realm of the primary underlying cause that precipitated the crisis. Though these very minor measures are immediately necessary, there is only one long term solution.

All people, everywhere; all shapes, sizes, colours, classes, castes, religious affiliations or disaffiliations, of either gender, must come to that point in their personal evolution where there can be change. A profound spiritual recognition of our interconnectedness with the creative life force that permeates all life forms on this planet must replace previously held assumptions that separate us from the Earth, our natural world and each other. We can no longer afford blindly to hold to false ideals of individualism, the self, or even altruism, which holds an inherent concept of self-sacrifice and moral good for *others*. We must change our perception of personal identity to encompass more than self as personality, enabling the experience of true empathy, true compassion and true identity. The suffering of a small child on the floodplain of the Brahmaputra-Jamuna river during monsoon season becomes our own suffering. She is no longer *other*, but is *us*, one within the web.

The proposals of the UNDP, and the promises of the World Summit for Children, if fulfilled, are a stepping stone toward a *first call for children*. But implementation of these modalities and a long term commitment to build a new reality necessitates a radical shift in the world's priorities: where a reverence for life underlies all relationships; where family security, informed choices and loving encouragement allows girls and boys to achieve their full potential as women and men; where governments and nations will work actively and effectively to allocate their resources in a sustainable manner; and where local and global economic policy will serve as the viable means to global welfare improvement. With achievement of such objectives, the security of future generations and indeed the continued viability of the biosphere we inhabit will be ensured.

References

1   J.P. Grant, **The State of the World's Children**. United Nations Children's Fund (Oxford University Press, New York 1992).
2   A. Vittachi, **Stolen Childhood: In Search of the Rights of the Child** (Polity Press, Cambridge, UK 1989).
3   United Nations Economic and Social Council. United Nations Children's Fund, Report of the Executive Director 1991.
4   Worldwatch Institute. **State of the World 1992: A Worldwatch Institute Report on Progress Toward a Sustainable Society**. ed. L. Starke (W.W. Norton and Co., New York).
5   J.P. Grant, **The State of the World's Children**. United Nations Children's Fund (Oxford University Press, New York 1993).
6   United Nations Development Program. Human Development Report 1992. Overview.
7   R.L. Sivard, **World Military and Social Expenditures** 13th Edition (World Priorities, Washington, DC 1989).
8   UNICEF. 1990. **Children and Development in the 1990s: A UNICEF Sourcebook.**
9   Statistics Canada. 1990. Leisure and Personal Services Report **63-233**.
10 Medard Gabel and Evan Frisch, **Doing the Right Things: What the World Wants and How to Get it** (World Game Institute. University City Science Center, Philadelphia, USA 1991).

CHAPTER 9

How to Enhance Democracy and Discourage Secession

Metta Spencer

Abstract. Historical studies have shown that partitions of ethnic groups within nations often bring an increase in violence, not peace. In a search for political solutions that would forestall secession and outbreak of civil war, a new structure for parliamentary representation is proposed whereby the constituencies are non-territorial. Minorities that are large enough to form such constituencies would need further protection from being totally overwhelmed by the majority groupings, so that additional steps would be required to ensure that their aspirations are not totally overridden; referenda and weighted voting schemes are two elements that must be considered.

Introduction

Framing a constitution is a fundamental means of preventing warfare, but when it is successful, the effect is invisible. Not only do certain wars not happen, but in the best cases, no one will ever realize that they *might* have happened. Because this is so, the formulation of voting systems is dismissed as an arcane irrelevance by those who care about *real* problems, such as military crises. In the worst cases, on the other hand, when a war begins no one can think of an acceptable way to end it. Witness especially ethnic wars, such as those raging now in the Balkans, the Transcaucasus, and Sri Lanka. The intractability of such secessionist wars can be gauged by the persistence of the conflicts in Northern Ireland, in Israel, in Pakistan and India, which may never end. The only solution to such wars is prevention, and the only practical preventive is a structural innovation that can solve the problems that cause them.

The dominant motivation leading to the partition of states is the aspiration for democracy. What will be proposed here is a system for reducing ethnic conflicts and, at the same time, increasing the political effectiveness of *all* members of the society. There is a common misconception that the quality of democracy varies little from one democratic society to another. Consider these questions: Why are nationalistic campaigns for independence surging at precisely the moment when previously totalitarian or authoritarian states are becoming democratic? Why do countries such as Yugoslavia, Czechoslovakia, and the Soviet Union, begin to break up as soon as their citizens glimpse the prospect of self-rule? Why are even long-time democratic societies, such as Canada and Britain, experiencing secessionist movements? The evident answer is this: *In a democracy, the majority wins and minorities lose. This creates a powerful incentive for each minority to demand its own sovereign state where, as the majority, it will always win.* As democracy spreads, secessionist nationalists look for other ways of attaining political potency; the first idea that springs to mind is to partition existing nation-states so that they can achieve self-determination, or sovereign statehood.

Instead of addressing this problem with internal structural reforms, it has become common form in political discourse to promote fragmentation by treating self-determination as a collective human right — which is generally interpreted as the right to secede. Let us consider instead a way of enhancing self-determination without partitioning states into new sovereign territorial entities.

Who is entitled to self-determination? Clearly, an individual does not have a right to reject his or her nation-state and form a private government; only groups have the right to self-determination. But to be entitled to that right, how large a minority does a group have to be? Why does speaking a similar language or sharing a common history give some groups this collective right? Should this offer extend to such groups as trade unions, churches, or other voluntary groups that people join and leave freely? (DeGeorge, 1991: 2-4) If not, why not? The usual answer: Only a "people" is entitled to self-determination. *But what is "a people"?* A tribe? An ethnic group? A linguistic community? A religious community? The question involves the relationship between parts and wholes. Is there such a thing as a "Canadian" people, a "Yugoslav" people, or an "American" people? Is there a "Russian" people? What about Russians who have lived all their lives in Estonia? When do they stop being "Russians"? Are the Russian emigrés who have spent most of their lives in Canada "Russians"? What about their children who have never been to Russia? Or their grandchildren who have married Italian immigrants?

A "people" is not a concept that can be defined operationally. Likewise, the notion of self-determination is a myth — an inspiring ideal, perhaps, but not a practicable rule. Still, some myths have value: they summon us forward. As a mythic ideal, self-determination offers much that is worth striving for — so long as it is voluntary and nondiscriminatory. Those two caveats make quite a difference.

As a practical principle, self-determination is not always accepted in a consistent way (see the section entitled the Post-Yugoslav carnage, Chapter 2). People outside a national struggle may accept it in one situation and reject it in another very similar one. Within a national struggle it merely depends which side you are on: the colonists who fought the American Revolution to free themselves from Britain would surely have disapproved their grandchildren's attempt to do the same thing by forming the Confederacy and seceding from the Union.

The liberation movements that brought colonialism to an end justified their actions in terms of the principle of self-determination. However, that myth today is used to justify (Buchanan, 1991) secessionist claims by the Catholics in Northern Ireland, the Scottish and the Welsh in Britain, the Bashkirs and Tatars in Russia, the South Ossetians and Abkhazians in Georgia, the Tamils in Sri Lanka, the Sikhs in India, not to mention the Quebecois, the Slovaks, the Basques, the Flemings — the list goes on. Often grave conflicts have arisen because liberal, progressive people have underestimated the destructiveness of partitioning nation-states, and have assumed that any group wanting its own homeland is, *ipso facto,* entitled to it. Ethnic groups have been encouraged to demand secession in the name of democracy by people who should have known that it would lead to what we have witnessed in Bosnia-Herzegovina: killing and expulsions that are called *ethnic cleansing.*

This outcome was predictable. Historically, secession has been disastrous in the great majority of cases. As Robert Schaeffer (1990) has pointed out, over 13 million people had died between the end of World War II and the late 1980s in fights preceding and following partition in Korea, Palestine, India, and Vietnam. When a nation is partitioned, war often breaks out; families, buildings, and farms are divided; millions become refugees; internal strife hardens into permanent international hostility; and the remaining minorities within each of the new states are even more abused than in the larger previous state. No effort should be spared to find alternatives to the manifestation of ethnic identity in the form of nationalistic claims for territory. Ernest Gellner's widely accepted definition of nationalism is "primarily a principle which holds that the political and national unit should be congruent" (Gellner, 1983: 1).

The reason for objecting to equating the political and national units is that in most cases, a mono-ethnic state is an unattainable dream. Less than ten percent of all existing states are ethnically homogeneous. Most of them have more than five major ethnic groups within their borders (Matthews, Rubinoff, and Stein, 1989: 91). Moreover, societies are becoming increasingly multicultural and more porous, as international migration increases (Taylor, 1992: 63). Rarely can there be found places to draw boundaries to split a nation into separate homogeneous new states; almost inevitably, minorities will remain in each of the new territories. Territorial expansion following the split of a nation-state is at best a zero-sum game; each group can gain territory only at the expense of another group's territorial claims.

Actually, the ideal is relatively new in history that nation-states should be composed of separate, distinct ethnic communities. Eric Hobsbawm (1990:19) attributes the rise of this aspiration to the rise of the nation-state: "The equation nation = state = people, and especially sovereign people, undoubtedly linked nation to territory, since structure and definition of states were now essentially territorial." In previous eras homogeneity was typical of isolated barbarian societies, not of high civilizations, which were poly-ethnic. William McNeill has traced the course of the idea that

> it is right and proper and normal for a single people to inhabit a particular piece of territory and obey a government of their own devising.

He continues,

> The idea that a government rightfully should rule only over citizens of a single ethnos took root haltingly in western Europe,

beginning in the late middle ages; it got into high gear and became fully conscious in the late eighteenth century and flourished vigorously until about 1920; since which time the ideal has unquestionably begun to weaken in western Europe, where it began, but in other parts of the world, especially in the ex-colonial lands of Africa and Asia, it has continued to find fertile ground. (McNeill, 1985: 6-7)

If writing today, no doubt McNeill would include in this fertile ground the countries that recently were in the Soviet orbit.

McNeill's historical account is consistent with the common assumption that ethnic consciousness peaks during an early stage of modernization, giving rise to "ersatz" or "imagined" communities — to use respectively the terms of Karl Deutsch (1969) and Benedict Anderson (1983) — and declines thereafter. And indeed, there is empirical evidence that ethnicity has ceased to be a permanently ascribed identity and has become a transitory, optional one. A citizen may pick up, drop, and even change ethnicity several times during a lifetime (Waters, 1990). This fact exposes the flimsy basis of nationalists' demands for undying loyalty. Instead of being natural or inevitable, ethnic identity is a precarious ideological construct of no assured duration. Collective national identities may be supplanted over time by new forms of interest groups and parties as people become integrated into mature democratic political systems.

Nevertheless, until ethnic consciousness diminishes — and that may not happen — new arrangements are needed to satisfy the demands of nationalists for self-determination in the least destructive way possible. Fortunately, there may be a way to meet those demands and simultaneously enhance, rather than undermine, democracy. In fact, the reason minorities are continuing to demand self-determination is that they are consistent losers under the rules of everyday democratic practice. Democracy is, by definition, rule by the majority, not by a minority. In the best of circumstances all citizens in a democracy take turns being outvoted. However, cultural groups that constitute permanent minorities can never expect to win any political contest. No wonder they want out.

Such groups may differ demographically in their distribution within a society. In one case, a minority group may be dispersed so thinly through the population that it is nowhere numerous enough to elect a parliamentarian of its own. In another case, a minority may be concentrated in a particular district where it constitutes a local majority; predictably, it is in the latter case that a group's members tend to regard secession as a solution to their problem. They recognize that it would enable them, no longer a permanent minority in a large state, to be a permanent majority capable of winning every political contest in their small new state. They may not see the disadvantages of this until later.

There is a need for democratic methods of protecting minority rights and enhancing self-determination without resort to secession. This need exists even in old democratic societies with well-observed charters of rights and with few minority problems.

Robert Dahl has written, "Whatever form it takes, the democracy of our successors will not and cannot be the democracy of our predecessors. Nor should it be." (1989:340) Luckily, not all possible forms of democracy have yet been tried. However, as political scientists Andrew Reeve and Alan Ware (1992:4) point out, although an infinite variety of democratic electoral systems could be devised, and though it can be shown that different variants will yield very different decisions, it is rare for the public to consider electoral innovations seriously. People tend to assume that if an existing procedure is "democratic", it is good enough. Improvements are neither needed nor possible.

My intention is to propose innovations that will suffice for a single purpose — to give minorities more democratic opportunities — while minimizing other changes in existing political systems. Thus these suggestions apply to both parliamentary and presidential systems. They could be adopted in nation-states, in non-governmental organizations, and in transnational or global organizations.

First, for ethnic communities to mobilize and seek representation without carving up existing states, it will be useful for *parliamentary constituencies to be defined on a voluntary, functional basis, not a territorial basis.* In this way, ethnic groups can form constituencies at will. However, this alone will not overcome the disadvantage of constituting a minority in the polling booths. More is required.

Second, for small minorities even to put their issues on the public agenda of the whole society, it will be useful for *constituencies to be guaranteed the right once a year to place a proposition on a referendum on which the entire electorate will vote.* However, even this innovation will not overcome the disadvantage of the group's minority status. More is still required.

Third, it will be useful for the referendum to allow for *weighting votes according to the intensity of preference.* I will show that these three innovations, if taken in combination, will enable minorities sometimes to win political struggles — at least on issues about which the majority of voters are comparatively indifferent.

Non-territorial constituencies

In democratic states, votes are usually aggregated in geographical districts of approximately equal population size, though there are exceptions. Some constituencies are not purely defined territorially. For example, in Ontario an enumerator comes door-to-door before each election to ask all voters to declare their religious preference: Catholic or any other faith. Catholics' property taxes support Catholic schools and they elect the trustees of the Catholic School Board. All other religious communities support the public schools with their taxes and vote for trustees of the Public School Board. Thus different constituencies occupy the same geographical districts, yet handle their own distinct sets of problems independently. This solution provides a measure of "self-determination" in a context of social integration.

Similarly, electoral reforms have been suggested in Canada that will reserve seats in Parliament for representatives of aboriginal Indians, in proportion to their numbers — almost 2 percent of the population. In the existing system of territorial constituencies, these indigenous peoples are too dispersed to be able to elect a representative to the House of Commons. The proposed reform is one of several measures designed to increase their self-determination without re-drawing any territorial boundaries. As we shall see, one can invent other possible ways of maximizing self-determination without partitioning states or segregating peoples.

Non-territorial constituencies already form the basis for electing legislators in a few countries, such as Malta and Ireland, where constituencies of farmers, university personnel, and other functional groups are allocated seats in the Senate in proportion to their numbers in the population. Likewise, in Amsterdam, city councillors are elected, not to represent particular districts, but to represent particular interest groups. The votes that they receive become the basis for allocating other benefits, including the content of television programming. Catholic voters not only elect a number of Catholic city councillors, but are given control over a proportional number of minutes of television programming per month. Anarchists, gays, Latin Americans, and other distinctive communities also elect their own city councillors and receive their proportional share of TV time. Reportedly, anarchists receive too few votes to elect a city councillor of their own, but they are allocated a few minutes of television time each month.

Thus it is possible for groups to form constituencies that are not defined territorially or by ascribed social traits, but voluntarily on whatever basis they choose. Such constituencies may *include* nationality groups — for as long as people identify themselves as such. However, if individuals gradually come to assign higher priority to a different group identity (e.g. trade union membership, religious affiliation, feminism, or vegetarianism) they can form a new constituency and re-register accordingly, regardless of where they live. No fights for turf will arise and no one will have to move away to win political representation.

What I am proposing is that *electoral districts be abolished (at least for one house of a bicameral legislature* [1]) *and replaced by non-territorial constituencies*, to be determined by voluntary registration, just as the Catholics in Ontario identify themselves voluntarily and may change their religious identity at will. No objective criteria for membership should ever be permitted, lest people be classified involuntarily, according to some racist scheme, for example. The number of deputies or parliamentarians to be elected by each constituency will be proportional to the number of voters registered in it. Communities can be represented politically, regardless of where their members live, though issues that are of local interest will predominantly attract the votes of local citizens.

What are the advantages of such a system in comparison to more common systems for aggregating votes? The chief advantage is similar to that of proportional representation (PR) in party systems: even small minorities will be able to gain some representation in parliament. The proposal should also appeal to a minority group that is clustered in a particular region where it forms a local majority. These are the most likely groups to become secessionists, and our scheme might be acceptable to them as a substitute for secession [2], at least in combination with the other two elements of this proposal.

Direct democracy

In every state there will always be a need for some type of legislature. However, true democracy also allows citizens to participate in decision-making directly and not only through their elected representatives. Referendums are well-established practices in certain polities, such as Switzerland and California, where political decisions seem to be no worse than those made elsewhere.

The effectiveness of referendums depends on the ability of citizens to study the issues. These opportunities can be increased by technological means. As Robert Dahl notes,

> By means of telecommunications, virtually every citizen could have information about public issues almost immediately accessible in a form (print, debates, dramatization, animated cartoons, for example) and at a level (from expert to novice, for example) appropriate to the particular citizen. Telecommunications can also provide every citizen with opportunities to place questions on this agenda of public issue information. (Dahl, 1989: 339-40)

One problem is that it is theoretically possible for voters to be confronted with two incompatible propositions on the same referendum. In reality however, this concern seems not to be warranted; in California, where approximately 30 propositions are placed on the ballot each time, two contradictory proposals are never adopted. And if this did happen, the Supreme Court would provide a judgment to resolve the question. Parties and interest groups distribute arguments for or against particular propositions. By no means can all decisions be made by referendum; the legislators, the judiciary, and the executive branches of government all have their parts to play.

As a guarantee that minorities will be able to place their concerns on the public agenda, I suggest that *each constituency that is sizeable enough to elect at least one parliamentarian should be guaranteed the right to submit one proposition to the electorate in an annual referendum*. If, say, there are 20 constituencies, each referendum will comprise 20 propositions [3]. It will become apparent that the revolutionary feature of the present proposals is the unusual way in which citizens will vote for or against those propositions.

Weighted voting

The preceding two proposals do not actually eliminate the most objectionable aspect of territorial democratic voting: the fact that minority cultural groups can always be outvoted. Rules are enacted by the majority and imposed on the minority. A *fair* system is needed that will give minority groups an opportunity to enact certain measures of their own choosing, with the approval of the majority. Happily, the proposed solution to this problem will benefit not only minority groups but all citizens alike. Although all voters have equal decision-making power, they do not all care equally about the same issues. Each citizen only wants to influence certain decisions that concern him or her, and would gladly let others decide the remainder. A system of weighted voting makes this feasible. The outcome will be determined both by the number of voters expressing their opinion on an issue, and also by the intensity of their opinion on the matter.

In the hypothetical annual referendum proposed above, each voter is entitled to cast 20 votes — one for or against each proposition. *With a weighted voting system, however, each voter may "spend" his or her votes in various ways, distributing them across the referendum as he or she likes* [4]. It is one shortcoming of all conventional democratic systems that one's vote on a deeply-felt matter will be "cancelled out" by other voters who have nothing at stake and who may even flip a coin to decide how to vote. The proposed system of weighted voting gives all citizens more opportunity selectively to influence the issues that are salient to them and to skip others. Decisions will sometimes be made by a small number of voters who care strongly about a given issue — a circumstance that will especially please minorities, while also augmenting the political power of *all* voters.

Let us consider, as an illustration, three hypothetical citizens of a democratic nation, Mrs. Urdoh, Mr. Ivanov, and Dr. Yang, who confront a referendum listing 20 propositions, each of which will be enacted by a simple majority of the votes cast on it.

Let us suppose that Mrs. Urdoh cares profoundly about an issue that her ethnic group placed on the ballot — a measure that would require that the nation's paper money be printed in her group's traditional Somali language. Mrs. Urdoh may "spend" all 20 of her votes to endorse this proposal, Proposition 4, though she must then forego voting on any of the remaining 19 propositions.

Another voter, Mr. Ivanov, may not care at all what language is displayed on the paper money. He decides not to vote on that item, thereby saving one vote which he uses by casting two votes against Proposition Eleven — a measure that would prohibit the sale of alcoholic beverages on Sundays. Apart from that, Mr. Ivanov casts one vote in favor of each of the propositions.

The third voter, Dr. Yang, is also indifferent as to which languages will be displayed on the national currency. She does have a firm opinion on the alcohol issue, however, and differs from Mr. Ivanov. Dr. Yang spends her 20 votes equally on four issues. She casts five votes against Proposition 5 (which would require women to cover the whole body with a veil whenever appearing in public), five votes for Proposition 11 (which would forbid the sale of alcohol on Sundays), five votes against Proposition 12 (which would authorize the construction of a hydroelectric dam on the country's largest river), and five votes in favor of Proposition 17 (which would authorize a system of alternative service for young men who are conscientiously opposed to military action).

Table 1 displays the results as far as these three voters are concerned, with respect to only five of the 20 propositions. (Since Mr. Ivanov voted on 19 propositions, his effect on the outcome of this referendum will not be fully apparent here.)

Table 1: Results of hypothetical referendum for five propositions and three voters.

Proposition	Result	for	against
4: Somali language on national currency:	passed	20	0
5: Veil in public:	defeated	1	5
11: Alcohol prohibition on Sundays:	passed	5	2
12: Hydroelectric dam:	defeated	1	5
17: Alternative service:	passed	1	0

It can be seen that the weighted voting scheme used in this referendum has an unusual consequence, namely that every voter can have more influence over the decisions that he or she cares about than would be the case given the usual system of voting. Everyone — not only minorities — will gain from this approach. However, minorities may be the most enthusiastic supporters of such an innovation because now they will sometimes win. No group will necessarily constitute a permanent minority any more, perpetually outvoted and unable to effect their cherished cultural goals.

Best of all, the rest of the society will be satisfied whenever the minority wins a proposition. In the example shown above, only one person voted on Proposition 1, which would print the country's money in the Somali language, yet that proposition received the most substantial victory of all, making Mrs. Urdoh a satisfied citizen. But Mr. Ivanov and Dr. Yang are also satisfied with this outcome; if they had not found it acceptable, they would have voted against it. The strength of their opinions is registered in the proportion of votes that each person casts.

The proposed system is egalitarian. All voters have the same amount of power. It is also a win-win solution, benefiting everyone and disadvantaging no one. Minorities will sometimes win political contests — at least when the majority does not disapprove. Not only minorities will gain political power through weighted voting; so will all other citizens. Everyone can influence the decisions that they most care about and allow others to do likewise.

However, a single referendum may not be the last word on a controversy. Issues that pass easily in one referendum may become sources of dissatisfaction later, and reappear on a subsequent referendum. For example, this voting scheme has been simulated in several settings, including a 120 member sociology class in Canada. Four of the students approached the referendum in a playful mood. They formed a constituency representing "anglo-Canadians" and put forward a proposition that all Canadian beer must have an alcohol content of at least 5 percent. In fact, they argued spiritedly before the amused class in favor of this legislation. They were the only students, in the end, who voted on it, and they "spent" all their votes supporting their proposition, with good results — it carried. At first glance this example merely seems to show that a silly measure can pass if too few people care enough about it to waste votes in blocking it. On the other hand, one can welcome this outcome as evidence that a minority group can win — at least on measures toward which others are indifferent. Conceivably, if this beer proposition were enacted by a real electorate, it might cause so many negative social consequences that another group might mobilize itself to put the issue on another ballot later.

Discussion

In a few rare cases, a case can be made for partitioning states. However, it is a dangerous expedient, to be avoided except when there is mutual consent among all the participants — including all minority groups. Since this degree of consensus is rare, political incentives will frequently be required to induce disaffected minorities to remain part of an integrated polity instead of demanding territorial independence. The incentives of conventional democratic electoral procedures turn ethnic groups in the other direction — toward separatism, since they must expect to be permanently outvoted, whereas by seceding they could become a permanent *majority* in their locality. What is needed is a way of giving minorities a chance to win sometimes, with the full approval of the rest of the citizens. We have considered several proposed advances in democratic practice that offer minorities the possibility of attaining some of their ambitions, while also increasing the satisfaction of the wider electorate.

The use of functional (instead of territorial) constituencies is a democratic version of "corporatism" or "neo-corporatism" that is rather widely used in some Western European nations. Its advantage is that fairly small minority groups could be represented in the legislature, and each would be guaranteed a right to place one proposal before the electorate in the form of a referendum proposition. This incentive would diminish the urgency to minority groups of having their own separate nation-states. Moreover, if (as many theorists have argued) ethnic identity will be salient only for a limited historical period, then it is important to define constituencies that will allow minority groups to express their concerns on a voluntary, changeable basis. It is a mistake to build permanent political entities that assign territory to particular ethnic groups, since minorities will still be found inside almost any boundaries that could be drawn. Besides, the longer-term trend is for more of the world's problems to be transnational in scope, which calls for polities that are more, not less, inclusive. The challenge at this historical moment is to find ways of satisfying local interests and of protecting local cultures without slicing the map into smaller units.

While most electoral theorists appreciate the value of functional constituencies, some of them are wary of giving up the territorial basis entirely, and their reasoning should be taken into account. Thus Andrew Reeve and Alan Ware, having discounted as specious a number of justifications for territorial subunits, submit that "it is important to retain structures around which potential opposition can mobilize. Local party organizations, centred on territorially-defined Parliamentary constituencies, constitute one of those structures." There is merit to this point, and it would be a mistake to take away all the functions of parties. In a parliamentary system, the administrative branch of the government is formed on the basis of the number of seats that each party wins. The political parties in Britain or Canada would lose their *raison d'etre* if constituencies were defined entirely on a functional basis.

For these reasons, the executive leadership should be elected separately through candidacy in parties. Functional constituencies could elect the legislature while territorial constituencies elect the chief executive. Indeed, a plausible case can be made for retaining territorial constituencies in one house of a bicameral legislature [5]. This would allow parties to continue to mobilize opposition against interest groups, and thereby prevent national politics from becoming dominated by single-issue campaigns.

All the functional constituencies would be allocated a number of seats in proportion to their size, and the political parties would name a list of candidates for each constituency. This would create a system of proportional representation of parties (Reeve and Ware, 1992: 69-93) which, for Canada, would be a significant and constructive change. Other than that, however, most nation-states could implement the present proposals with limited change in their existing constitutional structures.

The three proposals here, taken together, offer new hope for minorities who are otherwise disempowered in their own polities. If these initiatives toward greater self-determination are to be effective in forestalling secessionist movements, they must be undertaken well in advance of any nationalistic conflict. By the time partition is being promoted, it is probably too late for these innovations to reverse the tide.

The proposals have been discussed here with reference to nation-states. This problematic has been chosen from a concern for the urgency of preventing secessionist wars. However, these proposals were initially considered as a response to a different problem — that of forming democratic systems of governance for large transnational bodies. The problem of integrating large polities comprising diverse populations is the same, whether the polity is a nation-state, a province, a continent, the entire planet — or just a non-governmental organization such as a professional association.

Organizations that provide representation to large populations usually adopt a federal structure, with the top decision-making positions being filled by representatives of nation-states, which are the "basic units" of the whole organization. On what possible basis can votes be aggregated, except by the existing "sovereign" states? How can the larger region be integrated across the borders of these states? These difficulties can be seen in the case of the European Community, for which there is yet no blueprint that looks democratic. It is inherently hard for top decision-makers to remain responsive to individual citizens or small, grass-roots bodies far away. The larger the body, the less democratic it is likely to be — a fact that must worry anyone who sees the increasing need for world governance.

Instead of trying to weld together congeries of hard-shelled nation-states, it is more promising to begin new organizations whose constituencies are not territories or nation-states, but voluntary, transnational groupings formed without regard to geographical location. Multiple communities of like-minded planetary citizens, each unified by common identities and concerns, can elect delegates, hold referendums, and express their concerns through the means that have been outlined here. They need not attempt to supplant nation-states, but help fuse the cracks between them. Such international societies, thickened by frequent interaction and politically mobilized, can contribute informally to the integration of global society, countering the centrifugal forces of nationalism. And more formally, transnational decision-making bodies can represent flexible self-defining constituencies more democratically than do present structures, which are built on the system of nation-states.

Unfortunately, electoral innovations are rarely adopted. There are some valid reasons for conservatism in such a matter. Decision-making procedures in a nation-state are so fateful that it is often better to adhere to flawed ones than to adopt "improvements" that are untested. One cannot expect a set of proposals such as those presented here to be accepted by existing states. However, non-governmental organizations can use some of these ideas. If such experimental approaches do, as expected, advance democracy and empower both minorities and majorities, nation-states or inter-governmental bodies may subsequently adopt them.

Notes

1   In Canada or in Britain, the relevant House would be the Lower House, unless the Upper House became elected.

2   Trends in the direction of this system — called "neocorporatism" or "liberalism" — are observable in certain European countries, where interest groups cooperate with government agencies in the formation and administration of policies. Concerns have been expressed that this approach might take over some of the usual functions of political parties, but this is not regularly the case (Ware, 1986:126).

3   In some states that hold referendums regularly, groups of citizens collect signatures on a petition in order to place a given proposition on the ballot. In Switzerland, 100,000 signatures are required. This rather costly practice could be continued under the new arrangements. Alternatively, the parliamentarian(s) for each constituency might have the responsibility for formulating their group's proposition, and would doubtless be lobbied by the electorate. Yet a third approach might be to have each constituency elect a nonpartisan panel that would formulate its referendum proposition. The argument for this third approach is that it may be not be desirable for political parties (or their nominees) to formulate the propositions, since this would open the way for manipulation. The *combination* of propositions on any one referendum will sometimes affect the prospects for an individual proposition. It would be better, therefore, for all the different constituencies to formulate their items separately, so as to preclude manipulation.

4   The present proposal applies weighted voting only to a referendum, but the same principle is sometimes applied to elections of representatives. For example, in Switzerland in a ten-seat constituency, a voter may give a single vote to each of the ten candidates, or may divide his ten votes among three or four candidates from the same or different parties (Urwin 1977:21). Since Switzerland is taken as the best example of a successful multinational state with very little internal strife, it is worth paying particular attention to their innovative and highly democratic political structures, including weighted voting and the extensive use of the referendum, which seem to accommodate minorities extremely well.

5   In a parliamentary system, the party in power in either house might elect the prime minister, as in Britain. Alternatively, party leaders might continue to be chosen by party conferences, as in Canada, though this approach has its critics. Its main disadvantage is in stripping backbench parliamentarians of their power.

Bibliography

Anderson, Benedict. 1983. **Imagined Communities**. London: Verso.

Buchanan, Allen.1991 Secession: **The Morality of Political Divorce from Fort Sumter to Lithuania and Quebec**. Boulder, Colorado: Westview Press.

Dahl, Robert A. 1989. **Democracy and its Critics**. New Haven, Yale University Press.

De George, Richard T. 1991. "The Myth of the Right of Collective Self-determination," in **Issues of Self-Determination**, William Twining, ed. Aberdeen: Aberdeen University Press.

Deutsch, Karl. 1969. **Nationalism and its Alternatives**. New York: Knopf.

Gellner, Ernest. 1983. **Nations and Nationalism**. Oxford and New York: Oxford University Press.

Hobsbawm, E.J. 1990. **Nations and Nationalism Since 1780**. Cambridge and New York: Cambridge University Press.

Matthews, Robert O., Arthur G. Rubinoff, and Janice Gross Stein, eds. 1989. **International Conflict and Conflict Management** 2nd ed. Scarborough, Ont.: Prentice Hall.

McNeill, William H. 1985. **Polyethnicity and National Unity in World History**. Toronto: University of Toronto Press.

Reeve, Andrew and Alan Ware,1992. **Electoral Systems: A Comparative and Theoretical Introduction**. London and New York: Routledge.

Schaeffer, Robert 1990. **Warpaths: The Politics of Partition**. New York: Hill and Wang.

Spencer, Metta 1991. "Politics Beyond Turf: Grassroots Democracy in the Helsinki Process", **Bulletin of Peace Proposals** Vol. 22 (4): 427-35.

Taylor, Charles 1992. "The Politics of Recognition," in Amy Gutmann, ed. **Multiculturalism and "The Politics of Recognition"**. Princeton: Princeton University Press.

Urwin, Derek 1977. **Electoral Systems**. Bergen: Institute for Sociology and Political Sciences.

Ware, Alan 1986. "Political Parties" in David Held and Christopher Pollitt, **New Forms of Democracy**. London: Sage.

Waters, Mary. 1990. **Ethnic Options**. Berkeley: University of California Press.

Part III

TOWARD A SUSTAINABLE ENVIRONMENT

CHAPTER 10

Global Governance to Address the Crises of Debt, Poverty and Environment

Morris Miller

Abstract. The global economy is in a state of crisis posing the threat of economic and financial breakdown into a great depression, a future that promises growing inequities and environmental degradation. This paper identifies seven current trends and juxtaposes the objective of a *return to creditworthiness* and *normalcy*. Models have identified four necessary conditions for recovery: improving rapidly the prospects for developing countries to export to industrialized countries; lowering trade barriers and improving the terms of trade for developing countries; lowering the level of real interest rates and dampening the volatility of interest and exchange rates; and increasing the amount and improving the terms of official aid (ODA) and private capital flows for both developmental and environmental purposes. Systemic change is called for, requiring leadership (a fifth necessary condition) to establish a global system of rules of trade, capital movements and environmental protection. A *new Bretton Woods* is proposed along lines similar to the original agreement of 1944 that prevailed for a quarter of a century and helped close the gap between rich and poor countries, but with rules appropriate to the present situation.

The setting and the challenge

Crisis : i) a crucial point or situation in the course of anything, a turning point; ii) in political, international or economic affairs, an unstable condition in which an abrupt or decisive change is impending; iii) in pathology, a sudden change in the course of an acute disease, either towards improvement or deterioration; iv) in literature, the point in a story or drama in which hostile forces are in the most tense state of opposition.

— The American Heritage Dictionary [1]

As the 20th century comes to a close there should hardly be a literate person alive who is not aware that we are living through an historic watershed period of far-reaching dimensions. It is a time of transition or transformation. Powerful dialectic forces are at work, one of opportunity and hope and the other of breakdown and despair. On the one hand there is the avalanche of dazzling scientific and technological innovations symbolized by the computer chip and the laser beam and, on the other hand, the onset of a global crisis, or rather of three overlapping and mutually-reinforcing crises if we differentiate the interrelated aspects of finances, trade and capital flows (the debt crisis), of equity (the poverty crisis) and of ecology (the environmental crisis).

Heeding the lesson of the shepherd boy parable, there are, admittedly, very good grounds to be cautious about crying "crisis!". But if we define the concept of crisis as a condition in which the prevailing trends, if not stopped or reversed, will lead to breakdown, there should be little doubt that the current *problems* in their dynamic are of a nature and scale that warrants the warning cries of "global crisis!" The *ominous* trends are well documented; a few examples should suffice to make the point.

(i)   Immiserization.
      The *absolute poor* (roughly identified as those with incomes of less than $1 per day) have increased over the past decade from about 700 million to over 1 billion; this means that one in six who are living on this planet are unable to feed, clothe and house themselves in a manner that can sustain health and human dignity. To put this in graphic terms, leaving aside special tragedies due to droughts and war, such as Somalia, Sudan and Sarajevo, about 20 million persons are dying each year from hunger and poverty-related causes; that is, 40,000 per day or 1700 per hour! What makes this especially poignant is the fact that a very high proportion of these unfortunate victims are children. Yet the incomes of their families that are at the bottom half of the income scales have continued to decline over the course of the last decade, adding an incalculable psychological impact to the physiological one.

(ii) Population growth, polarization and the quality of life.
      Meanwhile, in the poorer developing countries particularly, the rate of growth of the world population continues to be high. On

the basis of present trends, world population will double by the middle of the next century with over 90 percent of that increase occurring in the developing countries — and particularly in their cities. The developing countries already face a situation where their average *per capita* incomes are about one twentieth that of the average in the industrialized countries. But the dynamic is even more discouraging: between 1960 and 1990 there was an eight-fold increase in the absolute difference in incomes between the richest fifth and the poorest fifth. The trend is continuing as developing countries find it extremely difficult to improve *per capita* income levels when population rates remain high and exacerbate their social and environmental problems.

Lest it be thought that this is a contrast between the industrialized countries and the developing ones, note too that the North has its own South: one fifth of the population in the industrialized countries are in dire poverty, suffering homelessness, malnourishment and all the ills of the culture of poverty, including the opiate of the hopeless and the alienated, addiction to drugs. Crime follows. Is it any wonder, then, that in the USA private security guards now outnumber publicly financed police? The rich, it seems, are not insulated from the decline when we look beyond the numbers to that elusive aspect we cannot measure, the *quality* of life.

(iii) Increasing pressure on the environment.

As population and incomes grow — and growth is necessary if sufficient employment opportunities are to be provided for the labour-age population that will be increasingly urbanized and seeking nonfarm jobs — environmental degradation is bound to mount to stressful levels. In the cities — to which the job-seekers gravitate in search of productive work — there will be mounting problems of disposal of urban waste and of rising carbon-emission levels from vehicles, power plants and the like. In the rural sectors beyond the electrical grid, the environmental problems stemming from the great reliance on fuelwood for heating, cooking and power will persist until affordable alternative stand-alone energy sources are made available. This is an unlikely development when only about 1 percent of global research spending is undertaken in the developing countries in response to their own priorities.

(iv) The changing nature of technology and employment and the growing educational gap.

With the changing nature of technology and of the structure of modern economies, a higher proportion of the working population in both the developing and industrialized countries can only find employment (if any) in lower-wage service sector jobs. As the labour input required per unit of output falls and the skills required of the labour force rise in complexity, the less educated and skilled are finding it more and more difficult to find productive employment. Given the population increases and the annual flow of new entrants into the labour force and given estimates that reducing the high unemployment levels calls for a sustained annual growth of the industrialized economies in excess of three percent — a difficult target to attain and maintain as current and historical records attest — high levels of unemployment and of underemployment will likely prove endemic, especially in the less industrialized countries.

(v) The growing inhospitable nature of the global economy.

In the meantime, the international economic scene has become less and less congenial for the developing countries as a group:

- real interest rates have remained at a level several times higher than their historical and sustainable range of one to two percent;

- the level of prices for most of their exportable commodities hit an historic low about a decade ago and have hardly improved since while the prices of the manufactured goods and the services that they buy have risen so that the losses from the deteriorating terms of trade in many years exceed the inflow of development aid;

- protective trade barriers (especially non-tariff barriers) imposed by the industrialized countries against the exports of Third World countries continue to remain high — and higher against the exportable products of the Third World countries than against those from other industrialized countries;

- exchange rates and interest rates have fluctuated in an exceptionally wide range and at exceptionally great speed ever since 1970 when the Bretton Woods agreement was effectively jettisoned by the actions of President Nixon in closing the so-called gold window that enabled bankers and individuals to exchange gold for their US dollars.

Any one of these factors would be sufficient to keep most developing countries locked into the poverty trap despite their best efforts.

There is a tendency to rationalize the immiserization process afflicting these countries as self-inflicted due to their institutional arrangements that severely constrain private initiatives of an entrepreneurial nature by too much governmental involvement and too little scope for market forces to operate, due to rampant corruption, etc. As convincing a case could be made that even if these institutional and policy and *cultural* faults were to be corrected by *structural adjustment*, the international milieu will remain uncongenial for the developing countries while the average real interest rates remain high, while the already adverse terms of trade continue to deteriorate or fail to improve, and while exchange rates and interest rates remain so volatile. The situation is recognized and ostensibly being addressed, but the failure so far to take adequately corrective measures raises the issue of leadership and a frightening thought that the will and capability to do so on the part of the major economic powers is not commensurate to the challenge.

(vi) The issue of control of global economic and financial forces.
The necessary degree of control to lower the historically high real interest rate levels and to dampen the extreme volatility of interest and exchange rates seems inadequate, especially in light of the developments in the global financial market place over the past two decades. There is reason to question whether it is within the power of the central bankers and finance ministers of the major industrialized countries to control the movement of capital adequately when, a) many of the operations of financial institutions have moved off-shore to be beyond the control of their respective central banks, b) the global volume of electronic capital transfers *has expanded* to a point where it now approaches $1 trillion each day, an amount that is equivalent to the total reserves of the central banks of the major industrialized countries, and c) the *nature and composition of the capital flows has changed* to a point where

about 5 percent is estimated to be for the financing of trade and less than 15 percent is attributable to investment flows for productive projects and the rest is almost purely speculative [2]. The policymakers of the major industrialized nations are finding that their ability to take controlling measures is limited and this has become a cause for serious concern as witness the call of the former US Secrerary of the Treasury, Nicholas Brady, for a special commission to deal with this issue. But this phenomenon with its speculative character and volatility is especially injurious to developing countries that do not have the financial resources to take hedging measures and are, as a consequence, unable to plan and are buffeted on the turbulent financial waves.

(vii) The growing internationalization of production and the commensurate increased power of the large transnationals.

As world economic and financial integration proceeds at an unprecedented speed, governmental policymakers, especially those in the developing countries, find themselves less and less capable of influencing the investment decisions of foreign firms, especially of powerful transational corporations that account for a very large proportion of the movement of investment capital [3]. This has great relevance for the capability of capital-hungry developing countries to set and enforce high regulatory standards for *health, safety and fairness* — and, of special importance of late, for maintaining environmental quality.

(viii) The socio-economic consequences of the decreasing competitiveness of developing countries.

With the exceptions of the newly-industrializing countries (NICs), almost all the developing countries are finding themselves less and less able to compete in world markets for both primary and manufactured higher value-added products, many of which are either substitutes for natural primary products (fiber optics for copper, nylon for jute, aspertane for sugar, etc.) or are being subsidized in the industrialized countries to support local producers with the effect of reducing their imports and increasing competition in other markets.

One result is the rapid growth of the so-called "informal sector" in the economies of the developing countries, a trend that has a devastating impact on the financial resources available to the governments of these economies. This, in turn, lessens their ability to finance the education, health and infrastructure programs that are necessary if productivity is to be raised. When housing, health and educational standards are declining the victims most severely affected are those at the bottom of the income and power scales, largely women and, in particular, peasant women. But with these changes in the economic and socio-political structure, the power of labour *vis-à-vis* indigenous and foreign capital is also being weakened. This exacerbates the vicious downward spiral, further widening the gap between the rich and the poor [4].

The bleak picture so briefly sketched here must be seen and appreciated in *dynamic* terms. The worrisome trends indicate not only a growing gap that is of concern on compassionate grounds but a gap that may already have grown to a point of no return for most developing countries. If the gap between the haves and have-nots cannot be made to move in the opposite direction of closing the income gap at a speed that offers hope rather than despair and dependency with all its attendant human costs, a grim future of global and historically unprecedented proportions can be foretold. When, to this dismal picture one adds the costs of the environmental imperatives that must be assumed by the poorer developing countries as well as the richer ones, the reasons for a change of direction of these trends go beyond compassionate concerns to a concern for long-term human survival.

On the face of it, if we juxtapose these trends with the tantalizing potential for improvement offered by trends in scientific and technological achievements, there would seem to be little reason to despair. It is not beyond the capability of this generation and the next to provide every living being the opportunity to enjoy a decent life, at least in terms of the provisions of basics — food, clothing, housing — and, as a precondition for all this, a quality education, health services and productive employment. This is a challenge that puts the spotlight on *social engineering*: how are global institutional arrangements and policies to be changed so as to address the many facets of the global crisis by arresting the deplorable and dangerous trends and then initiating trends to close the gap between what is happening and, given our scientific-technological knowledge, what could be made to happen.

The primary question is simply: how is this to be done?

Two points need to be made at the outset. *First*, it is necessary to identify a key factor abetting these trends, namely, the emphasis on the rights of property in the economic sphere and the rights of humans in the political sphere. This is reflected in the exaltation of the market process and the deprecation and weakening of regulations and of the social safety net. The prevailing dominant ethos over the past few decades has been that the road to salvation is paved with private bricks. This religious or ideological view is the hallmark of the catechism of what may be called *the new capitalism* as championed by Presidents Reagan and Bush and by Prime Ministers Thatcher and Mulroney. The comforting handmaiden to this approach has been the trickle-down hypothesis that has rationalized the degree of indifference to both the rapidly increasing polarization of incomes within and between nations and the glaring unevenness of opportunities and burdens [5].

This outlook is clearly epitomized by the approach of the governments of the industrialized nations — in which the creditor banks are domiciled — to the global debt crisis that erupted in 1982 and, at that time and for a few years after, posed a threat to the major banks and thus to the international financial system. The creditor banks have been saved from collapse by a process that has given them time and opportunity to build up reserves against defaults or writedowns, but that same process of debt rescheduling has not appreciably lessened the pressure on the debtors that has resulted in depressing the living conditions of those already desperately poor and dampening their hope of ever escaping from the poverty trap that over the course of time has grown deeper in most countries and for most people.

Thanks to communication technology, there has been a growing awareness both of the tantalizing promise offered by spectacular advancements in science and technology and of the riches beyond the power of imaging being amassed by the few. Is it any wonder then that, as the social and economic conditions of life continue to deteriorate for the poorer half of humanity, there has been growing alienation and disillusionment with the prevailing political structures and processes and its leadership? *Change* and *the economy, stupid!* have become the catchwords of the season; worsening socio-economic conditions and the fear of worse to come have given that message great resonance with electorates everywhere. While institutional and policy change is now on the political agenda, it remains to be seen whether the proposed *and the implemented* changes can be significant enough to arrest and reverse the prevailing trends that have brought on the present triple-headed global crisis. The process would have to start with changes that are systemic and structural if economic and political objectives and rights are to be melded.

This is a challenge that was identified and posed in 1930 after the onset of the Great Depression in a perceptive article in *The Economist*:

> The supreme difficulty of our generation ... is that our achievements on the economic plane of life have outstripped our progress on the politicial plane to the extent that our economics and our politics are perpetually falling out of gear with one another ... The tension between these two antithetical tendencies has been producing a series of jolts and jars and smashes in the social life of humanity. [6]

Will it take a series of shocks as traumatic as that experienced in the decade of the 1930s to bring the antithetical tendencies together? Out of the ashes of World War II there emerged the Bretton Woods era that began when *rules* for trade and capital flows were agreed upon and were adhered to for a quarter century. Thereby hangs a lesson that we would do well to consider — see below.

Second, one of the key trends over the postwar decades has been the increasing degree of interdependence of national economies. Accordingly, it is now recognized as never before that many of the most serious problems besetting humankind extend beyond the nation state and that the treatment to arrest and reverse the current trends must go beyond the scope of the nation state. This has put the spotlight on the international level of governance. Without diminishing the importance of the institutional framework and policies at the national and sub-national levels of governance, it is clear that in a world economy as interdependent as it is today, a necessary condition for national success is appropriately congenial international conditions for trade, capital flows, etc.

Placing a major onus for change on international policymaking and program-implementing and enforcing obliges us to examine the past and potential performance of (i) the leadership of the industrialized nations that, by virtue of their size and power of their economies, are forced to play the starring roles on the global economic and financial stage, and (ii) the structure and operations of the existing international institutional arrangements which have so far proven to be too weak in relation to the challenge. Having examined these two aspects, we can then turn to the ways in which the international institutions can be modified so as to achieve the desired outcomes. This will also call for an assessment of the leadership of the major economic nations that play leading roles in the design and operations of these institutions.

Leadership à la G-3 or G-7

> The broad transnational forces call for true leadership by the US President and Congress and their equivalents elsewhere. Such leadership would display three linked characteristics — understanding, explaining and carrying out intelligent policies to meet changed conditions — (without which) there is no prospect of progress ... If the response to the new global agenda is successful, it will indeed have demonstrated true leadership. But that is a big if.
> — Professor Paul Kennedy, "True Leadership for the Next Millenium", *The New York Times*, 1 March 93

Since the 1940s, and especially after World War II, the mantle of leadership responsibility has fallen squarely on the shoulders of US policymakers, both public and private (as transnational corporate executives), simply because the US emerged out of that war as the world's largest economy with industrial output greater than that of all other countries combined. By virtue of that dominance, it was also the country whose currency became the world's reserve currency with all the obligations and privileges that this entailed. While the leadership role was not discretionary, it was willingly assumed for self-serving reasons having to do with hegemonic power and the benefits that accrue to the powerful. The Americans were thereby better able to influence the post-war design of international institutions of governance in a manner that favoured the USA's continued unchallenged dominance [7].

By the end of the 1960s and early 1970s it became apparent that the USA had neither the capability nor the necessary trust of others to go it alone as the reserve currency country and take on the leadership role that goes with it. The overwhelming role gave way to a co-starring one. The hegemon had to cease acting as a sergeant-major and had to recognize that it had no option but to share the stage and, indeed, to plead for the co-operation of Germany and Japan (constituting the Group of 3 or G-3) and, to a much lesser extent, of the British, the French, the Italians and the Canadians who constitute the other members of the Group of 7 (G-7). The era of shared leadership was henceforth to be relied upon to provide the "international public good" of a global milieu characterized by the rule of law and the attributes of stability, openness and fairness in commercial and other relations between nations and fairness in international economic and socio-political relations that are so desperately needed [8].

Halting awkward steps towards concerted international action have been taken as awareness spreads that there is a very close connection between acute financial stress and instability, extreme and growing income disparities and life-threatening environmental degradation and that these symptoms of global disorder can only be treated effectively through some form of global governance. Since mid-1960s the political leaders of the seven most powerful industrialized nations have come together annually, claiming on each occasion to be grappling with the major problems besetting the world. While giving lip-service to co-operation and co-ordination these annual ritualized *summit* meetings have, in fact, demonstrated that not one of these governments is willing or politically able to march to any tune but its own. Not surprisingly, politicians — as differentiated from statesmen — have found it difficult, if not impossible, to look beyond the short-term and the parochial interests of their own national or regional constituents. The process, with its manifest failings, has raised questions as to whether and, if so, how these nations could be constrained so as to ensure *concerted* action for objectives that were longer-term and universal.

Shared leadership requires special conditions to succeed. Professor Stephen Marglin has observed

> the central issue is whether there [is] ... a set of practices, a system of behavior which one or more major powers can follow in order to induce co-operative behavior on the part of the others? [9]

The necessary conditions to induce or force co-operative behaviour have not been evident. The leaders of the major industrialized economies continue to rely on an ineffectual *ad hoc* arrangement of G-7 meetings. Not only are the agreements couched in highly generalized terms with rarely a reference to how they might be operationalized, but, in addition, there has been little follow-up action. Indeed, what the seven governments have done after these meetings has more often than not been at odds with the tenor of the joint communiqués. Neither the interests of the participants nor those of the global community at large seem to have been served by this ritual beyond the semblance of action that emanates from meetings to discuss action. The point is well expressed by Stephen Marris in a report of the World Institute for Development Economics Research of the United Nations University (WIDER):

> the most important collective decisions in international financial policy in recent years have all been of an *ad hoc* type — the Louvre and Plaza accords and the Baker Strategy on the debt problem — [involving] ... only governments of the large developed economies [that have the requisite] financial kind of clout ... *Yet the limitations of ad hoc co-operation as a means of running the world economy are becoming increasingly clear ... [with its] inevitable bias towards damage limitation and the short-term political interests of those currently in power.* [10] (emphasis added)

There seems general agreement on the need for the *formalization* of the process of co-ordination that would both guide and constrain the conduct of economic and financial affairs among nations, but there is a great divergence of views with regard to how the co-operation could be achieved, that is, the procedural and organizational specifics as to how to proceed. This assessment is widely shared and thus gives rise to calls for consideration of the potential roles of the established international agencies. Accordingly, before considering more radical proposals such as those implied in the calls for a *new Bretton Woods,* it would be appropriate to assess the roles of the established agencies *as a system* to see to what degree and in what manner they could provide the needed degree of global governance.

A panoply of international institutions was established over the course of the last half century in response to problems that were global in scope and required a level of governance broader than that of any single nation state. The principal ones in the economic and financial field are the United Nations system (comprising the UN itself and a wide range of specialized agencies) and the international financial and developmental institutions (IFIs) that include institutions such as the World Bank and regional banks (that are sometimes labelled the multi-lateral development banks, MDBs) and the International Monetary Fund (IMF). These institutions have become major players in the global economy and, by virtue of that fact, have to bear a considerable measure of responsibility for the emergence of the present troubling situation with all its fragility, instability, unsustainability and inequity. These institutions have been criticized for their policies and/or operations on the grounds that they have not been able to prevent the deplorable trends. The question before us is not one of recrimination but one of rectification: can these international agencies be strengthened in a manner and to a degree that would enable them to act much more *effectively* (and, with other agencies *as part of a broader system*, adequately) on behalf of the community of nations to promote their long-term interests for growth, equity and environmental quality?

Suggested approaches to improving the institutions and policies of global governance should be identified and assessed as to both desirability and feasibility on the basis of the understanding that the lessons of past history could provide. *Prima facie*, it seems clear that the desired system should be reformed within the framework of a concept or design that provides a holistic perspective. After all, in the real world we never can start with a clean slate. However, it is clear that the system of international agencies grew piecemeal over time in response to past problems and opportunities and is not only messy with gaps and overlapping jurisdictions but, more importantly, does not seem structured either to tackle effectively current problems that now merit priority treatment — and on an urgent basis given the prevailing trends and their crisis nature — or to take advantage of current opportunities. A broad brush history of the past roles of both the IFIs and the UN system would be helpful in pointing out some relevant lessons for those who would reform the current system of agencies.

The past, present and potential roles of the IFIs
and the UN as a system of agencies

This is certainly not the finest hour for multilateralism. But the fault is not that of the Bretton Woods institutions. They (the management) would have liked to do more, much more. They have often acted with rare courage ... The fault is really ours — the member governments and we, the Governors — for we have failed these institutions and betrayed our own heritage.

> — Mahbub ul Haq, formerly Pakistan's Minister of Finance,
> Planning & Economic Affairs [11]

The role of the IFIs

The World Bank and their regional counterpart banks (the MDBs) are funded mainly through borrowing on capital markets and are misla-belled as *banks*. They are development agencies that lend for long-term projects and programs. They have traditionally operated on the basis of lending for projects in different countries after intense national and sec-toral reviews and even more intensive project feasibility studies that on average have gestation periods of over two years. This project approach still remains their principal mode of operations despite the increase in nonproject lending in the form of structural adjustment loans (SALs) that now account for about one-quarter of the total lending programs of these institutions.

The IMF has a different mandate, namely, that of a lender of last resort helping countries when they have exceptional, that is, temporary balance of payment problems and thus the funds are ostensibly lent for a relatively short-term of five years or less. From the onset of the debt crisis in 1982 both the analytic and the field operations of the IMF have overlapped in increasing measure with the MDBs, principally since the *structural adjustment loans* (SALs) were introduced in the early 1980s.

There are understandable reasons for this trend of shifting a greater proportion of lending operations into quicker-disbursing SALs and IMF allocations. The USA has exerted strong pressure for this shift in lending on the grounds that the lending process needs to be shortened

(SALs can be processed in a few weeks as contrasted with the noted average gestation period of over two years for project lending). At the same time, in the eyes of the major donors it has been no small virtue that SALs and IMF allocations can provide a means of gaining greater policy clout over debtor developing countries, clout that could then be exercised for greater and faster debt repayments to creditor banks and for easier more favourable entry terms for foreign investors that is the result of the promotion of policies for privatization of government enterprises and greater freedom for the play of the so-called market forces. This approach is rationalized as a necessary element in the policy package for reviving the economies of the distressed near-defaulting borrowers.

These institutions have been subjected to great pressure to meet the short-term crisis conditions. Their interventions have had the explicit objective of restoration of creditworthiness as reflected by sufficiently improved reserves and balance-of-payments trends and by the restoration of an adequate rate of growth in *per capita* income. Judged on the basis of this narrow criterion, their record of achievement is quite impressive, but much less so when the *longer-term* development mandate is considered, that is, a perspective that places special emphasis on the equity and environmental aspects as integral components of the concept of development. Much of the criticism of these institutions revolves around the implications of their lending programs with respect both to the fairness of the distribution of the costs and benefits and to the impact on the environment of the recipient country and, when the projects are large-scale, of the planet.

The World Bank and the IMF have been operating within an international economic order that, to put the best face on it, has hardly been congenial for the Third World countries that they were striving to help. Their analytic output has been global in its scope but their operations have had a country focus. Dealing with each recipient country on a case-by-case basis has its limitations when global conditions are not congenial. The clearest illustration is provided by the export promotion policies almost always advocated in structural adjustment loans: if all or many of these borrowing countries were to heed the same advice, the *fallacy of composition* becomes operative — meaning there are no assurances that, on the other side of the trade equation, the industrialized developed countries are prepared to import the goods which the developing countries can export [12]. Thus, until there can be an appreciable World Bank and IMF influence *on the policies of the industrialized countries*, the feasibility and desirability of this kind of policy advice is very questionable. In a phrase, *as a prior condition it is the international economy that needs to undergo structural adjustment.*

As the responsible international *developmental* institution, it would be incumbent on the World Bank to take initiatives on such global and regional issues as the level of real interest rates, trade policies and other factors which are exceptionally critical in resolving the debt crisis and meeting the need for long-term sustainable capital flows on acceptable terms. Not to do so would be tantamount to accepting the *status quo* with all its fragility and inequities and leaving the way open for a diminution of the World Bank's role. In that case, the World Bank would clearly not be fulfilling the aspirations of the developmental mandate set out at its founding at Bretton Woods.

To fulfil this mandate some changes need to be made. It is not feasible to change the constitution of the IFIs (called Articles of Agreement) with their weighted shares and voting structure, but in any case, tinkering with their constitutions is not necessary since their management style, organizational structure and policies can be changed by other means. First of all, there needs to be a will to change things and the courage to act on this conviction on the part of the so-called middle powers, that is, the industrialized nations that are not members of the G-3, and of the major developing nations. This could be called *democratizing* these institutions. The process would call for concerted co-operation when some or all of these nations find themselves at odds with the policies being advanced by the G-3 on selected but significant issues. The challenges can begin in the deliberations of the Boards of these institutions when the Executive Directors and/or Governors (in whose name the shares are held) hold discussions and make decisions on policies and projects that come before the board for approval. The hope and expectation is that this process would help overcome the shortcomings of the policies and operations of the IFIs that now reflect short-term, narrowly parochial self-serving objectives of the major powers.

But this will not be enough to make these institutions truly international with a perspective that gives priority to spatial and temporal objectives that are global and long-term in scope. What is needed, in addition to a change in will and courage, is a drastic change in the over-arching framework of mutually agreed-upon conventions or regulations pertaining to trade and capital movements between nations, that is, *rules* operating in a manner analogous to the way nations adhered to the rules of the game for the international economy agreed upon at Bretton Woods in 1944 and operative until 1970; in a phrase, a *new Bretton Woods*.

The role of the UN system

There is a *prima facie* case to be made for periodic reviews of the structure and *modus operandi* of any institutions so as to assess its performance in relation to the mandate at its inception and the circumstances at the time of the review. This applies with special relevance to the international agencies that can date their birth from the end of the Second World War, almost half a century ago. The world has changed radically over the intervening years and the institutions have, of course, responded with some change, as witness the environmental initiatives. But the question is: have they been able to adapt enough, not only as individual entities but as a *system* of agencies?

With the advent of a new Secretary-General and in response to a long-felt need to enhance effectiveness, the rationalization of the UN system of agencies has now been placed on the agenda for immediate action. This calls for reorganization of departments and agencies so as to minimize overlapping responsibilities and to fill in the gaps that are not being adequately met. After all, the UN system was founded over four decades ago, long before the current crises were on the front burner. Its original structural features have been changed over time in response to a rapidly and profoundly changing world — but with a lag and with untidy ill-defined compromises made in deference to already established jurisdictional vested interests. There has been no overriding holistic vision in evidence in this process.

Relatively new agencies, such as the the UN Environmental Program (UNEP) and the UN Conference on Trade and Development (UNCTAD), were added to the system during the last few decades, but their assigned functions, their operations and their budgetary resources were constrained by resistance from the established UN agencies which would not give ground in the ensuing jurisdictional battles. It would be more accurate to rephrase that to put the onus on the governments since the resistance to co-operation has come as well — and more importantly — from the delegates on the governing councils of these UN Specialized Agencies who have a vested interest along the lines of their sectoral concerns and/or suffer from the narrowness of parochial vision whether it be that of the departments of agriculture (at FAO), of education and culture (at UNESCO), of industry (at UNIDO), or whatever. Coordination to achieve common agreed-upon objectives begins with the governments who must direct/constrain their delegates within the framework of an overarching policy towards the UN system *as a system* rather than as a collection of separate fiefdoms.

Achieving a more effective role for the UN calls for more than reform of administrative structure of the whole system and for more coherent policies: it calls for financial resources commensurate with the assigned responsibilities of its mandate. The financial constraints are much less severe for the IFIs that have been given access to capital markets for their lending through the so-called *hard window* (lending at rates slightly above the rates at which the Banks can borrow in order to on-lend). But the IFIs are in the same financial boat with respect to their capacity to make grants and non-interest loans to the poorer developing countries [13]. Despite some additional funding of about $1.3 billion for the newly-created Global Environment Facility (GEF), the UN system and the IFIs are severely constrained, particularly with respect to achieving equity and environmental objectives along with the developmental ones.

There is a further constraint brought on by the annual ritual of *summitry* when the leaders of a few nations come together for a few days and presume to talk for the international community. By this process the G-7 pre-empts the role of the UN in discussion of economic and financial issues of global scope. The authors of the WIDER report on *World Economic Summits: The Role of Representative Groups in the Governance of the World Economy* have perceptively noted the results of the G-7 summitry process on the UN system's objectivity and morale:

Many of the problems discussed at the Summit meetings fall within the competence of one or more of the relevant international organizations, as does the responsibility for carrying through the proposed solutions ... [But] in political terms, international organizations are in a subservient position vis-a-vis the Summit, and cannot help competing among themselves for its favours ... and, in doing so, be tempted to compromise their objectivity and their responsibility to the world community as a whole. [14]

Relegating the UN system to a tertiary policy role and routine administration leaves the non-G7 countries, and particularly the Third World countries, out in the cold. The situation has, therefore, evoked calls for involvement of the UN and, at the same time, calls for its strengthening so that it can merit such involvement. Concerns and suggestions for reform have been made for a long time, most notably, in the mid-1970s when the United Nations Group on Restructuring was established, but this effort, and many others afterwards, have come to very little [15]. To this day the UN system continues to suffer from divided jurisdiction with gaps and overlaps and to be regarded by knowledgable observers as weak in terms of such attributes as *realism and intellectual coherence* [16].

Proposals abound for major reform that rationalizes the multitude of agencies so as to enable the UN system (including the IFIs) to address the debt, poverty and environmental crises in a more effective and more democratic way. As a first step we could begin with the suggestion put forward by Professor Gerald Helleiner, who was the Chairman of the Commonwealth Secretariat's Study Group that prepared the 1983 report, "Towards a New Bretton Woods: Challenges for the World Financial and Trading System". He has proposed

a carefully planned World Economic Conference — what some are calling 'a new Bretton Woods' — [to] provide a framework and the beacon needed to give focus and a sense of overall direction to international economic reform. [17]

Whether or not a new Bretton Woods could emerge from a conference is a procedural issue. What is important is what could be achieved by an arrangement analogous to the original agreement forged at Bretton Woods in 1944 and what this implies with respect to the form that global governance might take if it is to be effective in addressing the current crises.

The *New Bretton Woods* as concept and reality

> The biggest politico-economic challenge to statesmen is to integrate national policies into a global perspective, to resolve the discordance between the international economy and the political system based on the nation state ... In [today's] circumstances the international economic system operates — if at all — as crisis management. The risk is, of course, that some day crisis management may be inadequate. The world will then face a disaster its lack of foresight has made inevitable ... *My major point is that the world needs new arrangements.*
>
> The spirit that produced Bretton Woods reflected the realization that in the long run the national welfare can only be safeguarded within the framework of the general [global] welfare. (Emphasis added).
>
> — Henry Kissinger [18]

The call for change in the prevailing global rules of the game for trade and capital movements is tantamount to a call for *systemic* change. This suggests that the objective is to go beyond the avoidance of catastrophic breakdown of the economic and financial system and the limited objective of a return to debtor's creditworthiness, to create conditions that are conducive to faster global growth in real incomes or well-being, a more equitable sharing of this growth, and a pattern of growth that is compatible with standards of environmental quality, locally and globally, that would enable such growth to be sustained over the long-term. Attaining this state of affairs with respect to trade and capital flows would, in the view of many analysts, call for the establishment of a global set of institutions and rules analogous to what was achieved at the conference held in Bretton Woods, New Hampshire, in 1944. It is important, therefore, to understand the original Bretton Woods agreement in terms of its genesis and its performance, if the calls for a *new Bretton Woods* are to have a resonance.

The agreement that emerged from the Bretton Woods conference addressed a key issue facing the post-war world, namely, the rules for international movement of goods and services and of investment. It was a system in the sense that the parties involved in across-border trade and capital movements were co-operants agreeing willingly or not, to conduct their affairs according to these rules. Professor Richard Cooper has, therefore, referred to it as *the Bretton Woods bargain* or an understanding whereby the USA was to take on the obligation to act as a stabilizer by exercising an overwhelming degree of control over key elements of the international financial system, money supply and exchange rates [19].

To carry through on this agreement there was a need for new institutions. Two were established: the International Monetary Fund (IMF) and the World Bank, often referred to as the Bretton Woods twins, and one, the International Trade Organization (ITO) was aborted through US opposition [20]. The Bretton Woods system's rules vested the IMF with the role, as one commentator so aptly put it, of "the champion of virtuous finance". But the IMF, despite its international board of directors and shareholders, had limited power since it was the US that was vested with the responsibility of *virtuousness* in keeping the US dollar, as the saying goes, *as good as gold* [21].

Under pressing circumstances, such as financing the expensive Vietnam war, US policymakers had to choose between adhering to the obligations the country had assumed under the Bretton Woods agreement by reining in the inflationary forces through the imposition of tough fiscal and monetary policy measures or breaking the agreement. The US Administration chose the latter course of action by *closing the gold window* in 1969 (to private individuals) and in 1970 (to central banks). Thus, after a quarter century, the Brettons Woods era came to a dramatic end — and, since the post-Bretton Woods period of a non-system was the gestation period for the debt crisis that broke out in the summer of 1982, a tragic end.

All this was avoidable. After the collapse of the Bretton Woods agreement in 1970 there was no longer an adequate *control* mechanism in place to prevent the chain of events that led to the enormous pile-up of the troubling mountain of debt. *Under a properly functioning global economic and financial system, the countries that went on a borrowing and lending binge in the 1970s would have been brought up short by the Bretton Woods reins.* But the basis for the advocacy of a new Bretton Woods is more than preventive; the days of Bretton Woods are being recalled with nostalgia when it is realized that during the period when its rules held sway there was an increase in the global flows of trade (by 250%) and of incomes (by 150%) and a greater degree of sharing of this increase of income as developing countries on average grew at a much faster rate than the industrialized ones.

Those who call for rules such as those that held sway for a quarter century from 1945 until 1970 — *but adapted, of course, to current circumstances* — have learned the lessons of the fragility of the Gold Standard and the Bretton Woods systems and of their limited achievement in terms of the sharing of the putative benefits of the large increase in global average *per capita* incomes. Thus, the envisaged change would focus on the objectives for the new Bretton Woods and its means of achieving them: the *objectives* would be broader than the narrow focus on increased trade and growth, and include greater emphasis on fairness and on maintaining environmental quality; the *means* would be co-operation that relies less heavily on one key player or one group of players such as the G-3 or G-7.

The challenge is to determine what *form* this system of co-ordination and constraint should take under present circumstances and the *process* by which the hoped-for agreement could be achieved. The world has long lived with indecision, inefficiency, and inequity. Few of the advocates of a new Bretton Woods would be moved to urge changes on that account, but they make common cause in feeling that as a matter of pragmatism and morality the present arrangements are unsustainable. The necessary policy and institutional changes will, therefore, be made by *volitional* decisions in a controlled and orderly way to take advantage of the greater integration of the global economies or they will be changed by *force majeure*, that is, in an uncontrolled and precipitous manner. Should the changes come about in the second manner, the solution or outcome is likely to be a retreat from the 40-year-old trend toward interdependence to autarkic policies as each of the industrialized countries endeavors to minimize the damage to itself by adopting *beggar-thy-neighbor* policies. The possibility of the last outcome gives the problem and the approach to finding a solution an element of urgency.

Accordingly, a broad agreement has seemed to emerge that, in a world of great interdependence, it is imperative that international co-operation be put on a *regularized* basis both for consultations and co-ordination of policies, and for securing the capital to sustain the necessary programs and projects. There is no evading or fudging the financial aspect. The essential element in such a co-operative arrangement is access to secure and plentiful sources of finance. Many proposals have been put forward; these include an expansion of the IMF's special drawing rights for developmental purposes and charging royalties and/or taxes for the use of *The Global Commons* as, for example, the rights to mine the seabed for manganese nodules in international waters, to position satellites in Earth orbit, and so forth [22]. To this list one can add many items such as a recent proposal to levy a small tax of 0.003% on each financial transaction of the global currency exchanges; such a tax would currently yield over $8 billion annually, enough to finance the UN system's obligations including peacekeeping [23].

If this implies new institutional arrangements to achieve the required global management on trade, capital and environmental issues, the newness should be understood to relate to the strengthening and expanding of the operations of the existing international agencies and/or the establishment of additional institutions on their own and/or as adjuncts to those already in operation. The first is clearly preferable since starting new institutions is a difficult and lengthy process and, in any case, the existing ones are amenable to change in their structure, their policies and their mode of operations.

The appreciation of the dire consequences of not rising to the challenge can, perhaps, be a forcing mechanism. The fear of mutual peril might have more persuasive power than the appeals to team work even in the cause of avoiding a world torn by poverty in the face of affluence and debilitated by environmental disasters and the prospects of a bleak, even tragic, future. Can we count on the intelligence and the resilience of humankind and on its basically decent attributes to sustain hope that we and following generations can forge a better future?

Let's hope so — but there's work ahead to make it so. This task would be tantamount to laying the foundation for a future characterized by international relations that reflect the most meaningful concept of national and planetary security.

Notes

1   For an elaboration of the concept of crisis as applied to the current situation, see Appendix A in "The Concept of 'Crisis'" in M. Miller, **Debt and the Environment: Converging Crisis** (UN Publications, New York, 1991) pp.277-280.

2   "Traders put daily net turnover in foreign exchange (including derivative products like futures, options and swaps) at about $900 billion, only $50 billion or so less than the total foreign-currency reserves of all IMF members ... [and] more than a third higher since April 1989 and double the previous survey's figure for 1986 ... Less than 5 percent relates to underlying trade flows, ... another ten percent representing capital movements." - "The last of the good times (for the principal participants of the world's foreign-exchange market)?", *The Economist*, 8(15) 1992, p.61.

In late August '92 the concerted intervention of the central banks of all major economies into foreign exchange markets failed to arrest the decline of the US dollar.

Summitry as a means of achieving co-operation has occasionally succeeded, but if judged on the basis of results, this process has fallen far short of expectations and, on the whole, merits a failing grade. Professor Paul Krugman has made a pertinent comment in connection with one "success" of the G-7:

> in retrospect, *the apparent success of the G-7 at enforcing target zones* after the Louvre meeting [of February 1987] appears to have been something of a fluke: the G-7's actions had a major effect only because the market expected them to, *not because they were powerful in their own right, (thus) meaningful monetary reform on a global scale remains to be achieved.*

— "International Adjustments 1985-90: What Have We Learned?: A Review of an IIE Conference", *International Economic Insights*, Inst. for International Economics, Washington, DC, November/December 1990.

3   In late September of 1992, a Reuters dispatch entitled "Brady Proposes Study of Global Capital Flows" reported that US Treasury Secretary, Nicholas Brady, "all but admitted that central banks were being overwhelmed by currency speculators, saying that [as] foreign exchange markets were approaching daily transactions of $1 trillion, [the action of speculators was] overpowering the ability of governments to intervene to protect their currencies. He concluded that 'new ways of co-operating must be developed to fit the changed circumstances of the new world'." — *The International Herald Tribune*, 24 January 1992.

4   The trends in the key indices of *the human condition* is graphically documented in the annual editions of the UN's *Human Development Report*, the World Bank's annual *Atlas.* and the World Bank's Social Indicators of Development, 1991-92 (The John Hopkins University Press, Baltimore, Md. 1992).

5   This faith in the market approach rests on the asssumption that *market forces* can be harnessed to the cause of reducing the inequity and instability of the global economy and the pace of deterioration of the planet's environmental quality. Those who pin their hope on the market approach would, in most cases, allow for government involvement for the sake of *health, safety and fairness* and for achieving non-economic objectives such as nation-building. But, as a generalized ideological proposition, they ignore or downplay the nature and significance of market failure even under idealized assumptions of *pure competition* that could put the best face on that process. They justify the growing inequities and the cyclical ups-and-downs of the market-economy on the basis of the logic offered by the *trickle-down theory:* a bigger pie to divide could make everyone better off; though some would be left better off than others, it is those who are the greater beneficiaries of the system that provide the dynamic required to assure a bigger pie because of their self-centred motivation and larger disposable resources.

6   From *The Economist*, October, 1930, quoted by Professor Kennedy in his op-ed piece in the 3 January 1993 issue of *The New York Times* entitled "True Leadership for the Next Millenium."

7   This dominance is reflected, for example, in the deliberations of the Bretton Woods meeting in 1944 where decisions were made with respect to such matters as the mode of operation, staffing and weighted voting structure of the Articles of Agreement of the International Monetary Fund, the International Bank for Reconstruction and Development (otherwise known as the World Bank), and the General Agreement on Tariffs and Trade (known by its acronym, GATT) — and as reflected in the institutional arrangements they vetoed such as the establishment of a proposed International Trade Organization (for which GATT was the anemic substitute proposed by the US delegation). For a full discussion of this meeting and subsequent negotiations on the issue of establishing and modifying the principal institutions of international governance in the postwar period, see Stephen Marglin and Juliet Schor, eds. **The Golden Age of Capitalism: Reinterpreting Postwar Experience** (Clarendon Press, London, 1990).

8   See Professor Kindleberger's presidential address to the 1986 annual meeting of the American Economic Association entitled, "International public goods without international government", *The American Economic Review* (March 1986) and M.Miller, *Debt and the Environment: Converging Crises*, UN Publications (NY 1991) pp.167-177.

9   Stephen Marglin and Juliet Schor, ed. *The Golden Age of Capitalism: Reinterpreting Postwar Experience* (Clarendon Press, London, 1990).

10 *World Economic Summits: The Role of Representatived Groups in the Governance of the World Economy*, WIDER Study Group Series #4, Helsinki, 1989, p.11.

11 In a speech at the 1985 World Bank/IMF Annual Meeting. Mr. Haq had served for many years within the World Bank, rising to the position of the Director of the Policy Planning Division. His comments derived from his working experience within the institution as well as from his vantage as governor.

12 This can be illustrated with the example of the outcome of petrocycling when lending and borrowing were carried to a point of crisis: "... loan pushing and subsequent pulling led to all lenders being on the run (at which time) the borrowing country has nowhere to borrow and no one can be repaid. Bankers forgot the sections in their elementary economics courses dealing with the fallacies of composition." — MIT Prof. Lance Taylor, "The Theory and Practice of Developing Country Debt: An Informal Guide for the Perplexed", *Journal of Development Planning*, # 16, UN, NY, 1985, p.205.

13 The tri-annual ritual of replenishing the funds for *soft* lending (through the International Development Association (IDA) in the case of the World Bank and in comparable entities for the other MDBs) involves very hard work. But what is most significant is the fact that the USA, by withholding its pledges is able to hold the World Bank up to ransom: we will provide the funds on condition that the policies of the Bank suit us. It is worth pointing out that over the 40-plus years of the Bank's operations the US contribution to the World Bank in encashment terms (as contrasted with its 'callable capital' contribution and with the funds paid into IDA) has been less than its annual payments in the military budget for lost and misplaced equipment. On this, see M.Miller, Coping is not Enough! ..., op.cit., pp.194-204.

14 *Op.cit.*, p.24. The report goes on to suggest the long-run objectives and strategy for achieving "genuine institutional reform ... ...ving the negotiation of new or amended charters, articles of agreement, conventions, etc., the downgrading or elimination of some organizations, and the strengthening — and possibly the merging — of others ... [as a way of] improving the existing UN policymaking system."

15 "A New United Nations Structure for Global Economic Co-operation", Report of the Group of Experts on the Structure of the United Nations System, UN, NY, 1975. There were also other groups charged with similar tasks, such as the Group on Supplementary Financial Measures arising out of an UNCTAD conference in the mid-1960 and the Committee of Twenty which was formed by the IMF and World Bank to consider reform of the international monetary system and which issued a report entitled, "International Monetary Reform: Documents of the Committee of Twenty

on Reform of the International Monetary System and Related Issues" -(IMF, Washington, DC, 1974).

16 See, for example, a recent study sponsored by the UNU's World Institute for Development Economic Research (known as WIDER) that contains the recommendation for the establishment of a World Economic Council that would undertake the necessary reform exercise:

> hammer out, through small negotiating groups, collective positions on specific and well-defined policy issues and to make agreed recommendations.. *of a more realistic and intellectually coherent nature* than those that have emerged from majority decisions (of the existing UN bodies)...and which therefore would carry greater weight. (emphasis added)

— WIDER Study Group Series #4, *op,cit.*, p.24. The study contains detailed proposals, particularly in the Appendices by Stephen Marris entitled "A Proposal to Create the 'Group of the Non-Five'" and by Lal Jayawardena entitled, "Towards Improved Decision-making in the UN System", pp.34-120.

17 Professor Gerald Helleiner, "An Agenda for a New Bretton Woods", *Foreign Policy Journal*, Winter 1984, p.374. He added, "this is one case in which the process may be more important than the ultimate destination ... The new Bretton woods should, therefore, be seen not so much as a conference but as the initiation of a *negotiating process* involving a re-examination of the world's financial and trading machinery in light of current and prospective needs ... in the same spirit of optimism and creativity as characterized the preparations for the original conference at Bretton Woods."In this article he summarizes the ideas contained in the 1983 Commonwealth Secretariat report "Toward a new Bretton Woods". He notes that "process must begin with or without the USA [but] to be sure, if negotiations are to succeed they must eventually include the USA."

18 "International Economic and World Order", the Motta Lecture, Washington, Sept. 24, 1984. Reprinted in op-ed page of the *Washington Post*, "International Trade: It's Time to Change the Rules of the Game" (22 November 1984).

19 Professor Richard Cooper, "A Monetary System for the Future", *Foreign Affairs*, Fall 1984. There are some, such as Anthony Solomon, formerly a governor of the Federal Reserve Bank of New York, who dispute the designation of *system* to this arrangement or agreement since it did not have an enforcement provision, that is, it was based only on an *understanding*.

20 A third institution, the International Trade Organization (ITO) was proposed and aborted by the US in favour of a truncated entity that was labelled, the General Agreement on Tariffs and Trade (GATT). In effect, as

Professor Heilleiner aptly describes it, GATT was "a small secretariat authorized to do little more than 'service' the 89 contracting nations (out of the IMF's 146)" and to do so with respect to only some of the trade-related issues since there were "major gaps in the coverage of GATT that were left out by [force of] political events such as the final defeat of the ITO." — Professor Gerald K. Helleiner, "An Agenda for a New Bretton Woods", *Foreign Policy Journal*, Winter 1984, p.367.

21 The US dollar as the reserve currency was to be backed by gold reserves in only a loose sense because the relationship of the US money supply was not, itself, fixed in relation to gold except in a figurative sense since Congress could — and did — change the legal *obligatory* connection between its gold reserves and money supply. But, nonetheless, US policymakers were expected to exercise the necessary discipline incumbent on a reserve currency country. To ensure this confidence, anyone could obtain gold bricks from the Fort Knox vaults in exchange for the paper dollars at a price set on the *free market* of the London bullion exchange. The Bretton Woods constraints obliged the US to maintain global *confidence* in the dollar, and there was thus a sense of limits to the permissible bounds of money supply expansion. In the late 1960s, at the time of the Vietnam War, US policymakers tested the limits of monetary expansion that was *allowed* under the Bretton Woods *rules* when they pursued domestic policies that brought on inflation at a rate that greatly exceeded that of the other major industrialized nations. Downward pressure was exerted on the dollar. By the end of the 1960s a gold rush was set in motion reflecting rapidly waning confidence in the dollar. This confidence factor was dramatically reflected in events that can be dated almost precisely: on 1 March 1968, the upward spiral of gold prices commenced, ending only after several years when the price per Troy ounce that had fluctuated in the $300-400 range reached its peak at a level in excess of $800.

22 Morris Miller, **Debt and the Environment**, *op. cit.* pp.185-91.

23 Martin Walker "Global Taxation; Paying for Peace", 1993, World Policy Journal X No.2: "The world has now spawned a huge global economy, a resource that is effectively untaxed ... In 1992, the total value of the transactions of the world's currency exchanges was some $280 trillion dollars (over $900 billion every trading day), or more than ten times the estimated value of the world's economic product. The scale is as glaring as the opportunity. A barely noticeable electronic deduction of 0.001% on each transaction would be nearly enough to pay the UN's peacekeeping bill ... 0.003% would be $8.4 billion, enough to finance UN peacekeeping and almost all other operations of the one club to which the whole world belongs. ... Technically such a tax would be remarkably easy to collect through the computer systems that record such trade ... An agreement by the [governments of the] dominant G-7 economies, backed up by the OECD, requiring their own banks and trading houses to comply, should suffice to police such a relatively painless system of exploiting this global resource."

CHAPTER 11

Reducing the Impact of Fossil-Fuel Burning — Steps Toward Environmental Sustainability

Eric L. Tollefson

Abstract. The next 30 to 50 years will see a dramatic shift from the present day heavy reliance on non-renewable fossil fuels to greater dependence on various forms of renewable energy. In the interim period, as that transition slowly occurs, there will be extensive dependence on fossil fuels which will have to taper off in an effort to control the *greenhouse effect* due largely to emissions of carbon dioxide. This chapter indicates the role of fossil fuels in this period and how the effects may be alleviated.

Introduction

The Brundtland Report [1] *Our Common Future* states, "Humanity has the ability to make development sustainable — to ensure that it meets the needs of the present without compromising the ability of future generations to meet their own needs." To "make development sustainable" it was recognized that limits would have to be imposed so that the biosphere would be capable of absorbing the effects of human activities. McLaren [2] (see also Chapter 7) noted that over the past 150 years, the world population has grown from 1 to over 5 billion with a current doubling time of 30 to 40 years, that a comparable increase in the usage of fossil fuels is leading to global pollution, to changes in climate and sea level and that destruction of the habitat of life is accelerating causing extinction of species. In McLaren's opinion the term *sustainable development* cannot be used while trends such as destruction of forests, soil erosion, overuse of ground water and the production of wastes are accelerating. Of all the factors opposing the sustainability of the environment, the buildup of carbon dioxide in the atmosphere is (apart from the disappearance of the ozone layer) the greatest environmental concern and will be the focus of this chapter.

In *State of the World 1988,* Brown and Flavin [3] provide data showing that carbon emissions (as carbon dioxide) from combustion of fossil fuels have risen from 1.7 billion tons in 1950 to 5.5 billion tons in 1988 while the world population grew from 2.5 billion to 5.1 billion. The Brundtland Report predicts a world population of 8.2 billion by 2025 which would imply that carbon emissions from burning fossil fuels will reach 8.8 billion tons per year by that time assuming that energy consumption patterns remain as they were in 1988 (see Figure 1). However, with increased industrialization in the developing world utilizing coal to a large extent it has been estimated that these emissions could rise to 10 billion tons per year by 2010 unless major steps are taken to reduce the consumption of non-renewable fossil fuels as energy sources and to reduce the CO_2 in the atmosphere by means such as growing biomass [4]. Some of the changes which can be introduced to reduce the load of carbon emissions from the consumption of fossil fuels are examined below.

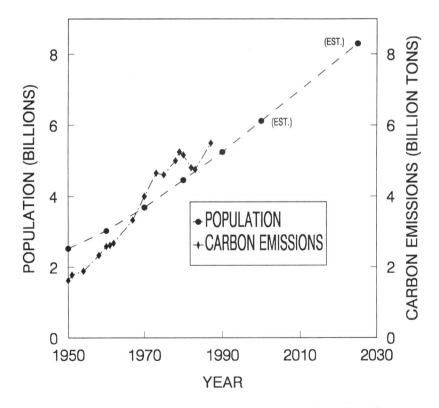

Fig.1 World population and carbon emissions from fossil fuels
as a function of year

If nothing is done to modify these trends, standards of living will sag, and will sag even further in the developing world; malnourishment, starvation and disease will become more widespread than they are today. Carbon emissions enhance the greenhouse effect, the thinning of the ozone layer, and consequent climate changes leading to drought may create conditions in some areas of the South such that the people will be brought to desperation; their fight for a greater share of the world's goods may well lead to many an armed conflict, thereby creating an even less secure world.

The greenhouse gases

Of prime importance among the *greenhouse* gases are carbon dioxide (CO_2), the chlorofluorocarbons (CFC's), methane (CH_4) and nitrous oxide (N_2O). They are distributed throughout the atmosphere and have the capacity to trap infrared radiation energy leaving the Earth's surface, causing the atmospheric temperature to rise. Carbon dioxide contributes 55% of the radiative heating while the others contribute 24, 15 and 6%, respectively [5]. Thus carbon dioxide is responsible for most of the heating effect although there is concern about the other gases as their concentrations increase. Cloud cover also plays a complex role in shielding the Earth from the Sun's energy, and in trapping radiation, although water vapour is not considered to be a greenhouse gas. The globally averaged surface temperature of the Earth could increase by 1.5 to 4.5°C, according to one estimate, if the CO_2 concentration in the atmosphere were allowed to double from its pre-industrial value of 280 parts per million (ppm) to 560 ppm [6]. The average CO_2 concentration in the atmosphere has increased from 310 ppm in 1950 to 350 ppm in 1990.

Schneider [7] shows the remarkable correlation of temperature with carbon dioxide concentrations in the atmosphere over the past 160,000 years, obtained by analyses of ice cores from Antarctica; the carbon dioxide in the atmosphere has been closely related to warming of the atmosphere in the past. There are those who are sceptical about such a correlation in today's world because, in addition to the old complicating factors such as dust from volcanoes, there are new ones, for example, sulfate aerosols in the atmosphere [8] which can reflect the Sun's energy back into space and prevent the temperature from rising even though the CO_2 concentration has been increasing steadily year by

year. However, the threat of global warming is real, even though clima-
tologists are not agreed on the rate of warming that the greenhouse
gases are making or will make as their atmospheric concentration
increases. Society has therefore much to gain by taking action now to
counter the *greenhouse effect*, by reducing CO_2 and other greenhouse
emissions.

Renewable and non-renewable energy sources

Renewable energy sources include those sources which daily derive their
energy from the Sun. These include hydro sources, wind, biomass and
the Sun itself. Biomass sequesters as much carbon dioxide from the
atmosphere as it releases at the end of its life cycle. Biomass sources
therefore do not add to the carbon dioxide content of the atmosphere
unless they are burned and not replaced by new plant growth.

Non-renewable energy sources include gas, oil in various forms and
coal, known as *fossil fuels*, as well as nuclear energy (which contributes
carbon dioxide insignificantly in fuel processing). The fossil fuel
sources have been stored in the Earth's crust for millions of years. When
they are burned the carbon present in them is added to the load of carbon dioxide in the atmosphere.

Flavin and Lennsen [9] have suggested that global emissions of carbon dioxide from fossil fuels should be reduced from the current rate of
approximately 6 billion tons of carbon per year to about 2 billion tons
per year to reduce the rate of global warming so as to forestall melting
of the polar ice caps and consequent inundation of coastal areas. To
achieve such a goal they proposed a scenario for the year 2030 which
might be accomplished by changes in the types and quantities of fuels
consumed compared with present day patterns. This scenario would
have the consumption of oil cut approximately in half by 2030, coal
consumption would be reduced to one-tenth of the present usage rate;
natural gas consumption would remain the same, while energy from
renewable sources would increase by a factor of four. For environmental
reasons nuclear energy would be phased out. The energy produced
from fuels consumed would be approximately 13% more than in 1989
but the world population would have increased by 58% (Table 1). Such
a great reduction in per capita energy consumption would be possible
only if major improvements could be achieved in the efficiencies with
which the energy sources are used. According to Amory Lovins [10],

large improvements in the efficiency of use of energy are already possible at relatively low costs. It may, however, be questioned whether Flavin and Lennsen's large projected increase in the use of renewable energy could be achieved on the given time scale. This paper introduces a modification of their scenario (Table 1), to answer some of the concerns arising from their projections. While the author accepts the assumption that consumption of oil from fossil fuels might be reduced to half of its present amount, it seems unlikely that coal consumption could be reduced to one-tenth of its present rate during the period in question, in view of China's great dependency on coal and its high industrial rate of growth. A goal of 27 percent of the present use rate corresponding to an annual energy output of 600 millions of tons oil equivalent of energy (mtoe) and a carbon emission rate of 647 million tons would seem more attainable. If China, with its large population, would continue to take steps to modernize its coal-burning power plants and would take other measures such as applying co-generation in power production as well as a program involving extensive insulation of buildings to provide higher efficiency in the utilization of energy, it would do much towards achieving the large reduction in the consumption of coal which is needed. Extensive action by other countries as well is necessary along these lines if less coal is to be consumed according to the modified goals in Table 1.

Table 1
World energy use and carbon emissions for 1989 with goals for 2030

	1989		2030 - Estimates by Flavin and Lennsen[4]		2030 - Modified by this author	
	ENERGY	CARBON	ENERGY	CARBON	ENERGY	CARBON
	(mtoe)[1]	(Million Tons)	(mtoe)	(Million Tons)	(mtoe)	(Million Tons)
Oil	3098	2393	1500	1160	1500	1160
Coal	2231	2396	240	258	600	647
Natural Gas	1707	975	1750	1000	1850	1057
Renewable[2]	1831	–	7000	–	6000	–
Nuclear[3]	451	–	0	0	451	0
TOTAL	9300	5764	10490	2418	10401	2864

1. Millions of tons of oil equivalent. 2. Renewable biomass energy results in net carbon emissions when mass is not replaced by new growth. 3. Fuel preparation leads to carbon dioxide production. 4. See Reference 9.

Providing energy for the increasing population

The 2.8 billion increase in the world population which is predicted to occur by 2030 will take place largely in the developing countries in the tropical regions of America, Africa and Asia which in 1991, together with other parts of East and South Asia, had a total population of approximately four billion people. According to Andreae [11] approximately 79 percent of the renewable fuels consumed in today's world is used in these areas. In other words, much of the 1813 mtoe of renewable energy/annum (see Table 1) is being utilized by people in the tropical regions. This breakdown in population by region and in biomass fuel consumption is seen in data excerpted from Andreae's paper shown in Table 2 which illustrates the distribution of the world's population in 1985 and the relative amounts of fuelwood, charcoal and agricultural waste that were burned in tropical and extratropical regions that year. The percentages of these three fuels consumed in the tropical areas were 88, 95 and 67 percent, respectively. Since the population of the developed world is projected to be fairly constant [12] these data strongly indicate that to supply the energy needs of the expanding world population in the period to 2030, great emphasis should be placed on growing biomass in tropical regions. While there will be a tendency to turn to the use of fossil fuels in these areas as a *quick fix* to solve the energy supply problems which will arise with the rapidly growing population, efforts should be made to avoid this approach so as not to increase the emissions of carbon from fossil fuels to the atmosphere any more than necessary.

The estimate of renewable energy usage in 1989 provided by Flavin and Lennsen (Table 1) of 1813 mtoe may be divided as indicated in parentheses as coming from wood (500), biomass (738), hydropower (538) and other (17) [13]. According to Andreae in Table 2 (and as noted above) 79% of the mass of renewable material consumed occurs in the tropical developing regions so that from the 1238 mtoe of energy from wood and biomass, approximately 978 mtoe is consumed by the population of 4 billion in these areas. Using the same rates of consumption for 2030 but with a population of 6.8 billion, the consumption of renewable energy in these areas would rise to 1660 mtoe in terms of wood and biomass. Hydropower production might be expected to rise to approximately 800 mtoe but is limited by availability of suitable rivers, capital and environmental factors. Subtracting these two items from the 7000 mtoe of renewable energy estimated by Flavin and Lennsen for 2030, leaves 4540 mtoe of energy to be produced to meet the goal. Part of this would come from wood and biomass to be consumed largely in the developing world, the remainder would be from solar, wind, and other, smaller sources. This quantity of energy is very large indeed, being equal to 2.5 times the present consumption of renewable energy.

Scott (see next Chapter) and this author doubt whether the consumption of biomass alone can be increased by an additional 4540 mtoe per year by 2030. It would necessitate the development of large tracts of land totalling approximately one billion hectares of biomass plantations and the development of means of harvesting and transporting the products to suitable industrial units which could utilize them as such or for producing energy in the form of gas, oil, coke or charcoal. While this would have to be a very large industry, it should be remembered that such an industry is in place but on a smaller scale and that it is spread out, requiring the dedication of much land and services to maintain it. The much larger industry that will be needed will require many years to build, and involve a lot more suitable land, capital and people to maintain it.

Table 2

Estimates[a] of fuelwood, charcoal and agricultural wastes burned in tropical and extratropical regions annually expressed in millions of tons of dry material

Region	Population (1985 in millions)	Fuelwood*	Charcoal	Agricultural Waste**
Tropical America	430	170	7.5	200
Tropical Africa	550	240	9.3	160
Tropical Asia##	2820	850	3.3	990
Oceanic	25	8	0	17
Total Tropics	3820	1260	20.0	1360
USA and Canada	260	80	0.5	250
Western Europe	380	40	0.2	170
USSR and Eastern Europe	390	50	0.2	230
World Total	4840	1430	21.0	2020

[a] Source — M.O. Andreae [11]
* Average values from data by FAO for 1989 and figures based on population and consumption per person per year at an efficiency of 90 percent.
** Based on total production of crops.
Includes nontropical East Asia and South Asia [editor].

In parts of India which have been greatly deforested the government has increased funding for forestry [14]. Massive tree planting programs [15,16] will be required to supply fuelwood, construction materials and other products to the additional 2.8 billion people expected in the tropical regions by 2030, and to help control erosion of soil in river basins and on farmlands. Some such projects are underway in India and China for example, but there is a great need for more in other areas such as in parts of Africa and Nepal. More on the growth of forests is given in the Annex to this Chapter.

We therefore do not see how the 4540 additional mtoe could be achieved solely from increased use of biomass, wind, hydroelectricity and photovoltaic sources by 2030. For this reason the renewable energy goal in the last column of Table 1 has been reduced to 6000 mtoe from the 7000 mtoe of Flavin and Lennsen. The shortfall is made up in our projection by increasing the coal mtoe to 600 from 240, the natural gas mtoe from 1750 to 1850, and by restoring the nuclear mtoe from 0 to 451.

A carbon tax on fossil fuels

In Chapter 12 the renewable energy future is discussed in some detail. To assist in the development of new technology, with a view to making renewable energy production economic, a dedicated carbon tax on fossil fuels could be a great help, if it were possible to direct the proceeds into relevant branches of research — toward the reduction of greenhouse gas emissions. A problem with national carbon taxes, of which there are a great many, is that the funds raised tend to be simply absorbed into the national budgets, without any regard for the goals discussed in this paper.

What is the future of nuclear power?

The reduction of the energy from nuclear power plants to zero by the year 2030 (Table 1) for environmental reasons may not be reasonable because this energy is contributing minimally to global warming. Therefore, though many may think a complete shut-down of nuclear power desirable, some measure of dependence on it is likely to continue. The United States, France, Germany, Japan, the United Kingdom, the countries of the former Soviet Union, Canada and several other countries are dependent to a considerable extent upon nuclear energy today and are not considered likely to decommission their plants and the nuclear industry unless a very strong need to do so can be demonstrated or the political pressure to do so becomes overwhelming. Not only does nuclear power provide energy with very low carbon emissions (essentially only those from fuel processing and the production of the steel employed), but also nuclear reactors could consume the plutonium that has been amassed in nuclear warheads. Reactors would convert the plutonium to end products that can be permanently disposed of, forestalling the danger of the material being put clandestinely into bombs. For these reasons it may be desirable to replace reactors now in operation, as they end their life cycles, with newer models that are fundamentally safer than the best of today's [17]. Thus, the energy per annum projected to 2030 by the present author has been left at 451 mtoe (Table 1) to allow for the great uncertainty in the future of nuclear power, and its possible contribution to the stemming of global warming.

A middle-of-the-road approach

The modified scenario (Table 1) would reduce the carbon emissions from the present estimated 5764 million tons from these sources to 2864 million tons, a reduction of 50 percent while the energy output would increase by 13 percent to approximately 10,400 mtoe per year. The reduction in carbon emissions is less drastic than the 58% reduction proposed by Flavin and Lennsen. However, in the transition period to the year 2030, the consumption of coal might be further reduced or technology might be developed which would enable the removal of carbon dioxide emissions from large coal-burning power plants (see below).

The modified scenario may be inadequate in the sense that the goals, if achieved, still may not create a sustainable environment. If, in the next decade, it becomes evident that the greenhouse effect is causing a sharper rise in the average global temperature than can be forecast now, then stronger countermeasures will be needed. Under such conditions it would be much easier to convince governments and industrial companies, especially those in the fossil fuels supply business, to take appropriate actions. In the meantime, research on the removal of CO_2 emissions following fossil fuel burning is surely needed.

The industrialized world has a tremendous opportunity during the transition period to increase efficiency in the use of energy which would yield three benefits: economy, a better environment, and protection of the standard of living which otherwise would certainly fall. Such opportunities can only be fully realised through adequate funding of research and development, as well as the adoption of existing technology for increasing efficiency. However, pressure will be brought to bear, and is already being brought to bear on the nations of the North to assist the nations of the South in achieving significantly higher standards of living by providing appropriate industrial technology. [The equally important matter of debt relief is dealt with in Chapter 10]. Many of these activities will be related to maintaining or improving the quality of the environment which in many situations has no boundaries and is, therefore, of interest to all nations.

In the short term many countries will no doubt attempt to fuel their industries by using oil and coal. This trend, however, must soon be reversed in favour of greater use of renewable energy in its various forms. It is apparent that countries such as Sweden, Norway, the United States, and Canada are rethinking their energy needs and that, through various improvements in the efficiency of use of energy, have been able to reduce markedly the predicted needs for power plants and refinery capacity. As Amory Lovins points out [10], [much] technology to increase efficiency in the use of energy is well known. It is now a matter of doing careful planning to provide modified facilities so as to take advantage of the savings that are possible.

While the industrialized countries have been very dependent on the use of fossil fuels, during the transition period many changes will be occurring in which the dependency on fossil fuels will be reduced or in which technology will be developed permitting continued use of these fuels coupled to permanent storage of the CO_2 emitted. A discussion of some of these approaches will follow later.

What should happen in the developed countries during the transition period

For the energy shifts indicated in Table 1 to happen, the Western world including Europe, the United States, Canada, and Mexico needs to reduce its consumption of oil and coal to **less than half** of present levels. While technology will play an important role in this (for example, trends toward even lighter and more fuel-efficient vehicles), the problem of achieving such a drastic reduction in fossil-fuel consumption must be to a large extent social. The difficulty of resisting the tendency to waste (in the current oil glut) illustrates the depth of the social dilemma: what realistic measures, to take one example, would effectively discourage the trend back toward larger, luxury cars? Renewed programs for insulation of homes and other buildings, the expanded use of co-generation in power production, and the use of power from wind farms and from the Sun (thermal or photovoltaic) should be encouraged actively by governments. For the most part, the essential reductions can be achieved by more efficient use of fuels [10]. Clearly the problems are not just technological. They are also very much the social products of the affluent society that has been developed in over twenty countries, with built-in wastefulness and insufficient regard for environmental factors. In a typical North American city, fossil fuel consumption could in principle be drastically reduced through a number of measures, none of them technical. Technological improvements could then bring in additional savings of fossil fuels. This paper is primarily concerned with the technological aspects.

Strategies for reducing carbon dioxide emissions during the transition period 1990-2030: use of high H/C (hydrogen/carbon) fuels

The data provided in Table 1 can be used to show that the energy available per ton of carbon emissions from natural gas, coal and oil is 65.2, 34.7 and 48.2 gigajoules (10^9 Joules), respectively. Energy available per ton of carbon emissions from natural gas is almost double the energy from coal and 35 percent greater than that which can be produced from oil. It is apparent that using fuels with high H/C atomic ratios such as methane, CH_4, with a value of 4.0 rather than oils or coals with ratios of 1.4 to 1.9 and 0.5 to 1.1, respectively, is an important means for reducing CO_2 emissions. A swing toward natural gas as a fuel is therefore to be expected. Fortunately, the world has sufficient natural gas reserves to last for many decades until renewable energy sources are more readily available. In a similar way the catalytic hydrogenation of low H/C hydrocarbons to give products with higher H/C values higher energy and lower CO_2 production on combustion is of major importance as part of the program to reduce CO_2 emissions.

Improving the efficiency of fuel consumption in automobiles

Increased efficiency in the use of fuels means that less fuel is burned and that less CO_2 is produced. According to Lester Brown et al. [4] in 1989 there were approximately 400 million automobiles around the world which released some 547 million tons of carbon per year, representing 10 percent of the carbon emitted by the combustion of fossil fuels. Recent trends suggest that this emission rate would double by 2010. However, great strides have been made in reducing the fuel consumption of automobiles, especially in North America where it was common to get 12-18 miles per US gallon in the early 1970s. The 1973 oil crisis and competition from foreign vehicle manufacturers started and entrenched the trend toward lower fuel consumption, now as low as 38% of the consumption 20 years ago, and therefore producing about 38% as much CO_2. With continued improvement in engine efficiencies, streamlined design to reduce air resistance, lighter vehicles, improved fuels and, it is to be hoped, the enforcement of appropriate highway speed limits, fuel economy should be further improved. Adherence to speed limits would also save lives. Passenger cars capable of 70 to 110 miles per US gallon (2 to 3 litres/100 km) are being tested according to reports in the Environmental Almanac 1992 [18].

The possibility of limiting the number of automobiles in the world to, for example, 500 million along with increasing their gasoline mileage on average up to about 50 miles per US gallon could reduce carbon emissions to about 275 million tons, half of the amount emitted to-day [4]. This socially improbable scenario nevertheless gives an idea of one kind of limit that is needed. If such economy is coupled to other trends (for example, the reduction of private motor traffic in large cities, and the encouragement of alternatives such as bicycles and public transportation, and improved traffic flow), a better idea of the possibilities emerges — some of these trends are already evident. As a beginning, strong measures are called for to discourage regular use of private cars carrying one person. The consumption of fossil fuels by truck transport also needs attention, as the volume of such traffic is not likely to decrease much in the short term.

The use of oxygenated fuels to reduce environmental pollution by automobiles

With the ban on the use of lead tetraethyl in gasoline in the USA, December 1990, along with a limitation on the proportion of benzene, a known carcinogen, allowed in gasoline, there has been a scramble to find replacements for these components to provide the desired performance in new engines. The Environmental Protection Agency (EPA) in the United States [19] has negotiated regulations under the 1990 amendments to the Clean Air Act which required certain urban areas with excessive ozone and carbon monoxide levels to start using oxygenated and reformulated gasolines in the winter of 1992-93. There are 41 cities with serious carbon monoxide (CO) problems which require oxygenated gasolines while nine with ozone problems require reformulated gasolines. Other areas not meeting the ozone air quality guidelines may use the reformulated gasolines.

The oxygenated fuels are produced by adding methanol, ethanol or methyl tertiary butylether (MTBE) to the gasoline at the refineries. Oxygenated fuels can be burned under leaner operating conditions and reduce the emissions of CO and CO_2 in cold or cool weather. The regulations require that the fuel contain an average of 2.7% by weight of oxygen. The EPA claims that this will reduce the CO_2 emissions by 17%. This implies a significant improvement in the efficiency of utilization of the fuels.

Regulations for reformulated gasolines are more involved. Refiners would provide new gasolines by January 1995 to meet the ozone guidelines in 87 cities. This would mean that about 55% of the gasoline used in the United States would have to meet these requirements. The requirements include an average oxygen content of 2.1% by weight, no more than 1.3% benzene by volume and an average Reid vapor pressure of 7.4 pounds per square inch. In addition, standards will be set on sulfur, olefins and the boiling point range.

Hall et al. [20] claim that methanol, which can be derived from biomass by thermochemical processes, and ethanol, which may be produced by enzymatic hydrolysis of lignocellulosic feed materials (biomass), could become competitive with gasoline by 2000 "if the necessary technologies are developed". Adding these alcohols to gasoline would reduce the non-renewable fraction of gasoline and thereby decrease the net CO_2 emission.

Production of MTBE to provide an octane boost along with the desired effect on the vapor pressure of the gasoline will require that several small production plants (each of about 12,000 barrels per day) be built at strategic locations. MTBE is made by the catalytic reaction of methanol with isobutene, the latter being produced by dehydrogenation of isobutane, a fraction which may be recovered in refining petroleum products.

The use of MTBE in gasoline initially began as a replacement for lead tetraethyl to boost the octane number. Its vapor pressure and oxygen content make it a desirable component to improve the performance of engines in cool weather permitting the use of leaner air-fuel mixtures and thus reducing carbon monoxide and carbon dioxide production. More complete combustion under these conditions and the lower vapor pressure of the fuel may reduce the smog-forming propensity of the gases released to the atmosphere.

The use of methane as a clean fuel during the transition period

While methane is normally considered to be a non-renewable fossil fuel as a component of natural gas, it can be produced by anaerobic digestion of wastes and is sometimes called *biogas*. Besides being available in many parts of the world in plentiful supply in natural gas, it is also present in association with beds of coal in very significant quantities. In addition, there are very large deposits of so-called *methane hydrates* which exist off-shore at the bottom of the ocean under pressure and where it is cool [21]. Deposits of the hydrate, a solid, also exist in the tundra regions. While the technology for recovering methane gas from these hydrates is not well worked out, estimates suggest that the methane trapped is about the same as or up to 1000 times more than the conventional methane reserves, indicating that it could be a large energy source. Concern has been expressed about the possible dissociation of these methane hydrates if the average global temperature should rise significantly, causing methane to be released to join other greenhouse gases, and to enhance the warming of the atmosphere.

Methane is a desirable clean fuel since it burns to produce water and carbon dioxide

$$CH_4 + 2O_2 \rightarrow CO_2 + 2H_2O$$

As mentioned earlier the energy released per unit mass of carbon dioxide formed is much higher than that from combustion of fuels containing less hydrogen such as coal. For this reason it is being used as a fuel to combat pollution of the atmosphere in some areas and to reduce CO_2 emissions. The production of the carbon dioxide in the reaction, of course, adds to the load of CO_2 in the atmosphere. In western Canada efforts are being made by the oil industry to recover this CO_2 and to use it to enhance oil recovery from depleted oil-bearing formations [22]. Once the oil has been recovered, the CO_2 may be permanently stored in the formation or in other formations which are porous and sufficiently well sealed to act as underground reservoirs.

The use of methane in hydrogen production

Methane is being *reformed* on a large scale by a catalytic reaction with steam to yield a product gas containing hydrogen and carbon dioxide thus,

$$CH_4 + 2H_2O \rightarrow CO_2 + 4H_2$$

The hydrogen is used extensively in the oil industry to upgrade heavy oil fractions into lighter liquid fractions and gases which may be used as transportation fuels.

Methods for separating CO_2 from hydrogen are being steadily improved. The hydrogen product, a clean fuel, can be used to power fuel cells which operate at efficiencies of approximately 60-70% and cause very little pollution of the atmosphere. Spurred by the Hydrogen Industry Council in Canada, a bus has been built which is powered by hydrogen using fuel cells and batteries to drive electric motors [23]. The bus will be used on a test basis in the public transportation system in Vancouver, British Columbia, Canada. It is hoped that this will lead to vastly expanded use of hydrogen for transportation and at the same time cause a reduction in atmospheric pollution in the cities following this approach.

Marchetti [24] has suggested the possibility of converting the methane in a pipeline running from the former Soviet Union to western Europe by catalytic steam-methane reforming in which the energy required would be supplied by a high temperature nuclear reactor. The carbon dioxide would be used for enhanced recovery of oil or permanently stored while the hydrogen would be pumped through the pipeline to western European consumers as a clean, non-polluting fuel.

Although the use of a nuclear reactor to supply heat is desirable because it would not produce carbon dioxide, it may not be acceptable on other social and/or environmental grounds. Heat, however, could be supplied by burning part of the gas being transmitted and the carbon dioxide produced could be recovered for disposal in a formation allowing for enhanced oil recovery. This strategy offers one means by which the oil and gas companies can remain active energy producers without adding to the pollution of the atmosphere.

Countering carbon dioxide production in power generation

Another strategy that has been suggested by power producers [25] as a means of countering CO_2 production from combustion of oil and gas is for the power companies to increase their energy utilization efficiency and to adopt conservation measures. Forestation projects are part of the strategy in that they counter CO_2 production through the sequestering action of the trees.

In the transition period it would help to control the CO_2 load in the atmosphere. In some parts of the world such action could produce much needed fuelwood or biomass which could be used for fuel thus alleviating the pressure on the forested areas which are being depleted to supply energy for cooking and for heating homes for about one quarter of the Earth's people [26]. Such a program could also assist with control of soil erosion and the control of flooding in river basins.

Increasing energy efficiency in the use of residential appliances and equipment

Data provided by Flavin and Durning [27] indicate that very substantial energy savings may be expected from the use of the most energy-effective appliances. Table 3 shows such a comparison between average 1985 consumption and what is technically possible. The higher cost-effective potential estimates were used to calculate the potential savings.

It is apparent that substantial energy savings can be achieved by adoption of these new energy-efficient appliances and equipment. New standards [28] being applied in some states in the United States will require adoption of these more energy efficient designs. By the turn of the century, it is estimated that the use of these standards in new appliances and equipment will have saved $28 billion in gas and electricity in the USA and reduced the carbon emissions to the atmosphere by approximately 342 million tons. According to Lee Schipper [29] similar improvements in energy efficiency of electric appliances are being achieved in Sweden and Germany.

Approximately 64% of the world's electrical energy generated today is produced by combustion of fossil fuels which account for 27% of the emissions of carbon i.e. 1.5 billion tons annually [30]. Assuming that the world could double the efficiency of lighting systems by 2010, the projected carbon emissions from lighting estimated at 450 million tons could be reduced to half of the value, a very significant reduction. However, there is again a social factor here; wastage is largely a matter of human habits, especially when it comes to lighting.

Table 3
Potential energy efficiency improvements for residential appliances and equipment compared with 1985 average values in the United States

Product	Average of those in use	Estimated cost-effective potential	Potential savings
(Kilowatts-hrs per year)			
Refrigerator	1500	200-400	73%
Central air conditioning	3600	900-1200	67
Electric water heating	4000	1000-1500	62.5
Electric range	800	400-500	37.5
(Therms per year)			
Gas furnace	730	300-480	34
Gas water Heater	270	100-150	44
Gas range	70	25-30	57

Efficiency improvements in various electric appliances, furnaces, refrigerators, air conditioners, electric motors and lighting devices offer opportunities for a great deal of activity in industries which would provide new models to the public around the world. Where it has not already been done, in countries manufacturing appliances, governments need to legislate against the production of appliances that are not energy-efficient. Such legislation necessarily requires the back-up of technical assessment to ensure that the newly legislated standards are complied with. It is to be hoped that the added industrial activity generated in the development and production of newer, more energy-efficient models could become part of a world-wide effort to convert industry from production of military to civilian goods, and could do much to solve unemployment problems.

Cogeneration of electricity and heat energy

Flavin and Durning [27] point out that one of the greatest opportunities to improve energy utilization efficiency is to use cogeneration which involves the combined production of heat and electricity. Instead of installing conventional steam boilers in plants to generate electricity alone, the waste heat from the electricity generation is used in various processes in industry or can be employed to heat buildings, greenhouses and shopping centres. By using cogeneration, factories have been able to raise total plant energy efficiency from the 50-70% range into the 70-90% range.

Using natural gas as fuel for a gas turbine producing electric power, the specific CO_2 emissions per kilowatt hour of energy produced are from 0.6 to 0.7 kg per kWh [31]. By using a combined cycle with a gas turbine providing heat to an unfired heat recovery steam generator in conjunction with a steam turbine, the efficiency rises from approximately 30% to 55% and the CO_2 emissions are reduced to approximately 0.4 kg per kWh. The potential for savings with lower CO_2 emissions is large using such approaches.

An example given by Brown et al. [30] describes changing from a conventional 1000 megawatt coal fired power station to a combined cycle system in which a 30% efficiency improvement is achieved and carbon emissions are reduced by 568,000 tons per year. Such combinations can offer tremendous savings. There may, however, be difficulties in finding locations in which the need for electric power and heat can be matched up. Many industries and some municipal operations such as hospitals are possible candidates if they are not already taking advantage of such opportunities.

Recently a novel concept has been described by Walker et al. [32]

for the generation of electric power utilizing the exhaust energy of a gas pipeline compressor to operate a Stirling engine system. A typical installation by elementary analysis would recover 9 MW of power from a gas compressor. There are 6000 gas turbine/compressor units in North America suggesting that as much as 54000 MW of electric power might be recovered.

Recovery use and disposal of carbon dioxide

In a number of industrial operations such as steam-methane reforming to produce hydrogen, the CO_2 produced is present in a concentrated form so that it can be recovered and used for other purposes such as enhanced recovery of oil. The idea of collecting these CO_2 streams and piping them to oil fields where they can be used is now being actively considered in some places and already utilized elsewhere [33]. For example, Vikor Resources Ltd. has produced over a million barrels of oil in its Joffre Viking pool in Alberta, Canada. The field had been abandoned because of uneconomic production. Additional production was established by injection of carbon dioxide. It is hoped to recover an additional 12 million barrels from the field.

The hydrogen produced in steam-methane reforming operations is at present being used in large measure to upgrade heavy oil to lighter petroleum products and to remove sulfur and nitrogen. The hydrogen itself could be used in many applications as a heat source and a fuel in fuel cells to produce electricity at high efficiency.

Various systems for removal and storage of carbon dioxide from waste gases were considered at a recent conference held in Amsterdam in March, 1992. It was sponsored by several governmental agencies and companies from the Netherlands, Belgium, France and the United States. It is apparent that much consideration is being given to research on this important topic.

Reducing CO_2 emissions by insulation of buildings

Much has been written about the very important contributions which insulation of homes and office buildings made in the 1970s and early '80s when the OPEC nations were able to raise the price of oil on the world markets. When the prices fell in the eighties as a glut of oil was created, this drive to improve insulation in older homes levelled off.

New building codes incorporate much better insulation standards so that their energy efficiencies are high compared with those of most older homes. Should the price of oil and gas rise again, the impetus to improve insulation to save heat energy would no doubt be reactivated and emissions of carbon dioxide would be reduced. The economic justification for improving older homes is weak as long as fuel prices remain low. Introduction of a new carbon tax, which has been discussed widely, could spur efforts to save energy being lost from older homes and commercial buildings.

The cost of increasing efficiency in the utilization of energy

The wide variety of options which can be developed in increasing the efficiency of utilization of energy create a difficult task in estimating the overall costs of such developments. Brown and Wolf have made a rough estimate of the cost for the period 1990 to 2000 which averages $30 billion per year for raising energy efficiencies [34]. A report from the World Game Institute by Gabel and Frisch [35] also recognizes the tremendous advantages to be gained and have estimated the cost at $33 billion per year for this period. This estimate includes the costs of increasing the efficiency of appliances, lighting, heating and cooling equipment, insulation and weatherizing of buildings, increasing the gasoline mileage of automobiles as well as expanding the use of cogeneration in various ways for power and heat production. If society moves positively in these directions, major reductions in carbon emissions will result creating a more sustainable society and environment.

Conclusion

Several ways of reducing carbon dioxide emissions have been considered. The use of methane as a fuel is likely to expand as one means of reducing carbon emissions over the next 30 to 40 years. Some of the most favorable possibilities for reducing hydrocarbon fuel and electric power requirements lie with increasing the fuel and electrical energy efficiencies of cars, electric appliances, heating and refrigeration equipment. Tremendous energy savings are also in principle achievable by a variety of changes in human habits. By banning the sale of appliances and other electrical devices with low energy efficiencies, governments could improve opportunities for relevant industries to develop and market energy-efficient equipment; this would create jobs and reduce the levels of unemployment in numerous areas. Cogeneration of heat and electric power also offers large energy savings and reductions in carbon dioxide production. Recovery, use and storage of carbon dioxide is under active consideration on an international basis. All of these efforts to reduce carbon dioxide emissions will help in a global sense to reduce the concentration of carbon dioxide in the atmosphere and hence are moves toward making the environment sustainable.

Military forces are major users of oil and are responsible for about 10% of the greenhouse-gas emissions world-wide. They have made a considerable contribution to the destruction of the ozone layer. Reduction of military budgets is thus an avenue of great potential in the struggle to preserve the environment.

Annex

Using Growth of Forests to Remove CO_2 from the Atmosphere and to Provide Fuelwood and Other Products

Norman Myers [36] in 1989 pointed out that to absorb half of the carbon emissions taking place i.e. three billion tons of carbon, 300 million hectares of tree plantations located in areas capable of supporting rapid growth such as the tropical regions would be required. Such areas can remove up to 10 tons of carbon per year per hectare. The cost for such an operation according Myers has been estimated at $120 billion (US) or $12 billion per year spread over 10 years. If this type of approach is not taken and the greenhouse effect begins to affect the climate, rainfall patterns, irrigation and hydropower operations, it may be necessary to spend much more on alterations and maintenance programs to counter these effects.

Houghton and Woodell [37] support this approach to removal of carbon dioxide from the atmosphere. They indicate that there may be as much as 800 million hectares of land which was once forested and which now could be reforested. In their opinion the retreat of glaciers is evidence of global warming and there is a need to stabilize the world's atmosphere by removing three billion tons of carbon per year. This they maintain, can be done by reducing deforestation and by reforestation.

As a result of a program of massive reforestation as implied above much wood could be made available on an annual basis to provide the energy needs of the growing population in the tropical regions particularly. The energy usage per inhabitant of the world is 1.8 tonnes of oil equivalent per year. Since the calorific value of wood is approximately 0.4 that of oil, on average an inhabitant would require four tonnes of wood per year. Since as much as 10 tonnes of wood can be produced per hectare per year in a tropical region, if as much as 800 million hectares of land could be reforested, this could provide eight billion tonnes of fuelwood sufficient to support the energy needs of two billion people. This would go a long way towards supplying the needs of the additional 2.8 billion people likely to be added to the world population by 2030. However, the need to develop other energy sources such as solar, windpower, and geothermal is very much evident.

References

1   Brundtland, G.H., "Our Common Future" The World Commission in Environment and Development, Oxford University Press, 1987.
2   McLaren, Digby, "Are Global Change and Sustainable Development in Conflict?" Proceedings of the Fortieth Pugwash Conference on Science and World Affairs, Egham, UK, September 15-20, 1990, p.493.
3   Brown, L.R. and Flavin, C., "The Earth's Vital Signs", in State of the World 1988*, pp.1-21.
4   Brown, L.R., Flavin, C. and Postal, S., "Outlining a Global Action Plan", in State of the World 1989*, p.177.
5   O'Sullivan, Dermot, A., C & E News London, Science Technology, October 29, 1990, p.29.
6   White, Robert M. "The Great Climate Debate", Scientific American, July (1990) p.36.
7   Schneider, S.H., Scientific American, Special Issue, September (1989) p.70.
8   Science and Technology Concentrates, C & E News, January 27 (1992) p.31.
9   Flavin, C. and Lennsen, N., "Designing a Sustainable Energy System", in State of the World 1991*, p.25.
10 Lovins, Amory B., "Energy, People and Industrialization" in Resources, Environment and Population edited by Kingsley Davis and Mikhail S. Bernstam, Oxford University Press 1991, p.95.
11 Andreae, M.O., "Biomass Burning in the Tropics: Impact on Environmental Quality and Global Climate" ibid, p.268.
12 Lee, R.D., "Long-Run Global Population Forecasts: A Critical Appraisal" ibid, pp.44-71.

13 Pease, Rendel, "The Prospects of Non-Carbon-Based Energy Sources" Commissioned Paper, 41st Pugwash Conference on Science and World Affairs, Beijing, China, September 17-22, 1991.

14 Pastel, S. and Heise, L., "Reforesting the Earth" Chapter 5 of State of the World 1988*, p.100.

15 Brown, L.R. and Wolf, E.C., "Reclaiming the Future" Chapter 10 of State of the World 1988*, p.175.

16 Li, Jing-Ning, "Comment: Population Effects on Deforestation and Soil Erosion in China" See Ref. 10, p.254.

17 Zumdahl, S.S., "Nuclear Power: Could It Stage a Comeback?" Chemical Principles, Chapter 21, D.C. Heath and Company, Toronto, p.914.

18 Environmental Almanac 1992. Compiled by World Resources Institute, Houghton Mifflin Company, Boston 1992.

19 C & E News, News of the Week, "Air Pollution Cleanup: Pact Set for Reformulating Gasolines", August 26 (1991) p.4.

20 Hall, D.O., Mynick, H.E. and Williams, R.H., Commentary, Nature, Vol. 353, September 5 (1991) p.11.

21 Sloan, Dendy Jr., "Clathrate Hydrates of Natural Gases" Marcel Dekker Inc. New York, (1990) p.393.

22 Bailey, R.J. and Logan, A., Canadian Heavy Oil Quarterly Meeting, Calgary, Canada, May 13 (1991).

23 Prater, K.B., "The Ballard Fuel Cell Bus Project," Tenth Anniversary Conference, Hydrogen Industry Council, Kananaskis, Alberta, Canada, May 20-21, (1992).

24 Marchetti, C., Int. J. Hydrogen Energy 44 (8) (1989) p.493.

25 C & E News, News of the Week, "Utilities to Cut CO_2 Emissions 20% by 2010," May 27, (1991) p.6.

26 Brown, L.R. and Flavin, C., "The Earth's Vital Signs," in State of the World 1988*, p.9.

27 Flavin, C. and Durning, A., "Raising Energy Efficiency", in State of the World 1988*, pp.45-61.

28 Flavin, C., "Creating a Sustainable Energy Future", in State of the World 1988*, p.30.

29 Schipper, Lee, "Improved Energy Efficiency in the Industrialized Countries - Past Achievements, Future Prospects", 41st Pugwash Conference on Science and World Affairs, Beijing, China, September 17-22 (1991).

30 Brown, L.R., Flavin, C. and Postal, S., "Outlining a Global Action Plan", in State of the World 1989*, pp.173-179.

31 Bohm, H., "Fossil Fuel Power Plants: Minimizing Emissions, Maximizing Efficiency" Siemens Review, Vol. 58, March-April (1991) p.18.

32 Walker, G., Krekmer, J., Reader, G., Fauvel, O.R. and Bingham, Dept. of Mechanical Engineering, University of Calgary, "Generation of Electric Power Utilizing the Exhaust Energy of Gas Pipeline Compressor Stations".

Presented to the 1992 ASME Cogenturbo Congress and Exposition on Gas Turbines in Utility, Industrial and Independent Power, Houston, Texas, September 1-3 (1992).

33 The Tar Paper - Published by the Alberta Oil Sands Technology and Research Authority, Vol. 13, December 4 (1990).

34 Brown, L.R. and Wolf, E.C., in State of the World 1988*, p.183.

35 Gabel, M. and Frisch, E., "Doing the Right Things", World Game Institute, University Science Center, Philadelphia, Pa (1991).

36 Myers, Norman, "The World's Forests and Human Populations: The Environmental Interconnections" See Ref. 10, p.237-251.

37 Houghton, R.A. and Woodell, G.M., "Global Climatic Change", Scientific American, April 1989, pp.36-44.

* A Worldwatch Institute Report on Progress Toward a Sustainable Society, W.W. Norton and Company, New York 1988.

CHAPTER 12

Energy Alternatives for Sustainable Environmental Security

Donald S. Scott

Abstract. If a change from carbon-based fossil fuels to greater dependence on renewable and sustainable energy sources is to take place as rapidly as possible, then it is imperative that these alternative energy technologies be developed to a technically and economically feasible stage as soon as possible. Of the various sustainable energy options, each has its own optimal circumstances for adoption. There is no single "best" alternative energy, but several have been developed to a point at which informed choices can be made. Some of these sustainable energy options are economically feasible in favourable situations even at the present time.

Introduction

As discussed in the previous chapter, the problem of the *greenhouse effect* is one which is of such potential for damage to our environment that it must be addressed in a constructive way in the next decade. One of the major ways to reduce significantly the amounts of carbon dioxide added to the atmosphere is to eliminate as completely as possible the use of fossil fuels. Indeed, a good case can be made that this store of carbon and hydrocarbons is, in the long run, too valuable to be used as fuel but should be conserved as a primary source for the manufacture of the many organic compounds which are essential to our present standard of living and are likely to remain so for a long time. However, if the cheap and presently abundant fossil fuels are to be replaced to a significant degree in the near future, there must be concerted political action to bring this about. Such actions cannot be expected to be implemented without nearly insuperable obstacles unless there are available alternative technologies which can be employed, and which are both technically and economically feasible without generating unacceptable risks or undue economic hardship. The present status of such technologies will be briefly reviewed in the rest of this chapter, and our ability to adopt such sustainable energy sources considered.

Renewable energy sources

The Sun is our only major source of renewable energy. Therefore, sustainable energy consists of the various ways to utilize the solar energy received by Earth. The energy utilizing processes can be categorized as "primary" if the radiant energy of the Sun is used or converted directly (as in photosynthesis) or is transferred first to the atmosphere and oceans and then converted. Such processes give rise to *sources* of energy, and such technologies as

- direct heating or cooling of water and houses
- photovoltaic and other direct means of energy production
- wind and wave power
- tidal power (gravitational in origin)
- hydroelectric power
- energy production from biomass

Energy from the above sources can be converted into other, more readily utilized forms of energy, such as methanol, ethanol, syngas and hydrogen. Because the production of these alternative fuels from solar sources requires more energy than they furnish, they are not primary energy sources, but rather *energy currencies*.

However, these alternative fuels or energy currencies can also be produced on a renewable and sustainable basis from the Sun's energy. Occasionally, the opinion is expressed that **all** carbonaceous fuels must be banned, but this is not a reasonable option. The processes of photosynthesis remove atmospheric carbon dioxide, so that the utilization of biomass, in whatever form, as a fuel source does not add any net carbon dioxide to the atmosphere as long as the growth/consumption cycle of biomass is at a steady state.

The variety of alternative energy sources, and their differences, implies that usually only one or two of these may be technically or economically feasible in any given set of circumstances. It is necessary, therefore, to investigate these technologies thoroughly and to make informed selections of the most suitable technology if alternative sustainable energy is to substitute successfully for fossil fuels in the near future. At the present time, some of the most acceptable renewable energy processes are those which yield a generally useful form, such as a storable and transportable liquid or gaseous fuel. Therefore, these will be discussed first.

Energy from biomass

The solar energy captured by photosynthesis in the form of biomass is estimated to be equivalent to ten times the world's present consumption of energy. However, the biomass which is available through cultivation or other forms of harvesting is only about 10% of this, or approximately equal to the world's annual energy usage. Much of this biomass must supply the food, fibre and timber for the world's needs. Consequently, while the amounts of presently harvested or potentially readily available biomass can form a significant contribution to total energy needs, biomass cannot be a sole source of the world's energy requirements. Of course, the supply of biomass available for energy use can be increased very greatly in several ways — by growing suitable *energy crops* on marginal or presently under-utilized land, by better harvesting and collection methods in forestry and agriculture, by increasing crop yields by better cultivation practices, and by the development of more efficient plant varieties using genetic engineering techniques. These options would all increase the potential supply of biomass as an energy source and give a sustainable energy system.

It has been estimated that the United States currently obtains about 4% of its energy needs from biomass, as does Europe. In both areas, it is estimated that biomass could readily supply 10% of all energy requirements by the year 2000. In some Third World countries, the use of biomass as a fuel is the primary energy source, supplying up to 90% of the energy needs of these economies.

Biomass can be burned as a primary fuel source. It is not an ideal fuel, because of the high moisture content and low available heat per unit mass — only from one-half to one-quarter that of fossil fuel. It is usually bulky and therefore costly to ship and to store and, for these reasons, it is used close to the source of supply. There is, therefore, considerable incentive to transform the biomass to more concentrated, and more easily used, shipped and stored forms of energy. The greatest amount of available biomass and the most convenient to harvest for energy is wood. Table 1 shows the distribution of the world's wood resources, and it is clear that substantial amounts are widely available, in both developed and developing areas. Most of the presently available conversion technologies for non-food biomass have been developed with surplus or waste wood as the intended basic feedstock.

The simplest and oldest technique for the conversion of biomass to a superior fuel is the production of charcoal. The yield is about 30%, but the heating value is high. Charcoal is produced in substantial amounts today, especially in less developed countries. It will continue to be a useful and relatively clean fuel, but the low yield and inefficient production processes make it relatively expensive. A wide variety of new conversion techniques to produce liquid or gaseous fuels from biomass have been developed in the last two decades. A summary of some of the available technologies is shown in Table 2 [1]. Many of these processes are only now entering full scale commercial operation in locales in which circumstances allow economics competitive with fossil fuels. Processes for conversion of biomass to liquid fuels, especially transportation fuels, are perhaps of the greatest current interest. This is usually accomplished by the production of alcohol, either by fermentation of sugars produced by the plant or formed by the hydrolysis of cellulose, or by synthesis

Table 1
World Forest Resources

Million m^3	Total standing timber	Total harvest	Industrial harvest**
Canada	19,100	149	145
USA	20,193	345	331
Western Europe	8,280	219	191
Eastern Europe	3,153	80	67
CIS	74,710	389	315
Latin America and Africa	176,000	263	67
		343	46
Asia	10,400*	735	204
Oceania	1,239*	31	24

* Minimum estimate ** Excluding firewood

from carbon monoxide/hydrogen mixtures obtained by biomass gasification. In the former case, the product is usually ethanol, and in the latter, methanol. Both can replace gasoline partly or completely in internal combustion engines. Mixtures of gasoline and ethanol (up to 20% ethanol) are already in fairly wide use in the United States and Europe. These *gasohols* give clean-burning and acceptable fuels which can be directly used in today's automobiles. With some modifications, 95% ethanol or 100% methanol can also be readily used for automobiles, although some minor technical problems remain to be overcome. Since about 50% of the carbon dioxide produced in North America comes from transportation fuels, replacement of 20% to 100% of present hydrocarbon liquids by ethanol or methanol derived from biomass would have a very significant impact on the *greenhouse* problem in our environment.

Among the newer technologies for conversion of biomass to an alternative fuel oil is the process now known as *fast pyrolysis*. A number of reactor configurations can be used, but all the methods are characterized by a high intensity heating rate in the absence of air or oxygen, and a short residence time for the biomass and volatile decomposition products. This approach results in liquid yields, typically about 75% from wood, with about 15% charcoal and 10% medium heating value gas [2]. The *bio-oil* produced is free of sulphur and can be readily burned, although its heating value on a volumetric basis is only about two-thirds that of fossil fuel. However, this type of pyrolysis accomplishes the aim of conversion of biomass to a storable and easily transportable fuel. In addition to its use as an alternative liquid fuel, the oil is also a source of organic chemicals, and could be an additional source of some petrochemicals now made from fossil fuels [3]. These pyrolysis processes are only now beginning to be commercialized, however. Costs of production of a bio-oil from wastes is estimated to be about the same as the present cost of conventional light fuel oil on an equivalent energy basis. The cost from energy crops might be up to 50% more [4], but in this case, a considerable job-creation factor for rural areas is gained.

With the current rapid scientific and technical progress on many fronts which will increase the available biomass for energy use, and improve its conversion to useful fuels, particularly liquid transportation fuels, biomass as an energy source has a very significant and important role to play in any system of sustainable energy production. Of all the alternative energy options, biomass conversion is the only one that can produce liquid fuels contributing no net carbon dioxide to our environment. Municipal urban wastes are 70% or more either biomass or biomass-derived products [5]. This source of renewable energy, particularly for conversion to more acceptable fuels, is just beginning to be exploited as sorted refuse-derived material becomes increasingly available. Because urban waste is generated in North America at a rate of about one tonne per person per year [5], this is a resource which must ultimately be used to the fullest possible extent if a renewable energy society is to be achieved, particularly if the forest resources per capita of the world continue to decrease.

Table 2
Bioconversion processes and products [1]

Class	Process	Initial product	Final product (energy content)
Aqueous	Anaerobic digestion	Biogas (2 parts CH_4 to 1 part CO_2; 22-28 MJ/m³)	Methane (38 MJ/m³)
	Alcohol fermentation		Ethanol (19 MJ/L)
	Chemical reduction		Oils (35-40 MJ/L)
Dry thermochemical	Pyrolysis		Pyrolytic oils (23-30 MJ/kg) Gas (8-15MJ/m³) Charcoal (19-31.5 MJ/kg)
	Gasification	Low-medium energy gas (7-15 MJ/m³)	Methane (38 MJ/m³) Methanol (16.9 MJ/L) Ammonia Electricity (3.6 MJ/kWh)
	Hydro-gasification		Methane (38 MJ/m³) Ethane (70.5MJ/m³) Charcoal
Direct combustion	Wood chips (18.6-20.9 MJ/kg dry weight)	High pressure steam	High pressure steam Electricity (3.6 MJ/kWh)

Energy from hydrogen

It is possible to conceive of a global energy system based on hydrogen and electricity which does not use carbonaceous fuel in any form, renewable or fossil in origin [6]. This is a very attractive idea and one which is enthusiastically championed by its proponents. However, the enormous cost and extensive remaking of the energy-consuming societies which would be necessary to accomplish the hydrogen economy will, no doubt, mean that introduction of such a scheme would be slow and difficult, if possible at all. However, this does not mean that there is not a real possibility of using hydrogen as one of several renewable and sustainable energy options in the near future.

Hydrogen has the unique possibility of being prepared from water through gasification or electrolytic processes, and of producing only water when it is burned. Any source of high temperature heat, or of electricity, can be used to manufacture hydrogen. Again, hydrogen is not a primary energy source, but an energy currency. It must be prepared from some other energy source, presumable solar in origin, such as electricity from photovoltaic systems, solar thermal generators, hydropower, etc. It will require more energy to produce than it will supply. However, hydrogen can be transported through pipelines and stored in a variety of ways, and can therefore have a very wide range of energy applications. Not only can it be burned as a transportation fuel, but it can be used in fuel cells for direct transformation to electricity with efficiencies that now approach 70%. The disadvantages of hydrogen as a universal energy currency are that it has a low volume energy density, and therefore is usually used as a highly compressed gas. Not only is the need for these high pressures costly but it is also hazardous and, coupled with the wide explosion limits of air-hydrogen mixtures, gives a requirement for stringent safety practices in equipment design and handling for hydrogen as an energy source. Nevertheless, the offsetting advantage of hydrogen as a clean, convenient fuel will, no doubt, ultimately lead to fairly widespread usage of this fuel, but its adoption will probably come more slowly than that of other renewable energy sources.

Photovoltaic energy

Photovoltaic energy is the production of electricity directly from sunlight by the use of solar cells. The development of this technology has been one of the success stories of the last 30 years. The original impetus came from the space program where panels of these cells supply the electric power for spacecraft. Early silicon-based solar cells gave a conversion efficiency of only 5% to 10%, but recent research has improved this performance to the 20% to 25% range, and 30% efficiency has been reported to be possible [7]. Very extensive research on both the solar cells as well as on system applications has been carried out in both North America and Europe. Photovoltaic systems have the following advantages [8]:

- highly modular, so a wide range of sizes can be used. Small scale experimentation is directly scalable to larger installations
- sunlight-to-electricity conversion is accomplished directly in equipment with few, if any, moving parts, leading to low operation and maintenance costs
- no pollutants are produced because no fuel is consumed. The only environmental impact is the considerable land usage required. However, it has been estimated that a land area equal to only about 20% of the size of the state of Nevada would allow enough electricity to be generated by photovoltaics to equal the current US electrical production [8].
- research is active and projected production costs of photovoltaic energy are continuously decreasing.

On the negative side is the fact that energy is produced efficiently only in sunny climates, and primarily in the summer months. For this reason, hybrid systems of photovoltaic units plus a complementary fuel source are usually planned in order to give an assured energy supply. The auxiliary fuel must be one that can be stored or transported, so that in a sustainable energy system, either biomass or hydrogen would be the logical choice to be coupled to a photovoltaic system.

For widespread use in both large and small installations for the generation of electricity, photovoltaic systems show one of the greatest potentials for energy-significant contributions.

Direct solar heating and cooling

In small scale applications, solar energy is used with a variety of collector designs to heat water or for heating and cooling of buildings. In large installations, steam is generated and used as the working fluid for power generation. In small applications, heat can be stored in devices such as hot water tanks for use when solar energy is not available. However, in large power systems, it is necessary to couple the solar-thermal system with conventional fuel burning equipment to guarantee an uninterrupted generating capability.

A great deal of experimentation has been done and full scale demonstration systems have been constructed and tested in the last two decades to convert solar energy directly to usable heat energy. Particularly for home heating or cooling use, a variety of systems are now commercially available which are very successful technically. However, the costs of installation and operation of these solar home heating systems, at present competing fuel prices, substantially exceed their economic benefits. As costs of more conventional energy supplies increase, these solar systems will become increasingly attractive.

Similar considerations apply to large scale solar thermal power generating stations. A high level of direct solar radiation is required, and although they are technically feasible, they are costly to construct, operate and maintain. Also, it would be advantageous to employ some form of large scale heat storage for such installations, such as liquid or salt baths or in underground formations. There is as yet little actual experience with such large scale heat storage technology. However, in the appropriate climate, and in localities with higher costs of conventional fuels, such solar-thermal plants are nearly economically viable at the present time.

Wind power

Clearly, the use of wind power as a primary energy source for the generation of electricity is very site-specific and its successful use can only be achieved in adequately windy localities. Early efforts to make use of large-scale wind turbines were often plagued with severe problems, and indeed, even at present, the available designs of large- scale turbines are too costly and unreliable. However, smaller wind powered generators have met with very considerable success, both technically and economically, for example, in the extensive installations in California, Denmark and Scotland [8]. If large numbers of such smaller sized units, each with a capacity of 100 kW or more, can be located on a single site, then the costs of operating and maintaining the installation can become very reasonable, and electricity can be generated at competitive costs. Several such installations presently exist, and undoubtedly more will be constructed in the near future as the technology matures. Considerable land area is required for such generating facilities, and there is little flexibility in siting the turbine assemblies. As a consequence, environmental or aesthetic concerns may limit the choice of possible locations for such installations.

Wave and tidal energy

Although this form of energy is a large diffuse global source, its practical availability is limited to coastal regions [9]. Tidal power is, in fact, a proven energy technology, with large pilot plants in Canada and France. Other test facilities have been constructed in several countries to attempt to use tidal or wave energy for electricity generation. Efficiencies are low, about 20% for tidal or wave energy conversion, and costs are high. Probably only tidal power in a few very favourable coastal locations has the potential for any larger scale use, and its implementation will come slowly. Therefore, despite the enormous amount of energy contained in wave or tidal motions, its availability is such that it will remain one of the costliest sources of renewable energy.

Summary

The nature of a renewable, sustainable energy system is beginning to emerge. Various demonstrated technologies are available, and further development and improvements are continuously occurring. The question remains — when will these technologies be implemented? It is not a simple question, for the cost-benefit relationships and their economic and political implications are complex. It is not our purpose to discuss these implications in this chapter, but only to try to assess the technical possibilities for a renewable energy system. However, it is interesting to consider the impact of the movement to global free trade and the influence it will exert on the adoption of alternative energy schemes. On the one hand, new energy technologies and the capital to construct new facilities may become more readily available, particularly to Third World nations. On the other hand, it will make it more difficult to control environmental pollution by fossil fuels, for major energy users can locate in regions where environmental regulations are minimal, and refuse to adopt renewable energy technologies.

It seems certain that a solar energy based system will be more decentralized and diverse than what we have now [10]. The mix of energy technologies used would reflect the climate and natural resources of each region. Smaller installations, adapted to be optimal for local conditions, would become much more prevalent. Because of the intermittent or seasonal nature of energy from solar sources, there will be a need to develop and have available adequate and appropriate conversion technologies to give more acceptable energy currencies, and to be able to store and transport this energy safely and economically. Such processes are presently available and new technologies are not needed, only modest continued development and improvement.

Any discussion of a renewable and sustainable energy system must recognize the fact that such a system will create many employment opportunities. The diversity of processes and the smaller size of the operations will result in much more labour-intensive and much less capital-intensive facilities. Both semi-skilled and skilled job opportunities will be created which are incremental to the present energy industry, which is based on very large capital-intensive units.

Table 3
Costs of selected renewable electricity sources, 1980-2030[1]
in 1988 cents per kilowatt-hour

Technology	1980	1988	2000	2030
Wind	32[2]	8	5	3
Geothermal	4	4	4	3
Photovoltaic	339	30	10	4
Solar thermal				
trough with gas assist.	24[3]	8[4]	6[5]	–
parabolic receiver	85[6]	16	8	5
Biomass[7]	5	5	–	–

[1] All costs are levelled over the expected life of the technology and are rounded, and assume a return to high government research and development levels.
[2] 1981. [3] 1984. [4] 1989. [5] 1994. [6] 1982. [7] Future changes in biomass costs are dependent on feedstock costs.

Principal source: Worldwatch Institute, based upon *The Potential of Renewable Energy: an Interlaboratory White Paper*, prepared for the Office of Policy, Planning and Analysis, US Department of Energy, by Idaho National Engineering Laboratory et al., in support of the National Energy Strategy [USA] (Golden, Colorado: Solar Energy Research Institute, 1990).

The final question which must always be answered is "what are the costs to society of a renewable energy system?" Leaving aside the possibility that the world may really have no choice, and considering only the quantifiable costs, it is plain that several renewable energy technologies are already competitive with fossil fuel energy sources, given the right set of conditions, which indeed do exist already in selected localities. Table 3 shows some estimates of the costs of producing electrical energy from various renewable resources, and projections of future costs for these alternatives, given reasonable expectations concerning their continued improvement. All of the more successful processes are projected to decrease significantly in costs of power production, with the greatest gains being made in the technology of photovoltaics [11]. By the year 2030 all are potentially competitive with fossil fuels.

The world has already embarked on the road to a renewable and sustainable energy economy. Even at the present time, it is estimated that about 20% of all energy is derived from solar sources. By the year 2030, over one-half of the world's energy requirements could be obtained from these sustainable technologies (see Table 1 of the previous chapter). It remains the major problem to see that this change comes about as rapidly as possible, and is not slowed by societal or economic pressures to the irreversible detriment of our environment.

References

1   "Renewable Energy Sources" Report No. 22, Watt Committee on Energy, Michael A. Laughton (Ed.), Elsevier Applied Science, NY, 1990, p.107.

2   "Liquid Products from the Continuous Flash Pyrolysis of Biomass" Donald s. Scott, J. Piskorz and D. Radlein, Ind. Eng. Chem. Process Design and Development, Vol. 24, 581-585, 1985.

3   "Fast Pyrolysis of Natural Polysaccharides as a Potential Industrial Process" D. Radlein, J. Piskorz and D.S. Scott, J. Anal. & Appl. Pyrolysis" Vol. 20, 41-64, 1991.

4   "Thermal Conversion of Biomass to Liquids by the Waterloo Fast Pyrolysis Process" D.S. Scott, J. Piskorz and D. Radlein, in Pyrolysis as a Basic Technology for Large Agro-energy Projects, E. Mattucci, G. Grassi, W. Palz (eds), 102-115, Commission of the European Communities (Luxembourg) 1989 ERU 11382 en.

5   "Feedstock Availability of Biomass and Wastes" J.W. Barrier and M.M. Bulls in Emerging Technologies for Materials and Chemicals from Biomass, American Chem. Soc. Symposium Series 4765, R.M. Rowell, T.P. Schultz and R. Narayan (eds), Ch. 23, 410-421, Amer. Chem. Soc. Washington, DC. 1992.

6   "The Coming Hydrogen Age: Preventing World Climatic Disruption" David S. Scott and W. Hafele, Inter. J. Hydrogen Energy, Vol 15, 727-737, 1990.

7   "High Efficiency III-V Solar Cells" John C.C. Fan, Mark B. Spritzer, and Ronald P. Gale, in "Advances in Solar Energy" Chap. 3, Vol. 6, Karl W. Boer (Ed.), Plenum Press, NY, 1990.

8   "The U.S. Electrical Utility Industry's Activities in Solar and Wind Energy: Survey and Perspectives" Edgar A. DeMeo and Peter Steitz, Chap. 1 Ibid. see [7].

9   "The Prospects for Non-Carbon based Energy Systems" Rendel Pease, Commissioned Paper, 41st Pugwash Conference on Science and World Affairs, 17-22 September, 1991, Beijing, China.

10 "Designing a Sustainable Energy System" Christopher Flavin and Nicholas Lenssen, in "State of the World, 1991" Chap. 2 — A Worldwatch Institute Report on Progress toward a Sustainable Society, W.W. Norton & Co., NY 1991.

11 Ibid, Chap. 2, p.27.

Part IV
COSTS AND BENEFITS

CHAPTER 13

Estimated Costs and Benefits of Proposals to Create a More Secure World

Eric L. Tollefson

Abstract. The preceding chapters contain estimates of some of the costs and benefits of the programs proposed. These are drawn together here and compared with those of two somewhat similar programs published by two respected organizations, the Worldwatch Institute and the World Game Institute. Such estimates are helpful in arriving at rough orders of magnitude. The programs put forward call for expenditures ranging from $125 billion (US) to $250 billion (US) per year over a ten-year period, equivalent to 12-25% of the annual global expenditure on armaments. Benefits of the proposed programs include enhanced security for future generations through measures to provide improved health, nutrition, education, family planning and clean water for all. Tree planting programs would be undertaken to reduce carbon dioxide in the atmosphere, to decrease soil erosion and to produce much needed fuel wood and building materials. Efficiency in the use of fuels would be increased to reduce carbon emissions. The debt load of poor countries would be reduced. These programs have the potential to create several million jobs.

Introduction

In 1991, the governments of the world spent approximately one trillion dollars (US) on armaments and support of the military [1]. With the end of the East-West Cold War, there is no justifiable reason to continue supporting the military at such high levels, especially in view of the need to create conditions that will raise the standard of living of those in need so that all people can live with dignity, including the basic needs of food, shelter, health care and education, and so that they can do so in a manner that maintains a quality environment. This chapter examines the cost of programs to fulfil the above objectives in a way that will make the future sustainable. While the cost estimates are mainly from North American sources, and many of the expenditures will be in the Third World, the author recognizes that the programs discussed here are matters for countries or regions to decide upon for themselves, and that such initiatives are likely to be taken up piecemeal. These are particularly matters where the developed nations must not preach "do as we say" or "do as we do", since our own practices are so often unsustainable in the long term — we need only look at the unsustainable agricultural practices in the West, or at the overconsumption of fossil fuels by the developed nations.

Though costly, many of the programs discussed here are of overriding importance for the world's future.

Proposals and estimates of the Worldwatch Institute

Estimating the costs of the programs required to attain these objectives is difficult because of the broad range of factors involved, the wide variations in the conditions prevailing in rich and poor countries as well as the range of quality standards that might be sought for the environment. Brown and Wolf [2], on the basis of many bold but reasonable assumptions contained in a program entitled *Reclaiming the Future*, have made rough estimates of additional expenditures for 1990-2000 to achieve sustainable development. The annual costs of their six suggested programs are given in Table 1. These programs relate closely to several topics discussed in this book, and are therefore discussed in detail here.

The first program would provide protection for river basins and farmlands against erosion of soil. The second would provide for removal of some of the carbon dioxide from the atmosphere and for the production of fuelwood desperately needed by 1.25 billion people in the developing world to cook their food and heat their homes [3]. These topics relate closely to those covered in Chapters 11 and 12 dealing with what needs to be done in the next 30-40 years to move from a society based largely on fossil fuels to one in which renewable energy sources will predominate.

Table 1
Rough estimated costs for sustainable development (from [2])

	Program	Annual Costs $Billions US
1.	Protecting topsoil and cropland	19.4
2.	Reforesting the Earth	5.4
3.	Slowing population growth	27.0
4.	Raising energy efficiency	30.0
5.	Developing renewable energy	15.6
6.	Retiring Third World debt	27.3
	TOTAL	124.7

The third program at $27 billion per year for slowing population growth, would be spent largely in the developing countries. It is discussed below under *Toward a sustainable society*.

Programs 4 and 5 outlined by Brown and Wolf would fund the many projects which can be undertaken to raise energy efficiency and to hasten the conversion from the present heavy dependence on fossil fuels to major dependence on renewable energy sources. These programs again are similar to those described in Chapters 11 and 12 which estimate what is likely to happen in the energy field between now and 2030.

Program 6 would provide assistance to Third World countries with heavy debt obligations that are in desperate need of low cost capital for development programs toward becoming self-supporting, and toward becoming viable trading nations.

All told, the estimates of Brown and Wolf add up to $125 billion per annum.

Proposals and cost estimates of the World Game Institute

The plan proposed by members of the World Game Institute, a non-profit educational organization based in Philadelphia, USA, is described in a publication by Gable and Frisch [4]. The list of strategies proposed by the WGI is somewhat broader than the outline of programs suggested by Brown and Wolf and is given in Table 2.

Table 2
Strategies proposed by the World Game Institute [4] and
their estimated annual costs over a ten-year period

Strategy	Description of Program	$US Billions	Millions of Jobs Created
1.	Famine relief Establishing farmers with sustainable agriculture Providing fertilizer for basic food production	2 10 7	0.3
2.	Providing health care for all • primary health care and health providers • health care for children (immunization and vitamins)	 15 2.5	1.5
3.	Eliminating homelessness - self-help housing	21	1.4
4.	Providing clean water for all • would provide clean water infra structure and adequate drinking water for 1.75 billion people as well as sanitation facilities	 50	5.0
5.	Educational use of satellites, television and radio	5	0.5
6.	Programs to increase energy efficiency	33	1-2
7.	Development of sustainable energy systems • use of biomass and solar energy	 17	0.4
8.	Retire Third World debt and preserve natural resources	30	–
9.	Stabilize the world population	10.5	1.3
10.	Regeneration of the environment. Preserve cropland • topsoil protection program • conversion of vulnerable land	 8 16	1.8
11.	Regeneration of the environment. Planting trees (150 million hectares) to slow soil erosion, provide fuelwood, sustain ecology, sequester carbon dioxide and protect rain forests	 7	1.0
12.	Would stop CFC production	5	⎫
13.	Would stop acid rain by removal of sulfur from fuels	8	⎬ 1.3
14.	Halt global warming - by increased energy efficiency, greater use of renewable energy sources and reforestation	 8	⎭
ANNUAL TOTAL		**$255**	15.5-16.5

Ten of the fourteen programs relate directly to topics discussed in the preceding chapters of this book. The other four items relating to famine relief, homelessness, stopping CFC production and acid rain also fit in well with the theme of this book.

It is useful to compare the cost estimates of the six program items from the list made by Brown and Wolf as given in Table 1 with those of the different strategies proposed by the World Game Institute. The total of the WGI estimates at $255 billion (US) is double the $125 billion of the earlier estimates. The difference lies largely in the WGI's inclusion of support for training and equipping farmers to do sustainable agriculture, in providing self-help to eliminate homelessness and in a much larger program to provide clean water and sanitation. According to the WGI publication [4], 1.75 billion people would benefit from such a program, especially in terms of health and general productivity.

The WGI list also would provide considerably more funding to regenerate the environment. Its Strategies 10-14, estimated to cost $52 billion per year, may be compared with the first two items of the Brown and Wolf proposal dealing with the protection of topsoil and reforestation estimated at $25 billion per year. These large extra costs are responses to the urgent need for action to halt the production of acid rain, CFCs and atmospheric pollution. Such actions would reduce the loss of forests, halt the thinning of the ozone layer, and decrease global warming.

Costs and benefits of a sustainable peace

The proposals of the Worldwatch Institute and the World Game Institute do not include programs to establish sustainable peace without which many of the proposals they have made could not be undertaken because of war, civil strife, and the lack of an infrastructure for such programs.

In Chapter 1 Douglas Roche makes the case for nations to move toward human security through sustainable development, the benefits of which would include security for education and health as well as security for the planet's life support systems. By the use of preventive diplomacy and confidence-building measures the need for armed forces would be reduced, permitting funds to become available as peace dividends. In the South, a $50 billion peace dividend could be created by cutting military spending and using the funds saved to promote human security with all of its benefits.

Chapter 2, by Carl Jacobsen, analyses the many problems of various trouble spots in eastern Europe. The New World Order he proposes must include a genuinely revitalized, more potent and more representative United Nations. In Chapter 6, William Epstein also describes a new role for the United Nations. In 1992 its regular budget was $1.03 billion not including the budgets of the United Nations agencies such as UNICEF, the United Nations Development Program, and the World Food Program which are supported by voluntary contributions from a variety of sources. The cost of peacekeeping jumped from $0.5 billion in 1991 to $2.7 billion in 1992. Support for this greatly expanded role for the UN will have to come from its members [5]. In Chapter 10 Morris Miller reiterates the suggestion [6] that the UN's programs could be paid for by instituting a tax of 0.003% on trade in international currency.

Chapter 3 depicts Canada's role for its military forces changing markedly as they become established in various UN peacekeeping operations. According to Leonard Johnson, an equitable burden for Canada to share in these activities is likely to be at least equal to what Canada has supported as a member of NATO in recent years. In his estimation, it is unlikely that we shall see a peace dividend from reducing Canada's support of its military. He sees the peace dividend as "the opportunity to advance the cause of collaborative security and thus to arrest the disintegration of civil order in the world".

William Epstein states, in Chapter 4, that the cost of maintaining armaments and armed forces in many countries could be greatly reduced following a comprehensive ban on nuclear testing. In the event of such a ban, development of nuclear weapons would likely also cease and the funds saved could again provide a peace dividend.

According to David Parnas, in Chapter 5, eliminating the space-weapons program formerly known as the Strategic Defense Initiative would yield a peace dividend of $6 billion/annum.

Toward a sustainable society

In Chapter 7, Digby McLaren provides a figure of $9 billion (US) per year as the cost of controlling population growth, based on a UNFPA

(United Nations Fund for Population Activities) figure that compares well with the $10.5 billion estimate by the WGI for its Strategy 9 (Table 2). These values are much lower than the $27 billion per year figure given for the period 1990-2000 by Brown and Wolf [2] in Table 1. The $27 billion estimate, however, includes $5.5 billion designated for family planning, $10.2 billion for education, immunization and health care of women and children. It also provides $11.3 billion for financial incentives to replace the need for large families as a means of old age security, thus encouraging birth control. The cost of population control given by McLaren is in line with these other estimates when the costs of similar programs are compared.

The 10-year program at $10.5 billion per year proposed by the WGI for stabilizing the world population would make family planning services available everywhere, provide financial incentives towards having smaller families, improve the education of women and provide prenatal and infant health care. McLaren provides a strong statement in support of these objectives at a somewhat lower estimated cost.

Job creation

It is difficult to estimate the number of jobs which would be created by a program on population control. However, if half of the $10.5 billion proposed were used to provide health care workers, family planning and health care education, it is estimated that approximately 1.3 million jobs could be maintained over the proposed 10-year period (Note 1 and reference [4]).

For each strategy proposed by the WGI, a rough estimate of the number of jobs that might be created has been made by this author (Table 2) on the basis of the assumptions in Note 1. The estimates are based on where such a program would likely be undertaken and depend strongly on the levels of training required to conduct the work.

Children, communities and health

The total cost of financing the goals set at the World Summit for Children in 1990 as reported by Collette Frances in Chapter 8 and estimated by UNICEF is $25 billion per year. This sum includes the costs of providing safe drinking water, adequate sanitation, maternal health, family planning education, and nutritional and supplemental feeding programs. In addition, it would cover community health measures, immunization and outreach health units as well as literacy programs. It should be noted that several of these items are included in the $27 billion program proposed by Brown and Wolf. (item 6 in Table 1.)

Strategy 2 proposed by the WGI would provide primary health care for *all* people, especially the approximately one billion people who lack it [4]. It would require the training and employment of 1.5 million health care workers. As indicated in Table 2 this would cost $15 billion per year for a 10-year period, assuming that much of the health care required would come from *Community Health Providers* who would handle the front-line defence against the spread of disease by means of vitamin supplements, immunization and vaccination. These workers would also play a role in giving advice on natal care, on contraception and, above all, on the prevention of AIDS. With the additional $2.5 billion per year they estimate for immunization and vitamins for children, their program extends well beyond the UNICEF program as outlined in Chapter 7 which is dedicated largely toward the health of children.

Clean water and sanitation

While the UNICEF program described by Frances is largely directed towards children, its rather minimal program for supplying clean water could be expanded to the WGI proposal in Strategy 4 if funds were available. In this connection, Gabel and Frisch [4] of WGI have pointed-ed out that 1.75 billion people have drinking water of poor quality.

WGI's Strategy 4 which would provide clean water for *all* of humanity, has been estimated to cost $50 billion per year for ten years. This program would include the installation of wells, water and sewage pipes, water purification systems and sewage treatment. Many people would be required for building such installations and for maintaining and operating them later. The availability of water would make the development of small industries possible and the combination of clean water and sewage treatment would reduce the incidence of disease. If half the $50 billion per year were used to provide labour and administration, these funds, employed largely in the developing world, would support about five million workers providing these services over the ten-year period. Costs would vary widely depending upon where the work had to be undertaken and the expertise required. Provision of these jobs would do much to establish the necessary infrastructure for building up local industries and making it possible to build towns and rural dwelling places. In Canada, for example, this program could mean supplying clean water and sanitation facilities for isolated populations that do not already enjoy these benefits.

Eliminating famine

Strategy 1 of the WGI proposals provides for famine relief and the development of sustainable agriculture and production of fertilizers. It would require the establishment of food reserves for periods of famine, and fertilizer distribution and production facilities to assist farmers with increasing food output. With the education of farmers in methods of sustainable agriculture the WGI would hope to wipe out starvation and malnutrition in large measure.

Eliminating homelessness

Strategy 3 of the WGI deals with the elimination of homelessness, in part by providing self-help housing. It aims to make housing available to roughly 100 million homeless people. The plan suggested would provide building materials and tools to the people who lack proper housing and train them in construction of homes.

Wiping out illiteracy

Illiteracy is another problem that is likely to be solved through different initiatives in different countries, possibly at quite low cost. Strategy 5 of Table 2 proposes the installation of satellites and television which, although it may be seen as a typically North American solution, could teach nearly one billion illiterate people to read. Education is the key to sustainable development. Installation of television and satellites on a large scale for educational purposes goes far beyond teaching people to read and could be of value in making technical education widespread. For example, a televised educational system could give useful instruction in the skills necessary to develop sustainable agriculture, control pollution and population, protect the environment and control the spread of disease. Development of the communications network required, if operated by solar power, would create a major stimulus in the photovoltaic industry, with predictable reduction in per unit costs and acceleration of the more widespread introduction of photovoltaics as renewable energy sources. Such a development is not likely to occur until the people in these areas have acquired sufficient technology to be able to maintain and operate the systems. Acceptance of an international code of conduct would seem to be a necessary precondition to prevent these systems from being used for inappropriate purposes.

Referenda

Chapter 9, by Metta Spencer, suggests new forms of parliamentary constituency coupled to the holding of plebiscites or referenda on various issues on a national or regional basis. The proposal offers the hope that enough of the demands of minority groups may be met so as to obviate partition of a country. Since the end of the Cold War secessions have become some of the more difficult problems of our time. The costs of referenda would have to be borne by the participating countries, or possibly by the United Nations if the voting populations of more than one country were involved. The recent referendum on the constitution in Canada cost about $100 million [7], not a trivial matter. However, costs could be kept down by holding referenda in conjunction with general elections or by using inter-active communication technologies. If the UN became involved in such activities, its budget would have to be expanded accordingly.

Third World debt

In Chapter 10 Morris Miller describes the need to reduce the intolerable debt load of the developing countries. The Worldwatch Institute's proposal to spend $27.3 billion per year over the period 1990-2000 [2] to reduce the debt load of developing countries was intended to give them a reasonable chance to rebuild their economic infrastructures and again become viable, self-supporting trading nations.

The World Game Institute under its Strategy 8 has estimated the need for $30 billion per year for 10 years to retire enough of the Third World debt to make their economies sustainable and to allow real development. In return for the debt reductions, natural resources such as the rain forests would be preserved in the interests of all nations.

Of course, total debt forgiveness would be preferable to either of the above proposals but it is not likely to be acceptable to the banking community.

Toward a sustainable environment: global warming

If the threat of global warming is to be reduced, it will be necessary during the transition period to the year 2030 that as many corrective actions as are reasonably possible be undertaken. One of the key issues is to reduce carbon emissions (as carbon dioxide) from combustion of non-renewable resources such as oil, gas and coal. This can be done in several ways. Instead of depending upon fossil fuels as is done today for approximately 80% of our energy needs (Chapter 11) strong efforts should be made to develop other energy sources.

Table 3
Actions that may be taken to reduce the greenhouse effect

a	Planting trees and other biomass as a means of short term removal of carbon dioxide from the atmosphere.
b	Increasing the gasoline mileage of cars as much as is reasonably possible, for example, up to 75 miles per gallon (US), through improved design of cars and fuels, improved car maintenance and lower speed limits in some areas.
c	Increasing the efficiency of lighting systems by using new designs of lights capable of saving 75 percent of the power for a given light output.
d	Decreasing the loss or gain of heat in housing and other buildings by proper insulation, design and construction.
e	Increasing the efficiency of energy utilization from the combustion of gas, oil, coal or biomass by applying the principles of co-generation of electricity and heat wherever it is reasonable to do so.

f   Using fuels such as methane with a higher energy output per ton of carbon emissions than is obtained from fuels such as oil and coal.

g   Where it is reasonable to do so, permanently burying carbon dioxide extracted from combustion and other processes in depleted gas and oil reservoirs, in other such empty geological formations or in the oceans at the necessary depth to contain it.

h   Burning renewable biomass in its various forms in place of non-renewable fossil fuels.

i   Developing the use of hydrogen as a clean-burning fuel which can be produced from renewable sources or from methane, the CO_2 produced with it being permanently stored.

This transformation will take several decades and will be expensive but it is a necessary step toward a sustainable environment. Several actions which may be taken to lessen the greenhouse effect are presented in Table 3. Four of the nine actions relate to removal from or reduction of CO_2 in the atmosphere, four are concerned with increasing efficiency in the use of energy, while the last may be classified as both a means of increasing efficiency and reducing CO_2 emissions.

Energy utilization efficiency

In support of research and development aimed at increasing the efficiency in fossil-fuel usage, the Worldwatch Institute and the World Game Institute have proposed, respectively, that $30 and $33 billion per year be spent for ten years [2,4]. Estimates by Flavin and Durning [8] indicate that the spending rate on such programs in the late eighties was between $20 and $30 billion annually and that it had been higher. If half of the amount proposed by the two institutes for increasing the energy efficiency, that is, $16 billion per year, were to be spent providing jobs to instal energy-saving equipment worldwide, between one and two million jobs would be created and supported over the ten-year period of the program.

Controlling soil erosion

In Strategy 10 it is proposed by the WGI that 128 million hectares of the world's most vulnerable cropland be converted to woodland and pasture so that topsoil erosion can be significantly reduced. About 1.8 million jobs could be created. The program would provide means of conserving valuable topsoil so that agriculture and forestry would be placed on a more sustainable footing.

Planting trees

In Strategy 11 of Table 2 it is proposed that 150 million hectares of trees be planted over a decade. The program has been estimated by the WGI to cost $6 billion per year for ten years. Another $1 billion per year would provide financial incentives and protection for rain forests. Half of the carbon emissions from fossil fuels into the atmosphere could be sequestered by photosynthesis by planting 300 million hectares of trees [2]. Norman Myers [9] estimated that this could be done for $120 billion (US) or $12 billion per year over 10 years. The two estimates are in reasonable agreement. The above strategies offer quick and effective means of reducing net carbon emissions during the transition period until solar photovoltaic, geothermal and biomass energy sources can provide a large enough supply of energy to greatly reduce fossil-fuel consumption.

The predicted population increase of two billion by the year 2030 greatly emphasizes the need for tree-planting programs.

Renewable energy systems

The basis of the $17 billion average annual outlay for research and development on sustainable energy systems (Strategy 7 of the WGI proposal) is attributed to Brown and Wolf [2] who recommended a doubling of the investment in development of renewable energy sources during the nineties in view of the tremendous costs which might have to be borne if climate change were to be greater than the minimum anticipated. In comparison with the proposed funding for increasing energy utilization efficiency and considering the tremendous possibilities if solar photovoltaic and solar thermal sources could be made more competitive with fossil-fuel sources, the figure proposed is a reasonable estimate.

Other strategies for a quality environment

The last three strategies, 12, 13, and 14 have been estimated by the WGI to cost $5 billion, $8 billion, and $8 billion each for periods of 20, 10 and 30 years respectively. The objectives are to stop the decrease in the ozone content of the upper atmosphere, to reduce emissions of sulfur dioxide from combustion of fossil fuels and to reduce the release of carbon dioxide, methane and CFC gases into the atmosphere. Tollefson and Scott discuss these emissions in Chapters 11 and 12 in relation to the greenhouse effect, energy efficiency studies and the use of renewable energy sources.

How to pay for the proposed programs

At this stage it is not possible to say which countries would adopt portions of the programs discussed above if funds were available to bear the very considerable costs. In today's world of economic stress there is only one area of human activity that expends hundreds of billions of the world's limited credit annually and where very significant cuts could be made, and made with concomitant gains in world security. If those nations that purchase armaments and maintain military forces were to reduce their military budget by 25% of the 1991 level and maintain that reduction, applying the savings to programs of the types and magnitudes discussed in this chapter, then all of them could be set in motion and continued. Additionally, nations that have borne relatively small or no military expenditures might be convinced to support such programs in the interest of improving trade and doing their share toward the common good.

A new and positive relationship between the nations of North and South would likely be created from which all nations could benefit. In particular the general health of the peoples of the South would improve and their economies would be enhanced. Hopefully, many of the programs suggested would improve the economies of the developing countries so they could handle the cost of maintaining the programs beyond the suggested ten-year period. A major role of the North would be the provision of technical education and basic technology, as well as some goods and services as requested by the nations of the South.

It would be necessary to have a strong UN or NGO component to monitor the administration of the programs in order to avoid the misuse of the resources for political purposes rather than for the welfare of the people. Corruption by those in control could destroy the programs.

Conclusion

There is little time left to sit back and contemplate these matters. A great deal needs to be done in the next two decades to avoid tragedies that are visibly imminent in so many places. Overall, the dominant problem driving many of the others will be the world population, predicted to be 8.2 billion by 2030. What kind of world will it be? Does humankind have the will to co-operate and to create a sustainable peace, society and environment for the benefit of all? We think that these things can be achieved.

Notes

1   In most cases estimates of the number of jobs which might be created were calculated by assuming that half of the proposed expenditures would be for labour. If the jobs were likely to be done in the developing world, labour costs would be low except where high technology would have to be employed in which case developed world labour rates were used. The average yearly wage of workers in the developing world was assumed to be $4000 US while that in the developed world was assumed to be $20,000. These estimates are based on what teachers on the average received in the developing world in 1987 (Sivard, World Military and Social Expenditures, 1991) and what production workers received in the USA in 1991 corrected to 1993, according to figures given in the World Almanac 1993.

2   Three hundred million hectares is about one third of the area of continental United States excluding Alaska.

References

1   The Defense Monitor (ISSN 0195-6450), (Center for Defense Information, Washington, DC, 1992) **XXI**, No.6, 4.

2   Lester R. Brown and Edward Wolf, "Reclaiming the Future" in State of the World 1988, a Worldwatch Institute report on Progress Toward a Sustainable Society (W.W. Norton and Co., New York) pp.170-88.

3   L.R. Brown and C. Flavin, "The Earth's Vital Signs" references 1, 9.

4   Medard Gabel and Evan Frisch "Doing the Right Things" (World Game Inst., Philadelphia 1991) pp.1-27.

5   Barbara McDougall, Secretary of State for External Affairs, The Disarmament Bulletin (External Affairs and International Trade Canada) No.19, winter 1992-3, 5.

6   Martin Walker "Global Taxation; Paying for Peace", 1993, World Policy Journal X No.2.

7   Personal communication with P. Hurtubise for the Chief Electoral Officer, Government of Canada, Ottawa, Canada, June, 1993.

8   Christopher Flavin and Alan Durning "Raising Energy Efficiency", references 1, 59.

9   Myers, Norman "The World's Forests and Human Populations: The Environmental Interconnections in Resources Environment and Population" edited by Kingsley Davis and Mikhail S. Bernstam (Oxford University Press 1991) pp.237-51.

About the Authors

William Epstein, LLD, OC, graduated from the University of Alberta and served with the Canadian Army in World War II. He was appointed Chief, Middle East Section of the Political and Security Council Affairs Department, UN Secretariat, 1946-50; Senior Political Officer, UN Palestine Committee, 1948; Director, Disarmament Division (UN) and Chief of the Disarmament Group (UN) 1950-72; He represented the Secretary-General at a number of disarmament conferences and at the negotiations for the 1963 Test Ban Treaty, the 1967 Treaty of Tlatlolco, the 1968 Nuclear Non-Proliferation Treaty, the 1971 Sea-Bed Treaty and the 1972 Biological weapons convention. He has been Senior Fellow, United Nations Institute for Training and Research and Special Consultant on Disarmament to the Secretary-General since 1973. He has been a member of the Canadian Delegation to six sessions of the UN General Assembly. He was a member (1984-6) of the Board of Directors of the former Canadian Institute of International Peace and Security and is past chairman of the Canadian Pugwash Group. He wrote **Disamament: twenty-five years of effort** (Canadian Institute of International Affairs, 1971), **The Last Chance: nuclear proliferation and arms control** (Free Press, 1976), **The Prevention of Nuclear War: a United Nations perspective** (Oelgeshlager, Gunn and Hain, 1984) and has co-authored and/or edited several other books. He has published more than 200 articles on disarmament, international security, and the role of the United Nations.

Colette Frances is an analyst, specializing in microbial research and development. She is a graduate of the University of Calgary and former director of Canadian Student Pugwash. She has worked on a variety of studies in several disciplines: the assessment of science and technology education in Canada, including gender issues, technology transfer and the economics of research and development; redefining security in the post-Cold War global village; the biodiversity crisis; and the Canadian Prosperity Initiative. She has led workshops on communication and group facilitation skills and assisted the Canadian Youth Working Group to formulate their statement on the environment and development for the Brazil Earth Summit. She is married with two sons and lives in Calgary, Alberta, where she is an active volunteer with the Calgary Science Fair Society and the Science Hotline.

Carl G. Jacobsen completed a PhD on Strategic factors in Soviet foreign policy at the Institute for Soviet and East European Studies at Glasgow University. He is Professor of Political Science specializing in Soviet/Russian and Strategic Studies at Carleton University, where he is Director of Eurasian Security Studies. He has also taught at Miami, Harvard and Columbia universities, at Glasgow University, and at Acadia and McGill. He was Director of Carleton's Institute of Soviet and East European Studies 1990-2; Senior Research Officer and Director of Soviet Studies at the Stockholm International Peace Research Institute, 1985-7; and Director of Soviet and Strategic Studies at the University of Miami, 1980-5. He has published over 100 refereed or commissioned academic journal articles. His books include: **The Soviet Defence Enigma: estimating costs and burden** (Oxford University Press 1987), **The Uncertain Course: new arms, strategies and mindsets** (Oxford University Press 1987); **Soviet Foreign Policy; new dynamics, new themes** and **Strategic Power: USA/USSR** (Macmillan and St Martin's Press, London and New York 1989 and 1990) and **The Nuclear Era; its history; its implications** (O. G. and H., Cambridge, 1982).

Leonard V. Johnson, Major-General (retired), joined the Canadian Army (Reserve) at an early age and later graduated as a pilot in the Royal Canadian Air Force. Having gained extensive experience in staff and command positions, he was appointed Coordinating Member, Canadian Section of the US-Canadian Permanent Joint Board on Defence (1978-9). After serving four years as Commandant of the National Defence College of Canada, the senior educational institution of the Canadian Forces, he retired in 1984 with 34 years of active service on his record. He is a member of Generals for Peace and Disarmament, Veterans against Nuclear Arms, the Pugwash Conferences on Science and World Affairs, and the Group of 78. He is Chairman of Project Ploughshares, and serves on the Boards of

Directors of Energy Probe Research Foundation and of the Defence Research Education Centre. He is on the Military Advisory Board of the Centre for Defense Information. Along with service on several other national and international committees, he has contributed numerous articles, interviews, letters, reviews and editorials to Canadian periodicals and books. He has written an autobiographical study **A General for Peace** (James Lorimer, 1987).

Digby J. McLaren obtained an MA degree from the University of Cambridge (England) in 1946 and a PhD from the University of Michigan in 1951. He was a member of the Geological Survey of Canada and its Director-General (1973-80). Active in Devonian geology and paleontology of Western and Arctic Canada, international correlation and boundary definition, global extinctions and asteroid impacts, and global change, he was a founding member and chairman of the ICSU/UNESCO International Geological Correlation Program. Recently he convened and edited (with B.J. Skinner) the the final report of the two Dahlem Conferences on Resources and World Development, and (with Constance Mungall) a book **Planet under Stress** (La Terre en Peril). He is a Fellow of the Royal Society of London, a foreign associate of the National Academy of Sciences (USA), and a past president of the Geological Society of America. He was President of the Royal Society of Canada from 1987-90.

Morris Miller, PhD, graduated from McGill University, Harvard, and the London School of Economics. He has taught at McGill, the University of Maryland, Carleton University, and the World Bank's Economic Development Institute, University of Ottawa. He has worked for the UN in New York, the UN's Food and Agricultural Organization in Rome and the World Bank in Washington. He is currently Executive-in-residence and Adjunct Professor at the University of Ottawa. He consults on international development issues which include aspects such as the environment, river basin planning and debt management. He founded Tele-Teaching International Inc. to advise developing countries on the use of the most advanced informational and instructional technology. He has completed a term on the Board of the World Bank as Executive Director representing Canada, Ireland and Carribean countries. He served for several years with the UN as

Deputy Secretary-General concerned with preparation for the 1987 Conference on New and Renewable Energy. He has written several books and articles dealing with the current global economic situation, including: **Coping is Not Enough: the international debt crisis and the roles of the World Bank and the International Monetary Fund** (Dow Jones-Irwin, 1986), **Resolving the Global Debt Crisis** (UN Development Programme, 1989), and **Debt and the Environment: converging crisis** (UN Publications, 1991).

David Lorge Parnas, born 10 February 1941, is a professor in the Department of Electrical and Computer Engineering at McMaster University in Hamilton, Ontario. He has taught at Carnegie-Mellon University (where he received his PhD), the University of Maryland, The University of North Carolina, the University of Victoria and the Technical University of Darmstadt, Germany. He has also consulted for leading US military suppliers and was a part-time employee of the US Navy from 1973 to '86. While working for the US Naval Research Laboratory, he instigated and led a major project on software for aircraft navigation and weapons delivery. Author of over 150 papers and reports, he has made a number of fundamental contributions to concepts of software engineering. He became well-known outside his profession after he resigned from a committee advising on the Star Wars project, explaining why he felt that the project was fraudulent and dangerous. He received an honorary doctorate from the ETH (Federal Institute of Technology) in Zurich. For his deep concern that technology be applied for the benefit of human society he became the first winner of the *Norbert Wiener Award*, given by the Computer Professionals for Social Responsibility. He is a Fellow of the Royal Society of Canada, past president of Science for Peace, and an officer of Canadian Pugwash.

Douglas Roche was a member of the federal parliament from 1972 to 1984. Retiring from politics, he was appointed Ambassador for Disarmament in 1984, a position that he held until 1989, spending much of that time with the Canadian delegation to the UN in New York. He has served as President of the United Nations Association of Canada, as Honorary President of the World Federation of United Nations Associations, and was the founding President of

Parliamentarians for Global Action. In 1989 he was appointed Visiting Professor at the University of Alberta where he teaches *Canada's Role in Global Peace and Security*. He has been the recipient of many awards for his national and international service. His many books include: **The Human Side of Politics** (Clarke, Irwin, 1976), **Justice Not Charity: a new global ethic for Canada** (McClelland and Stewart, 1976), **What Development is All About: China, Indonesia, Bangladesh** (NC Press, 1979), **Politicians for Peace: a new global network of legislators working for human survival** (NC Press,1983), **United Nations: divided world** (NC Press, 1984), **Building Global Security: agenda for the 1990s** (NC Press,1989), **A Bargain for Humanity: global security by 2000** (University of Alberta Press, 1993).

Donald S. Scott graduated from the University of Alberta in Chemical Engineering and received an MSc in Chemistry from the same institution. He was awarded a PhD in Chemical Engineering from the University of Illinois. His early teaching career began at the University of British Columbia. Since 1964 he has been at the University of Waterloo as a Professor and Chairman in the Chemical Engineering Department, Acting Dean in Engineering, and Associate Dean in Graduate Studies. Since 1989 he has been an Adjunct Professor. He has received many awards, one of the most prestigious being the R.S. Jane Award from the Canadian Society of Chemical Engineering. He has published about 80 refereed journal papers and two books. He also has eight patents to his credit. He has been a consultant to numerous companies and government agencies. His research in recent years has emphasized the conversion of biomass to liquid and gaseous fuels.

Metta Spencer, PhD, graduated from the University of California, Berkeley, and shortly afterwards became Assistant Professor at the University of Toronto, Erindale College. She now holds the Associate Chair of Sociology at that institution and is coordinator of the undergraduate program in peace and conflict studies. Over the last decade she has made more than 100 presentations at professional meetings. She is founder and editor-in-chief of *Peace Magazine*, and is a member of the editorial board of *Peace and Change*. She has served on the Consultative Group of the Canadian Ambassador for Disarmament, the Canadian Commission to UNESCO regarding the International

Peace University in Schlaining, and with the Canadian delegation to the UN during the Third UN Special Session on Disarmament (1988). To keep abreast of the East-West peace dialogue and new political thinking she made several visits to the (former) USSR for the purpose of interviewing, and is writing a study of the effect of the dialogue of the peace movement upon Soviet policy during the Cold War. Her well-known textbook **Foundations of Modern Sociology** (Prentice-Hall) is now in its ninth edition (sixth Canadian edition).

Eric L. Tollefson was awarded degrees in Chemistry from the University of Saskatchewan and a PhD in Physical Chemistry from the University of Toronto. During his career he has worked at the National Research Council in Ottawa, in industry in the USA and in Canada, and has been teaching at the University of Calgary for 25 years. For a ten-year period he was Head of the Department of Chemical and Petroleum Engineering. From 1982 to 1987 he was the Alberta Oil Sands Technology and Research Authority (AOSTRA) Professor in the department. He has published numerous technical papers, and reports and has sixteen patents to his credit. His recent research has dealt with upgrading of bitumen, heavy oil and sour gas. He was co-author and winner of the Best Paper Award from the Canadian Journal of Chemical Engineering in 1986 and recipient of the Canadian Society of Chemical Engineering, Esso Petroleum Canada Award in Industrial Practice in 1987. He was awarded a Fellowship in the Chemical Institute of Canada and is a registered Professional Engineer in Alberta.

INDEX